MAUREEN GILMER

the gardener's way

a daybook of acts and affirmations

CB
CONTEMPORARY BOOKS

Library of Congress Cataloging-in-Publication Data

Gilmer, Maureen
The gardener's way : a daybook of acts and affirmations / Maureen Gilmer.
p. cm. — (Contemporary gardener)
ISBN 0-8092-2389-9
1. Gardeners—Prayer-books and devotions—English. 2. Gardens—Religious aspects—Meditations. 3. Devotional calendars. I. Title. II. Series.
BL625.9.G37 G55 2001
242'.68—dc21 00-31555
CIP

Interior design by Diane Jaroch

Published by Contemporary Books
A division of NTC/Contemporary Publishing Group, Inc.
4255 West Touhy Avenue, Lincolnwood (Chicago), Illinois 60712-1975 U.S.A.

Printed in the United States of America
International Standard Book Number: 0-8092-2389-9

01 02 03 04 05 06 LB 18 17 16 15 14 13 12 11 10 9 8 7 6 5 4 3 2 1

IN MEMORY OF MY GRANDMOTHER,

Mary Benita Esnard

THE CONTEMPORARY GARDENER

Other books in The Contemporary Gardener *series*

Gaining Ground: Dramatic Landscaping Solutions to Maximize Garden Space
Maureen Gilmer

Gardening Wisdom: Time-Proven Solutions for Today's Gardening Challenges
Douglas Green

Growing Perennials in Cold Climates
Mike Heger and John Whitman

Growing Roses in Cold Climates
Jerry Olson and John Whitman

Growing Shrubs and Small Trees in Cold Climates
Nancy Rose, Don Selinger, and John Whitman

The Landscaping Revolution: Garden *with* Mother Nature, Not Against Her
Andy Wasowski with Sally Wasowski

Native Landscaping from El Paso to L.A.
Sally Wasowski with Andy Wasowski

CONTENTS

Copyright Acknowledgments

Grateful acknowledgment is made for reprinting artwork from the following:

Matteo Capcasa, *Il libro della agricultura*. Published 1495 by Petrus Crescentius. Library of Congress, Washington, D.C.

Francis Marion Crawford, *Ave Roma Immortalis*. Copyright © 1900 by The Macmillan Company, London.

Jacopo di Carlo, *The Florentine Fior di Virtu of 1491*. Library of Congress, Washington, D.C.

Peter Drach, *Ruralia Commoda*. 1491 by Petrus de crescentilis zu teutsch, J. Rosenwald Collection, Library of Congress, Washington, D.C.

G. F. Scott Elliot, *The Romance of Plant Life: Interesting Descriptions of the Strange and Curious in the Plant World*. Copyright 1907 by Seeley and Co. Ltd., London.

Rodney Sydes Ellsworth, *The Giant Sequoia*. Copyright © 1924 by J. D. Berger, Oakland, CA.

J. N. Fradenburgh, *Departed Gods: The Gods of Our Fathers*. Copyright 1891 by Cranston & Stowe, Cincinnati, OH.

Carol Belanger Grafton, *Old-Fashioned Christmas Illustrations: Copyright-Free Designs*. Copyright © 1989 by Dover Publications, Mineola, N.Y.

Carol Belanger Grafton, *Old-Fashioned Floral Illustrations: Copyright-Free Designs*. Copyright © 1990 by Dover Publications, Mineola, N.Y.

Carol Belanger Grafton, *Medieval Life Illustrations*. Copyright © 1996 by Dover Publications, Mineola, N.Y.

Jim Harter, *Animals: 1419 Copyright-Free Illustrations of Mammals, Birds, Fish, Insects, etc.* Copyright © 1979 by Dover Publications, Mineola, N.Y.

Jim Harter, *Plants: 2400 Copyright-Free Illustrations of Flowers, Trees, Fruits and Vegetables*. Copyright © 1988 by Dover Publications, Mineola, N.Y.

Richard G. Hatton, *1001 Plant and Floral Illustrations from Early Herbals*. Copyright © 1996 by Dover Publications, Mineola, N.Y.

Johann Georg Heck, *Heck's Pictorial Archive of Art and Architecture*. Copyright © 1994 by Dover Publications, Mineola, N.Y.

E. W. Hilgard and W. J. V. Osterhout, *Agriculture: For Schools of the Pacific Slope*. Copyright 1911 by The Macmillan Company, New York.

Edward F. Hulme, *The History Principles and Practice of Symbolism in Christian Art*. Copyright 1891 by Macmillan and Company, New York.

F. Schuyler Mathews, *Field Book of American Trees and Shrubs*. Copyright 1915 by G. P. Putnam's Sons, New York.

John Parkinson, *A Garden of Pleasant Flowers, Paradisi in Sole Paradisus Terrestris*. Copyright © 1976 by Dover Publications, Mineola, N.Y.

Mary Elizabeth Parsons, *The Wildflowers of California*. Copyright © 1897 by California School Book Depository, San Francisco, CA.

Johann Petri, *Herbarius Latinus*. Published 1486 by Passau, Germany. The Dumbarton Oaks Collection, Library of Congress, Washington, D.C.

Jose Guadalupe Posada, *Gran Comeliton de Calaveras*. Antique broadsheet, Mexico, 1910.

William Rowe, *Floral Illustrations: A Treasury of Nineteenth-Century Cuts*. Copyright © 1990 by Dover Publications, Mineola, N.Y.

Heijiro Saita, *Chasitsu Kojo*. Copyright 1905, Tokyo.

Dorothy Smith Sides, *Decorative Art of the Southwestern Indians*. Copyright © 1961 by Dover Publications, Mineola, N.Y.

Emnanuel Sweerts, *Early Floral Engravings from the 1612 Florilegium*. Copyright © 1976 by Dover Publications, Mineola, N.Y.

The Yearbook Committee, editors, *Trees: The Yearbook of Agriculture 1949*. U.S. Government Printing Office, Washington, D.C.

Preface

Unless the god, whose temple the whole of this is which thou beholdest, shall release thee from the bonds of the body, thou canst enter here . . .
—Cicero

Every culture on earth maintains its own unique relationship with plants and the places where they grow. The root word of culture is *cult*, which is defined as a single unifying belief system that unites the people. These systems are invariably religious, with a thousand different paths to enlightenment, consciousness, and eternal life.

If you take a peek under the circus tent of world religions, each invariably has roots in plants and gardens. These origins might be traced back to creation myths, the proverbial paradise garden, or recognition of the divine powers that control planting and harvest of food crops. Peoples devised earthy rites and rituals that governed their tasks in the fields and appealed to the spirits of the plants to grow and fruit abundantly.

In recent years the world of horticulture has lost many of its connections to culture. Even more important, the age-old celebrations that connect people to their spiritual cults through plants have disappeared. This book is designed to rekindle this daily relationship to botanical spirituality. It guides you along a path of days, months, and seasons of the year in an ongoing celebration of plants and an exploration of the peoples who cherished them. It covers both the major religions and lesser-known forms of spirituality, showing that all share a reverence for nature and provide equal contributions to the spiritual culture.

In essence this is a bridge-building book designed to illustrate through season and celebration how the garden provides the single common ground in which all faiths meet. Leave dogma outside the garden gate, and open your mind, for here you will find that the gardener's way is the way of the soul. There are no divisions—only unity.

Acknowledgments

I wish to express my heartfelt thanks to those who made the dream of this book into a reality. My deepest appreciation to my friend and agent Jeanne Fredericks, who helped me develop the idea, and editor Anne Knudsen, who saw its value in print. With thanks to project editor Julia Anderson, whose tireless attention to detail is admirable, and copyeditor Elaine Robbins who worked so hard to make my prose read far better than it was written. *Gratia pro rebus merito.*

Our calendar year begins just after the winter solstice with the rebirth of the sun. It is a time when agricultural people of the Northern Hemisphere and their lands quietly rest and build energy for the demands of the coming season. It is the season of reflection, both on the events of the previous year's growing and on how the coming year might be better. It is also a time of study, for we may spend hours reading about plants and gardens from volumes old and new. The imagination is unleashed as, seed catalogs on our laps, we see in the mind's eye how this plant or that might be arranged in the field or landscape. Winter is a seasonal metaphor for sleep and recovery that illustrates to us that no matter how dark and colorless our landscape may appear, there is indeed life sequestered in those roots and twigs.

Winter

THE TIME OF REST

january

The name of this month is derived from the Latin *janua*, meaning "door." This is appropriate for a month that opens the new year. It is also named for the Roman god Janus, the doorkeeper, whose two-faced countenance looked both to the past and to the future. Janus was also believed to open the gates of heaven in the morning and close them again at dusk each day. Ancient Teutonic people called January the wolf month, because at this time the starving wolves ventured out from their forest lairs in search of dwindling prey.

The snowdrop is the old flower of January because it blossoms almost in midwinter. It was believed to have grown on Mount Hymettus in Greece as early as 100 B.C. The snowdrop became the first harbinger of spring, even though it blooms in the cold of winter. It is believed that St. Francis of Assisi called this old flower a symbol of hope, rising in pure white at the darkest time of the year.

ARAPAHO MOON: WHEN THE SNOW BLOWS LIKE SPIRITS IN THE WIND

The carnation is also an official flower of the month due to its resistance to frost and its tendency to bloom over winter in warm climates. The early wild carnations were pink or flesh-colored, and named for the Latin word for flesh, *carnis*. The carnation (and its cousins the pinks) was native to the Mediterranean and not introduced into Britain until the tenth century, when it was commonly called gillyflower.

january 1

NEW YEAR'S DAY

For hundreds of years, this association of religion and solitude, of nature and art, of legend and love, and a real or fancied connection between the plants of the field and God, has led holy men, prayerful laity, and repentant sinners into the wilderness of the world to build their shrines.

—ADELMA GRENIER SIMMONS, *Saints in My Garden*, 1932

The association of religion, solitude, nature, art, legend, and love is the sum of the garden. The great mysteries and truths are expressed equally in both the wild garden of nature's hand and the cultivated plots of our own. The garden itself is a living shrine that we create to capture that essence of nature in plants and space. Tending it is a sacrament that demands our attention and offers rewards of the spirit. Let us then go out into the garden and consecrate it as a shrine that exists both on the land and on a more ethereal plane lodged deep inside the temple of our humanity.

ACTS AND AFFIRMATIONS

If you do not have a special sacred place or shrine in your garden or home, it is time to create one. Locate it in a secluded part of the garden away from more active areas. It should have a flat place to make offerings and burn incense or candles. It should have a background or enclosure to define the limits of the sacred space. Above all, it should be a beautiful and intimate expression of your personal spirituality.

(*CALENDULA*)

pot marigold

The beautiful yellow and orange pot marigolds have been grown in Europe since ancient times. The Celts regarded this daisy as the flower of the sun god, for its "days eye" opened with the morning sun. The botanical name is linked to the Calends of ancient Rome, which were the first days of the new year when the flower blooms. Medieval Christians renamed it marigold after Virgin Mary, to whom they dedicated the first day of every new year. A flower for all faiths, it may have the richest spiritual history found in the Western world.

january 2

But a thing that is incarnate with the life of the soul—like the little flower—you can reach out and look into and suddenly find that you are taking hold of the things that lift you up and carry you along and make people love you and give you the joy of life and the joy of living and the joy of having come into the place God has for you, and the exuberance of filling that place in life.
—Henry David Thoreau, *Journal*, 1906

The things that lift you up from the mundane and carry you along on an elevated plane are your most valuable experiences, whether they are the expression on a child's face, the discovery of a wildflower, or a particularly vivid sunset. How often do we trudge through life rarely pausing to relish these simple beauties? It is the little things that fill our life that are God's greatest gifts, for these are many and everywhere, waiting patiently for our attention. The filling of your place in life is directly linked to these subtle beauties and experiences, and until we learn to acknowledge and enjoy them we can never grow to fulfill our ultimate destiny.

Acts and Affirmations

In all but the coldest climates, late winter is the time to sow annual wildflowers. These quick-to-germinate seeds should be in the ground before the temperature warms up. Purchase mixtures of annual wildflower seeds that feature those native to your region. This ensures that they will be perfectly adapted and successful in the long term. And as the patch grows and flowers this spring, each little flower will become a well of joy into which you may dip as often as you wish.

january 3

When a man looks out from the living room of his house into his small garden, he is reminded of mountains and their forest cover, of a mountain stream, and perhaps of the sea nearby. Thanks to his garden, the peaceful reassurance of nature will not escape him even in the heart of the city.

—TATUSO ISHIMOTO, *The Art of the Japanese Garden*, 1958

The gardens of Asia are a microcosm of nature, and their designers work by a set of ancient rules related to balance and harmony of elements in the landscape. All the components—such as trees, water, stone, and small scale. Similarly, a bonsai tree evokes the feeling of great old forests despite its minute size. Though we may not be able to live in the mountains or on the banks of a river, we learn from Japanese garden design how to create a small garden that inspires in us the spirituality and healing power of nature without ever leaving home.

ACTS AND AFFIRMATIONS

Japanese have been taking tea in their gardens for many centuries. The layout of the garden is related to the tea ceremony, which is a symbol of the spiritual path for many. When you want to relax, either in your garden or in a room that looks out onto the winter garden, do so in a slow and deliberate manner. Use teacups instead of coffee mugs. Make tea in a pot, not with a tea bag in your cup. Always have a few almond cookies on hand to go with the tea, and discover the serene magic of this age-old ritual drink.

january 4

It is under God's rule that the work of creation revolves in its evolution, and we have earth, and water, and ether, and fire and air.
—Svetasvatara Upanishad, Part 6, 600–900 B.C.

The single most common thread that links all faiths is a belief in a supreme intelligence or consciousness that is manifest in every thing on Earth. Though the specific form of the supreme may change from faith to faith, it is always expressed in beautiful passages in religious texts that remind us there is a sacred presence that exists all around us. It is manifest in the air, the sun, the earth, plants, and animals. To learn to see your everyday world as holy, find the sacred presence in your garden, thereby seeking the divine in all things.

Acts and Affirmations
Ayurvedic healing is an ancient medicinal approach used for over five thousand years in India. It integrates the mind, body, and soul for a more holistic approach to natural healing. If you have access to jasmine flowers, you can create a homemade ayurvedic headache remedy. Combine twelve flowers for each ounce of sesame oil. Heat the oil gently, and when it is very warm, submerge the flowers in it. Allow to cool completely. Strain out the flowers, and apply the oil to your temples.

january 5

Twelfth Night

Here's to thee, old apple tree! Whence thou may'st bud and whence thou may'st blow. And whence though may'st have apples enow!
—traditional sixteenth-century English toast

The taking down of Christmas greenery that decorated houses was once a solemn occasion treated with surprising care. The plants could not be taken down until either Twelfth Night or Epiphany. If left longer or removed prematurely, the house and its people would be haunted for the coming year. The material could not just be thrown away; it was ceremoniously burned or buried in the garden. This practice was a legacy of pagan times, when spirits were believed to dwell in vegetation, even after it was brought indoors.

Acts and Affirmations

The tradition of Twelfth Night included the toasting of the apple tree with hot cider in a big joyous party. If you have an apple or crab apple tree in the garden, brew up a potent batch of spiced cider, drink heartily, and go out into the night to *waes heil* your trees with this traditional toast.

january 6

EPIPHANY

And behold, the star they had seen at its rising preceded them, until it came and stopped over the place where the child was. They were overjoyed at seeing the star, and on entering the house they saw the child with Mary his mother. They prostrated themselves and did him homage. Then they opened their treasures and offered him gifts of gold, frankincense, and myrrh.
—MATTHEW 2:9–11

Of the three treasures offered to the Christ child, two, frankincense and myrrh, were plant products. These ancient incenses were the crystallized sap of trees that grew from Asia Minor to Northern Africa. They became valuable substance in ancient times because of their association with religious rites. Frankincense and myrrh were melted into oils to create potently scented salves used in holy anointing. People of many religions, from the Hebrews to ancient Egyptians, burned them on altars. These incenses are still a part of Catholic and Jewish rituals. Both were traded on the famous perfume trade routes across the Sahara Desert. What more historic and auspicious gift could one give to a child who would so completely change the face of the Western world?

ACTS AND AFFIRMATIONS

Nothing smells quite like raw frankincense and myrrh. Cone and stick incenses named for these originals are nothing like the real things, which are sold at New Age stores and occasionally at Catholic supply shops. Be sure to buy fresh round charcoals, which are necessary for burning, or you will never get the incenses started. Put a charcoal on a ceramic plate and about one-quarter to one-half teaspoon of incense granules on top. Light the charcoal (a lighter works best), then watch it burn to ignite this pungent incense—the most marvelous in all the world.

january 7

The Australian aborigines have a World Tree that supports heaven. The stars stud the branches, drawing spiritual sustenance from Nature and Earth. The natives celebrated the land and their closeness to it, even oneness with it, through various ceremonies that bound them together on the deepest religious level. Their strength was bringing the people of the present into contact with their past and their dreamtime.

—Judy Griffin, *Mother Nature's Herbal*, 1997

Indigenous people the world over have developed integral relationships with plants of all kinds. The Aborigines lived in a unique landscape populated by species that adapted to the very dry climate. Australia can be a very hostile environment during the wet and dry seasons, when trees provide the shade and shelter that are essential to survival. It is no wonder that Aborigine spirituality is integrated into the land and its plants: they are an environmental continuum shared by people of the present and those who came before them.

Acts and Affirmations

The aromatic eucalyptus tree is the dominant forest species of Australia. Its willingness to thrive in hot, dry climates has made it ubiquitous in parts of America, where we take it for granted. Let us remember that the value of the eucalyptus is often overlooked in days of plentiful resources. It is maligned as a scruffy child of a lesser god, while we turn away to lust after more succulent green plants. But when challenges of drought threaten our homes and communities, the muted foliage of the eucalyptus promises beauty and its canopy a life-giving shade while thirstier species die out. Give thanks to that child of a lesser god for the gift of its pungent aroma to add a soothing fragrance to the warm evening breeze.

january 8

The system of the world is entirely one; small things and great are alike part of one mighty whole. As the flower is gnawed by frost, so every human heart is gnawed by faithlessness. And as surely—as irrevocably—as the fruit-bud falls before the east wind, so fails the power of the kindest human heart, if you meet it with poison.

—John Ruskin, *Modern Painters*, 1843–1860

Had Michelangelo been discouraged from painting, he might never have found the courage to create the artwork on the ceiling of the Sistine Chapel. Failure to support each other's dreams and aspirations can destroy great potential in children or adults trying to develop new creative skills. It is not so important whether our efforts result in great accomplishments but that they expose us to life lessons of infinite value. Let us never respond with negativity to sincere attempts to reach beyond the ordinary. There is no telling what end may be achieved!

Acts and Affirmations

God: Allow me to let go of every discouraging word I received in my past. Help me to rise to challenges in life and in my garden, and help me to weather the inevitable failures. When I fail, remind me that it is part of the learning process, so that next year I will not make the same mistakes.

january 9

To know someone here or there with whom you can feel there is understanding in spite of distances or thoughts unexpressed—that can make this life a garden.

—Johann Wolfgang von Goethe, 1798

To thrive, the plants in a garden must have similar climate requirements. They should also look attractive as a group, complementing one another. To make your life a garden, surround yourself with all sorts of people who thrive in the same environment as you do. Gather kindred spirits as your best friends, for exchanging thoughts and emotions is an act of love. Whether they are far away or next door, cultivate these friendships to enrich the soil of your spirit and add flowering beauty to your soul.

Acts and Affirmations

Writing letters is a lost art these days, yet old letters can be our most endearing mementos. The art of the letter can be expanded to become a visual feast, with the page decorated with things of the garden such as pressed flowers or color pictures clipped from outdated gardening catalogs. To receive a decorated letter from a long-lost friend or relative is a tactile experience that conveys more than just a greeting—it is an expression of love and the garden. During these long winter days, avoid the doldrums by creating a winter garden of letters to those we care about but communicate with rarely.

january 10

We believe that God hath made all things out of nothing: because even although the world hath been made of some material, that very same material hath been made out of nothing.
—St. Augustine, *Of the Faith and of the Creed*, 397

When you explore the idea of a divine source of all things, it leads to ever deeper levels of spiritual contemplation. The real question comes down to not whether God created the flower but whether God created the cells that make up the flower. Then we ask who created the DNA in the cell, and then who created the atoms in the DNA, and then the atom's nucleus. Perhaps someday, when the final question is answered, we will discover the true nature of God.

Acts and Affirmations

Discover the world of plants through a microscope. A student microscope or even an antique model that uses mirrors and sunlight will open up a new realm of creation. Through it, you may discover the nature of a thousand different species of algae, the tiny parts of fungi and lichens, or the reproductive organs of a wildflower. This primitive cellular material is the foundation on which the higher plants evolved. To witness this truth on a microscopic level is to truly grasp its awesome magnitude.

january 11

No two trees are alike. And their individuality is no imperfection. On the contrary: the perfection of each created thing is not merely in its conformity to an abstract type but in its own individual identity with itself. This particular tree will give glory to God by spreading out its roots in the earth and raising its branches into the air and the light in a way that no other tree before or after it ever did or will do.

—Thomas Merton, *Seeds of Contemplation*, 1949

The sanctity of individual life is among the most beautiful creations of the world. Whether it is a tree or a child, each has a destiny, each is recognized by its unique strands of DNA. This suggests that every one of us should make the most of our talents and abilities, cultivating them as deeply and thoroughly as we cultivate the kitchen garden. We must add good compost in the form of spiritual attention and exercise to fertilize our potential and bring forth a good crop. And whether that crop is a quiet, contemplative life or one steering a revolution for the good of humankind, it is of equal value, for it is the result of vigorously living out our greatest potential.

Acts and Affirmations

If you strive to view each and every plant in your garden as an individual, you will be able to nurture it to its greatest potential. Each plant is slightly different, and these nuances become clear only when you learn to view them individually. While beginning gardeners often see only the most general of distinctions, this recognition of uniqueness is what makes a great gardener so successful.

january 12

Slave to no sect, who takes no private road,
But looks through Nature, up to Nature's God.
—ALEXANDER POPE, *An Essay on Man*, 1733

The beauty of finding God in nature is that you need not become a slave to any particular religion or sect. The spirituality of the garden is certainly rooted in many religious paths, but to tap into its wellspring is to draw from the best of all faiths. It helps us create our own private road that promotes peace and life through respect for the Earth and her cloak of green growing things. In addition, we may sanctify all organisms, from bacteria in the soil to the mighty forest trees, and find our church all around—wherever there is earth, plants, and sun.

ACTS AND AFFIRMATIONS

Take up your magnifying glass and follow the mosses as they grow in the cool damp of spring. They will turn green and grow vigorously in wet weather and are easily transplanted to other suitable places in the garden. Become aware of the mosses that live in your landscape and discover a microscopic world of fabulous plants. The reproductive structures are even more fascinating, appearing as if by magic with the coming of the rainy season.

january 13

A thin coat of ice covered a part of the [Walden] pond but melted around the edge of the shore. I threw a stone upon the ice which rebounded with a shrill sound, and falling again and again, repeated the note with pleasing modulation. I thought at first it was the 'peep' 'peep' of a bird I had scared. I was so taken with the music that I threw down my stick and spent twenty minutes in throwing stones single or in handfuls on this crystal drum.
—Ralph Waldo Emerson, journal, 1836

Nothing is as eerie and beautiful as the sound of ice, with its range of tones so like the haunting melodies of migrating whales. Emerson discovered he could make the ice sing and tested the range of Walden Pond's voice that winter afternoon. This is one of the hidden beauties of winter we miss when we hide indoors where it is warm or fly past the landscape in heated cars. Yet when we hike in the country during this quiet season, we discover much more than the view, for it is the greatest therapy for aging. The body loosens up with every step and the mind is awakened with sounds of breaking surf, crunching leaves, the rustle of tall grasses, and the singing of the ice.

Acts and Affirmations

If you live where it is cold enough for lakes and ponds to freeze, take a trek out to hear the ice sing. Do as Emerson did and throw stones at ice in smaller ponds, or, on larger lakes, find spots where the ice is thick. The ice is more vocal during slightly warm periods, when it is expanding and contracting. Sit and listen to the beautiful melody, and share the magic with your children and grandchildren.

january 14

RICE HARVEST FESTIVAL OF SUN GOD SURYA

> *Whom dost thou worship in this lonely dark corner of a temple with doors all shut? Open thine eyes and see thy God is not before thee! He is there where the tiller is tilling the hard ground and where the pathmaker is breaking stone. . . . Meet him and stand by him in toil and sweat of thy brow.*
>
> —RABINDRANATH TAGORE, *Giotanjali*, 1913

God is in the field, in the garden, in the meadow, and in the woods. He is everywhere: in the sun and the moon, in the wind and the ice and the winter barren trees. Though temples and churches have their place, the great apparitions of gods and goddesses have occurred in nature, not indoors. This alone should speak volumes about the value of spending time in the garden to renew the soul. For there, as tiller, path maker, and laborer, we are blessed.

ACTS AND AFFIRMATIONS

India's Rice Harvest Festival marks a change in winds, the shift of the sun from the Tropic of Cancer to the Tropic of Capricorn, and the start of the harvest. It is traditional to celebrate with sesame cakes and other sweets and decorations of fresh flowers. To celebrate the rice harvest festival at home, burn Indian incense and prepare a meal of curry and brown rice. Finish it off with sesame seed candy, which is found at most health food stores and organic groceries.

january 15

Let him establish a steady seat in a clean place, neither too high or too low, covered with a cloth or a deer-skin or sacred grass. Sitting there let him concentrate his mind on a single point, restraining the activity of thought and sense, and practice Yoga to purify himself.
—*Bhagavad Gita* 6, 11–14

Everyone deserves a special place to sit in the garden. This contemplative space should be beautiful, quiet, and comfortable. It should be far away from active places in the garden such as patios and play areas, surrounded with lots of plants for a cool, green, and fragrant environment. You may want to add a comfortable chair, lounge, or bench to rest on for long periods of time. And above all, it must feel good to you in an intuitive way. Over time, when retreating to that place, you will discover a conditioned response, a subconscious relaxation as mind and body recognize it as sanctuary.

Acts and Affirmations

If you have a contemplative garden space or are planning to create one, furniture is crucial to your comfort. If you are uncomfortable, it's likely you won't spend much time there. Invest in a very good chaise lounge, perhaps one of hardwood, like the deck chairs on old-fashioned ocean liners. Wood retains an even temperature, so it won't be too hot or too cold to sit on without cushions. A folding model is easy to take out during a winter warm spell and then bring indoors when you're through. Remember that, whether you sit on a lounge chair, lawn, deerskin, or blanket, just being there is the most important thing.

january 16

I am always most religious upon a sunshiny day . . .
—Lord Byron, *Detached Thoughts*, 1821

It is now widely recognized that Lord Byron was a manic-depressive personality. Like many artistic people, he suffered from excessive highs and overwhelming lows. In recent years it has been shown that many people suffer another malady, seasonal affective disorder, which makes them depressed when there is an absence of sunlight. This is particularly true when fog or overcast skies linger for many weeks at a time. There is little doubt that the weather influenced Byron's mood, and that a sunny winter day with the bright glare of newly fallen snow was the best therapy he could hope for. It is truly remarkable how much sunshine influences our state of mind, which suggests that gardeners working outdoors may be self-medicating with a prescription of solar therapy.

Acts and Affirmations

The easy way to bring the sunny taste of fresh sprouts into your winter diet is to grow them in your kitchen cupboard. Use a wide-mouth mason jar with just the band part of the lid. Place two teaspoons of dried mung beans or alfalfa seed (available at organic food stores) into the jar, then stretch a square of pantyhose material over the mouth and secure with the band. Fill the jar with water and let stand a few minutes, then pour it out. Put in a dark cupboard. Each day fill the jar with water and immediately pour it off again. In a few days you will enjoy a jar of fresh sprouts for a more diverse cooking experience and improved health.

january 17

Sit down before fact like a little child, and be prepared to give up every preconceived notion, follow humbly wherever and to whatever abyss Nature leads, or you shall learn nothing.

—Thomas Henry Huxley, *Zoological Evidences as to Man's Place in Nature*, 1863

As we grow older, we become more and more controlled by preconceived notions. Unlike children with no frame of reference for what they encounter, some older adults allow their perspectives to be jaded by experience. This less-accepting outlook colors simple wonders of nature in a way that destroys their mystery and magic. To return to the open-minded innocence of childhood means that as each new seedling or flower presents its lesson, our intellect must be free to grasp and hold it for gentle contemplation. This is the secret to continual growth. Never stop learning no matter how old you become, for learning keeps the brain active and alive.

Acts and Affirmations

You can learn the entire history of Western civilization through plants. Look for the human aspects of botany that make plants meaningful to us. For example, in wildflower folklore you will learn why early farmers named lupines "wolf flowers," or *Lupus* in Latin, because they grow where other plants will not. The red scale insect of the prickly pear cactus, once thought part of the plant itself, was made into a potent red dye by the Aztecs and later became a coveted tribute to the kings of Spain. From the gourd pots of Africa to the herbs and plant incenses that disguised the odors of the human body, there is a story behind most plants in your garden that will entertain the mind and enlighten the soul.

january 18

THEOGAMIA (CELEBRATION)
OF THE GREEK GODDESS HERA

I will sing of well-founded Gaia, Mother of All, eldest of all beings, she feeds all creatures that are in the world, all that go upon the goodly land and all that are in the paths of the sea, and all that fly: these are fed of her story.

—HOMERIC HYMN, seventh century B.C.

Hera, one of the first five great gods of the early Greeks, represented the fruitful earth. She was married to Zeus, god of thunder, and the couple represented the union between heaven and earth. Since Zeus was notoriously unfaithful, Hera later became patron of wives and marriage. She reminds us that in the wake of failed marriages, we may go back into our gardens to ease the pain. Life without a partner need not be so empty if we fill it with nurturing earth. For when we are alone to wander among our well-loved plants, their dependency is somehow comforting, and perhaps Hera lurks there to offer age-old whispers of empathy.

ACTS AND AFFIRMATIONS

God: Help me through the empty moments when I feel the loss of a partner or spouse. Remind me that relationships come and go, but the earth is ever-faithful and always there to absorb my tears. Fill the holes in my heart with warm fertile soil and an abundance of blooming flowers.

january 19

MARTIN LUTHER KING JR.'S BIRTHDAY

All my life I have risen regularly at four o'clock and have gone into the woods and talked with God. Alone there with things I love most I gather specimens and study the lessons nature is so eager to teach us all.
—GEORGE WASHINGTON CARVER, *The Man Who Talked with Flowers*, 1939

On this day we reflect on the life of this great leader and the history of African Americans. George Washington Carver was clearly among the greatest names in modern plant science. He devised the system of crop rotation that preserves soil fertility, a method we practice even in the smallest home vegetable garden. But above all, his life teaches us that the earth and gardens offer everyone, no matter how poor their beginnings and circumstances, an opportunity to achieve great things. Most of all, this former slave did not wallow in the injustices of the past but looked forward to see God in all his plants, in the earth, and most of all, in his fellow man.

ACTS AND AFFIRMATIONS

God: George Washington Carver saw you in every living plant he encountered. Help me to find my plants as inspiring so that I may grow spiritually as I garden. Let me see your face in every flower, in every bright new leaf, in every snow-white root, but most of all let me see you shining through the eyes of every human soul.

january 20

God sent thee Hart's-Ease. For it is much better with poverty to have the same, than to be King with a miserable mind. For from these springeth either felicity or adversity, and image of heaven with joy, or else with inward horror of mind and vexation, pray God give thee but one handful of heavenly Hart's-Ease which passeth all the pleasant flowers that grow in this world.

—William Bulletin, *Doctor of Phisicke*, 1562

The English cottage gardens we so admire are a true legacy of the black plague, an epidemic that killed off big landowners in Great Britain, making it available for the working class to finally own their own cottages. Though penniless, they planted the dooryard with every free plant possible, creating a whole new style of garden. They harvested seed from wild and cultivated flowers. They dug roots and ferns from the forest and grasses from the meadows. They even recycled leftovers from wealthier gardens and traded with one another. The cottage gardens prove to us that God has provided the opportunity for everyone to enjoy a garden, if only we discover the miracles of plant propagation.

Acts and Affirmations

Plant propagation is the art of working with God's free gifts to create a garden. When you learn how to grow plants from scratch, you gain more independence. A package of a hundred pansy seeds is about a dollar, while a single pansy plant at the nursery can easily exceed that price. Whether you practice voluntary simplicity or are dealing with a cash-flow crisis, propagation not only offers you a free garden but allows you to share in the sacrament of creation, working hand in hand with God.

january 21

Round the spruce top the blue was deepened, concentrated by the fixed point, the memory of that spot, as it were, of the sky is still fresh—I can see it distinctly—still beautiful and full of meaning. It is painted in bright color in my mind, color thrice laid, and indelible; as one passes a shrine and bows the head to the Madonna, so I recall the picture and stoop in spirit to the aspiration it yet arouses. For there is no saint like the sky, sunlight shining from its face.
—Richard Jefferies, *The Open Air*, 1863

Winter skies are among the most expressive, for they change so dramatically from day to day. From the inky dark before a snow or rainstorm to the incredibly bright, clear air of a cold winter day, there is always something to admire. Yet we tend to take the sky for granted until autumn fires cloud our view or summer humidity lays a haze on the land. Only in winter do we find skies almost fluid, like clear water flowing from under the snow. When coupled with evergreens, the startling contrast can arouse in us something close to religious devotion.

Acts and Affirmations

As children we had no sense of time and were rarely in a hurry. In those innocent days, we would lie on the spongy litter to gaze up lazily at the sky and the swaying treetops. When was the last time you took the time to lie down in the forest? If it has been too long, risk becoming a little damp and rekindle this early life experience. As an adult, it will truly touch your soul.

january 22

Hard frost. The market gardeners felt the severity of the weather—it stopped their labours, and some of the men, attended by their wives, went about in parties, and with frosted greens fixed at the top of rakes and hoes, uttered the ancient cry of "Pray remember the gardeners! Remember the poor frozen out gardeners!"
—*Morning Herald*, London, January 1826

Hard frost will never cause us to starve, but it shows us that in the garden there will always be surprises. Extreme cold, drought, heat waves that never seem to end, and a dozen other anomalies make each year's garden a fresh and new experience. It is so much like the twists and turns of daily life, the unexpected challenges that appear without warning. Over time what you learn about the flukes of weather and the unpredictability of living will yield wisdom—which in turn reminds us that troubles are but a bump in the road, and both we and our gardens shall eventually recover.

Acts and Affirmations
The consciousness of a gardener is dominated by weather. In winter we tend to ignore the garden, yet snow and ice can do terrible damage to our evergreens, particularly those under the eves of the house. Go out periodically to embrace the cold, and while there brush snow off your evergreens. Mere inspection of your plants is the perfect excuse to get outside for a while and kiss nature after being cooped up for what seems like an eternity.

january 23

There is a rhythm, then, in the weather, or at least a sort of rhyme, a repetitive sequence. All those folk rules that attribute weather changes to the phases of the moon, or to some other simple periodicity are not so far from the mark after all.

—Wolfgang Langewiesche, *What Makes the Weather*, 1943

Our greatest mistake is to view the universe in our own terms. The Earth has existed for so many millennia, but it is difficult to imagine time outside the brief life of a human being. We view natural changes in climate as dramatic and fatal, when in the larger scheme of things, they are just a small anomaly in an extended history of cataclysmic change. Experienced gardeners tend to take the variations in weather in stride, for over the years they accumulate a body of knowledge that predicts how plants will react to these annual changes. While young in garden terms, we must all learn to become keen observers of weather and how the earth and its botanical inhabitants respond. Thus we too shall earn the wisdom to understand this often unpredictable heavenly behavior.

Acts and Affirmations

In Tibet, colorful prayer flags in vivid yellow, red, blue, and green are hung everywhere—on buildings, trees, or poles. Prayer flags are available in this country from import stores and New Age shops and bookstores. About a foot square, they are very beautiful and festive in our own gardens summer or winter. If you have a petition, offer it in your garden, then hang the flag to flutter in the breeze as a symbolic continuance of the prayer.

january 24

You never enjoy the world aright, till the Sea itself floweth in your veins, till you are clothed with the heavens, and crowned with the stars: and perceive yourself to be the sole heir of the whole world, and more than so, because men are in it who are every one sole heirs as well as you.

—THOMAS TRAHERNE, *Centuries of Meditations*, seventeenth century

To become truly earth-centered, you must learn to feel more at home in gardening clogs than high heels or spit-polished wing tips. You must relinquish the idea that fingernails are to be long, painted, and manicured. You must grow strong enough to lift the stone, carry the wheelbarrow, and plant the tree. The rite of passage that all true gardeners experience at some point is the realization that all these preoccupations with beauty mean nothing, and that your work-worn calluses are among the greatest trophies in life.

ACTS AND AFFIRMATIONS

Calluses are God's natural way of helping us grow closer to our garden. Hardened skin allows us to use tools aggressively and plunge our hands directly into the soil in a tactile sacrament that brings us so close to the earth. It is so intimate we come away united, with some of it lodged under our fingernails. Though the soil does not remain there, those dark crescents are a sign that we have undergone the second most intimate communion with the soil besides the final rite of being buried in it.

january 25

Every day a new picture is painted and framed, held up for half an hour, in such lights as the Great Artist chooses, and then withdrawn, and the curtain falls.
—Henry David Thoreau, *Journal*, 1906

Light is the source of all color, and painters indeed see light very differently than the rest of us do. The challenge of painting a landscape is that outdoor light is continually changing, at one point lighting one part of a plant, and later another. The quality of light changes through the day, through the seasons, and through the year. We know instinctively that winter light is different than summer light, and morning light differs from afternoon light. What a great gift it is, for God has granted us a garden that is more than a static place for plants, one that is ever-changing as the sun travels its daily passage through the southern skies.

Acts and Affirmations
Now is the time to become more familiar with the position of the sun in your garden. With the sun low in the southern sky, it will set to the southwest, but in summer when it is farther north, it sets closer to true west. Mark sunrise and sunset with an existing tree or structure for reference, and in June mark them the same way. These positions tune us in to the celestial events that govern life on the planet. They make our garden a tiny extension of an infinite universe of natural wonders.

january 26

Chinese New Year

Of the things that are purely good without accompanying evil are: study, the love of mountains and rivers, taking pleasure in the moon, the breeze, flowers and bamboos, and sitting in an upright posture in silence.
—Chinese proverb

It is human nature to struggle with our desires. Many of them are compulsive, desires for material things that we think we want, but once obtained forever fail to satisfy. It is human nature to want what we cannot have, and in a sense this is what drives our compulsive desires. Many worldly and intellectual people have chosen to give up desire to pursue the simplicity of monastic life. In a way our gardens become a sort of monastic haunt. When we enter a garden, we leave behind the house and car, the fancy clothes and jewels to don our "grubbies" and root around in the dirt. It is a simple act of monastic simplicity that gives us a tiny glimpse into the contemplative and spiritually wealthy life of the monastery.

Acts and Affirmations

It is difficult for the Western mind to conceive of the utter peace achieved through meditation. In Buddhism, the emptying of the self to create a perfect void is the spiritual process used to help us rise above our compulsions and desire for material things. If you have never experienced the deep relaxation of meditation, consider taking a class to learn how. Many have found meditation a crucial skill for weathering the pressures of work, illness, family conflict, and the everyday stress of a chaotic life.

january 27

And again tobacco smoke rises. We ask that it will continue in the same manner. That the wind will be just so strong we are content. We are happy; the wind is just so strong and we are happy. And we ask that it will continue in the same manner in future days. And your mind will continue to be so.

—INVOCATION, midwinter Huron Feast of the Dead

Canadian winters of the Huron homelands are long and extremely cold. This beautiful invocation illustrates how much the Huron value contentment and predictable weather. Native Americans knew how to preserve their vegetable food supply, but the winter was still an ordeal. Many tribes lived at the brink of starvation when provisions dwindled toward spring. No one has ever looked forward to the thaw more eagerly as the Huron, and though we tire of cold and dreary weather, we must be thankful that starvation is no longer a threat in our age of abundance.

Acts and Affirmations

To avoid succumbing to cabin fever, always keep plenty of quality reading material around. Be thankful we may enjoy and support public libraries that bring the great authors of history to our towns however small. Use these long days to explore spiritual writers, from Seneca to Pliny and naturalists such as Thoreau to the myths and legends of Native Americans and writings of religious leaders around the world. As you wander the stacks in search of wisdom, you'll find a whole library of reading just waiting for you.

january 28

Live in each season as it passes; breathe the air, drink the drink, taste the fruit, and resign yourself to the influences of each. Let them be your only diet drink and botanical medicines.

—Henry David Thoreau, *Journal*, 1906

In winter we long for summer, and in the heat of the summer we dream of the cool days of winter. It is the same with age: the old long for the strength of youth, and the young are impatient for the freedom of adulthood. The art of peaceful living, as Thoreau so aptly says, is to live each season for its own unique qualities, without always wanting something different. In this season savor the scents of burning wood in the hearth, feel the icy wind on your bare cheeks, and marvel at the beauty of the frozen landscape. For only when you have reveled in the depth of winter, resigning yourself to its influences, will you discover the tranquility of your spirit and the soul of this quiet season.

Acts and Affirmations

Make a pact with yourself to avoid negative thoughts about winter. Look for the beauty that lurks in this dormant landscape, in the colors, textures, scents, temperatures, and light. Live in the season both indoors and outdoors, and enjoy each day for what it brings without being impatient for spring.

january 29

In the cooing of the doves, in the hovering of birds, in the pasturing of cattle, in the excellence of the strong, in the might of the full-grown, in the sleeping of slumberers, in the brightening of the morning, in the murmur of the winds.
—Sufi prayer

The divine exists in all things. This beautiful prayer reminds us to wake up to find that divinity in the animals, in our own strength, in the bright morning, and in the wind. It exists in our little gardens—in the soil, in the seedling, in the flower and vine—and when we go there we are surrounded by holiness. It is so easy to lose this sense of divinity and see our surroundings in the harsh reality of a man-made world. Yet to obtain deep spiritual consciousness, we transcend things of man and finally glimpse the infinite signs of God.

Acts and Affirmations

Sunrise in winter is most apparent because the darkness lingers late into the morning. All the deciduous trees are leafless and allow us to see a far greater horizon. Though you may be rushing to go to work this early, take three full minutes to stop and witness the morning sun as it first appears over the horizon or the neighbor's roof. These moments of first light are magical, the divine presence so palpable it will energize you naturally for the coming day.

january 30

SENEBTUVAE, THE ROMAN FESTIVAL OF SOWING

The three goddesses to the Latin mind distinct, Tellus being a personification of the earth itself, Ceres of the productive power of nature, which brings forth fruits out of the earth, and Ops of the human labor without which the productive power runs waste, and is insufficient for the sustenance of life.
—J. N. FRADENBURGH, *Departed Gods*, 1891

High atop the Chicago Board of Trade building stands a thirty-foot bronze statue of the goddess Ceres, with a large bag of corn in her arms. Erected in 1930, the statue of the ancient Roman goddess became a contemporary symbol of Chicago's deep link to midwestern agriculture, particularly corn. Though corn was unknown in Europe during classical times, Ceres was the Roman protector of all grains. The importance of bread and pasta in modern Italy shows how much the Roman Empire depended on grain crops. During the Senebtuvae festival, Ceres—from whose name we derive the word *cereal*—was honored as the fields were sown with wheat, rye, and barley.

ACTS AND AFFIRMATIONS

During this festival Romans fashioned little figures called *oscilla* to hang in tree branches and swing with the wind. Their turning was thought to suggest the nodding or rippling of mature grain plants as breezes run over the fields. The following ancient prayer to Ceres, recited while sowing, recalls the transition from a hunter-gatherer diet of acorns to the dependence on agricultural grains:

Partners in labor, Ye who reformed the days of old, and who replaced the acorns of the oak by better food. O satisfy the eager husbandman with boundless crops, that they may reap the due reward of their tilling!

january 31

We ourselves feel that what we are doing is just a drop in the ocean. But if that drop was not in the ocean, I think the ocean would be less because of that missing drop. I do not agree with the big way of doing things.
—MOTHER TERESA, *A Gift for God*, 1975

Each of us with our tiny plots of earth is part of a much larger community. Our soil is a portion of an enormous colony of living organisms that reside with particles of minerals and organic matter to cloak the globe. Growing plants links each of us to gardeners and farmers on nearly every continent and within every culture. No gardener is alone nor a single entity, but part of a collective consciousness. Perhaps this is why gardeners who share no common language understand each other. Together, like a great ocean, each of us in his or her little way becomes a vital part of a much larger earthy realm, the collective consciousness of the botanical spirit.

ACTS AND AFFIRMATIONS
To share in the worldwide cultivation of the ancient plant amaranth, plan to grow at least one of the more ornamental varieties in the summer garden. The two most beautiful varieties are tall ornamental Love-lies-bleeding (*Amaranthus caudatus*) and the more compact, but no less dramatic, elephant-head amaranth. Both are available through heirloom seed catalogs.

february

This month was named after the Latin verb *februare*, which means "to expiate or purify." It was the holiest month of the Roman year, when people repented their sins and made sacrificial offerings to the gods. It is also the month of the sabbat Imbolc, a Celtic ritual that celebrated the first awakening of the spirits of the vegetation. The Roman Empire's great rite of atonement combined with the pagan nature celebration combined with Candlemas, the feast of Christ as light of the world, is a buildup to the season of Lent, the forty days of fast and abstinence preceding Easter. At this time of year all faiths celebrate the dying winter and the miraculous birth of spring.

The tribal peoples of old Europe named this the month of cabbage, because February was when cabbage began to sprout and became the featured food of the season. It was a time when highly variable weather could yield a false spring or a deep freeze. To somehow divine the coming weather, superstitions, such as watching for groundhogs or sunshine on the second day of the second month, were considered reliable predictions. The little violet is the flower of this month because these wild plants are likely to blossom in the woodlands if temperatures are warm enough.

PREPARING FOR REBIRTH

february 1

Feast of St. Brigid

May the blessed sun shine upon you and warm your heart until it glows like a great peat fire—so that the stranger may come and warm himself, also a friend.
—Irish blessing

St. Brigid was an early Celtic saint of the fifth century who became known as "Mother of the Gaels." She founded a great monastic community in Kildare, Ireland, at a place that had previously been the temple and well of the threefold goddess of the Druids. This goddess represented the trilogy of healing, fertility, and knowledge and the life cycle of the grain divided into three phases—maiden, mother, and crone. The maiden, often called the "bride," is the virgin earth ready to be planted, as it lies during this season ready to accept the seed. This day was the pagan fire festival of "Bride," later given over to the Christian St. Brigid. Brigid means "fiery arrow," the reason a perpetual fire is kept burning to this day at the monastery. Therefore, the celebration of February 1 may be interchangeable between the pagan Bride and Christian Brigid, both of whom represent the universal mother of all Celtic peoples.

Acts and Affirmations

It is traditional to make a *bogha* Bride, or St. Brigid's cross, on this day. They are made out of bundles of reeds or straw lashed into a cross shape. More elaborate versions utilize old-fashioned wheat-weaving patterns. The cross is hung in the thatch roof, or under eaves above the front door, or, if you live in an apartment, on the back of the door. The above blessing from the *Carmina Gadelica* may be invoked to imbue your cross with power before hanging. The cross must remain in place a full year before removal.

(*Anemone coronaria chrysanthemiflora*)

st. brigid anemone

This poppy anemone is native to the Mediterranean and has been grown in European gardens since the sixteenth century. In Britain, *A. coronaria* was bred into a new form, with larger double flowers bearing more petals in mostly red or white. These improved plants were dubbed the "St. Brigid" strain anemones. Most were grown as bedding plants that produced far more attractive flowers than the wild species.

february 2

IMBOLC

If spring came but once in a century, instead of once a year, or burst forth with the sound of an earthquake, and not in silence, what wonder and expectation there would be in all hearts to behold such miraculous change!

—HENRY WADSWORTH LONGFELLOW

The ancient Celtic festival of Imbolc marks the awakening of the earth evidenced by the first signs of spring. The Celts did not see the winter solstice as the birth of the sun, because the land showed no signs of the transition, but by February, life was visibly awakening. Imbolc is also a goddess festival in which the aged crone of the old winter vanishes and the new virgin spring or the maiden bride is born. It is a time when we as gardeners are more acutely aware of this stirring of life than anyone else. While those not tuned to the earth grumble over dreary skies, slush, and mud, we see the buds begin to swell and rejoice.

ACTS AND AFFIRMATIONS

The tradition of Imbolc and—also today—Candlemas is to light candles as a symbol of the sun's return. Believers bring beeswax candles to the church on the Feast of the Purification to be blessed, then take them home to relight in times of sickness, when purification from disease was desired, or for protection during storms. Buy a large, fragrant green candle to light on this day—green for the spirits of the vegetation and fragrant as the spring flowers to come. Light it this evening to burn for a while, then save it for special days throughout the year to invoke the powers of the sun, the virgin, and the threefold goddess.

february 3

Setsubun-No-Hi: Shinto Festival of the End of Winter

And whoever loves this Way follows the laws of nature and becomes the friend of the season. Whatever he sees turns out to be flowers. Whatever he feels turns out to be the moon. When there are no flowers in what he does, he is like a barbarian. When there are no flowers in what he feels, he is like a wild beast. Forsake the barbaric, cast aside the brutish, follow nature's laws, return to her again.

—Matsua Basho, *U-tatsu-kiko Travel Journals*, seventeenth century

This day is celebrated in Japan as the official end of winter and a time for purification. It is a time of rejecting bad influences and encouraging the good. One way to do this is through the tea ceremony, which is an exercise in controlling barbaric human impulses. The tea garden becomes an environment of *precise* beauty at every turn. The implements of tea making become holy relics. The art of making and serving the tea is a calming, deliberate act. As we all celebrate the transition from winter to spring, let us make each small act a blossoming of kindness. For only when we forsake the barbaric do we discover the sanctity of flowers in everything we do.

Acts and Affirmations

In Japan the people celebrate this day by writing prayers on little pieces of paper, which are cast off bridges to float away on the rivers. They also use twigs to purify the house and then leave them by the doorway to prevent the return of winter. In the warmth of the home, the buds on the twigs invariably begin to swell as a sign that spring and life are dominant in the house and that winter need not enter again. Follow this example by cutting twigs from your garden to arrange artfully in a ceramic vase close to the front door. Then watch as the buds begin to open as a sign of the gradual weakening of winter.

february 4

When a man dies, his voice goes into the fire, his breath into the wind, his eye to the sun, his thought to the moon, his ear to the heavens, his body to the earth, his ego to the ether, the hair of his head and body to the plants and the trees; his blood and his seed flow into the waters.
—The Upanishads, 600–300 B.C.

Cremation, long practiced by the Hindus, has gained increased popularity in America, and there is a profound beauty in the ability to spread ashes into nature. When ashes are spread onto gardens, bodies of water, or other wild places, the remains are released with a sense of completion. For humanity came from the earth, so it is right we should be returned to her in death. And so we come to understand the fact that as children of the Earth, part of us exists in the wind, sun, earth, water, plants, and trees. While living we experience them, and after death as we become one with them.

Acts and Affirmations

For people looking for a meaningful way to honor the ashes of their deceased loved ones, there is no better place than in the garden. Place an urn filled with the ashes in a spot protected from the weather by a small structure and surrounded by beautiful plants. The shrine should be open to allow the ashes to be moved if the owner does. This garden shrine is a beautiful place to reflect and remember the departed on special days and seasons throughout the year.

february 5

I want to realize brotherhood or identity not merely with the beings called human, but with all life, even with such things as crawl upon earth. I want to realize identity with even the crawling things upon earth, because we claim descent from the same God, and that being so, all life in whatever form it appears must be essentially one.

—Mohandas K. Gandhi, *Works*, 1948

It is only through gardening that we attain a glimpse of the holistic nature of life. We learn that all crawling things are not bad—no matter how visually offensive we find them. Many are good insects that prey on the bugs that eat our plants, and when we begin to see them that way, we gradually change our attitude. When we become better identified with all the earthly organisms that exist in our garden, we discover how rich with life it truly is. And to spend time there is to recognize that all creatures are deserving of equal amounts of respect.

Acts and Affirmations

Strive to realize your kinship with all life on Earth by discovering more about the processes going on unnoticed in your garden. Pay special attention to the relationships of birds and insects to certain flowers. Birds eat fruit and the seed that passes through them is transported far from the mother plant to expand the range of the species. Insects are drawn to flowers by specific colors and nectar, and after feeding they carry pollen to the next flower. Each plant has evolved to appeal to certain forms of wildlife. It is these interspecies connections that speak most boldly to our spirits and fascinate the mind, for nothing so perfect could ever be the result of chance.

february 6

There are cedars on Lebanon which the axes of Solomon spared, they say, when he was busy with his Temple; there are olives on Olivet that might have rustled in the ears of the Master of the Twelve; there are oaks in Sherwood which have tingled to the horn of Robin Hood, and have listened to Maid Marian's laugh.

—Alexander Smith, *Historic Trees*, 1863

It is unlikely a cedar or olive survived since the time of Christ, but the great ages of some trees seem miraculous just the same. Some old trees are landmarks known by whole communities, with a deeply powerful presence. We as gardeners feel that power, for we know how many things can quickly kill a tree. Old trees are living miracles of nature, and our relationship with them makes us far richer in spirit.

Acts and Affirmations

Become more aware of the Famous and Historic Trees program of American Forests, the oldest conservation organization in the United States. This program allows you to purchase the progeny of very important trees to imbue your garden with special meaning. You are awarded a certificate of authenticity that shows family and children how tactile and alive their heritage can be.

Shrines blossomed like flowers along the highways and furnished places of peace and sanctuary where the traveler could rest. Monasteries furnished food for the hungry body, as well as calm for the tortured soul, and so the gardens grew and the number of plants multiplied. Thus gardening became an important part of monastic life.
—Adelma Grenier Simmons, *Saints in My Garden*, 1952

The great monastic traditions are inextricably connected to the history of gardening, for it was the Italian Benedictines who protected the ancient herbal books written in Arabic and Greek. These books would later be translated to provide the basis for modern pharmacy. In the fortresslike monasteries of the Middle Ages, the apothecary gardens served as protection for many species that had long been abandoned in fields outside the walls. As gardeners we enjoy a living religious legacy, for many of our flowers, herbs, and old roses would have been lost forever without these communities of men devoted to religious life.

Acts and Affirmations

Share in the monastic traditions by adding an espaliered, or cordoned, fruit tree to your garden. These are grown with a central trunk and lateral branches on a single plane that can be pressed up against a fence or wall without sacrificing space. Some come preattached to a trellis that you can simply mount on your wall, or you can use another trellis of your own design. It's possible to directly attach the plant to a wooden surface using nails and plant ties, or use masonry anchors for walls. As easy to grow as a standard tree, you need only give it basic care and plenty of sun for success. Apple trees are the most common choice, as the apple tree was the favorite tree of Eden and apples among the monk's most cherished fruits.

february 8

More things grow in the garden than the gardener knows.

—Spanish proverb

We as gardeners cultivate far more than plants. Each moment spent outdoors digging and weeding is a moment of contemplation. For during the routine physical tasks of gardening, we have the luxury of hours of rumination for pondering questions and mulling over decisions. When the body is fully active, the mind is able to relax and be free—and capable of its greatest revelations.

Acts and Affirmations

Whenever you have a difficult problem to solve, take time to think about it while working in the garden. It can be wonderfully productive because your mind won't be distracted by work, family, household chores, or other interruptions. With the sun on your back and a hoe in your hands, deeply mull over your choices. You will discover that gardening is more than just creating beautiful flowers—it is a true therapy that helps us cope with the challenges of life.

february 9

So often the forces of nature and all the natural phenomena of spring pass unnoticed. We take for granted and hardly look. Why should I not devise my garden deliberately as an act of appreciation to the forces which bring about this ardent growth.

—William Tyler Page, nineteenth century

The forces that bring about the "ardent growth" of spring are invisible and elusive. Yet the first glimmerings seem the greatest miracles, for they rise up out of the cold heart of winter. Plan early color in your garden to experience this most satisfying of moments, when early quince, lilac, and witch hazel blossom. When we plant for the earliest spring color, we also nurture our spirituality, for both provide invaluable respite from the inevitable and unexpected return of winter.

Acts and Affirmations

Make a special effort to notice the tiny bulbs this spring, those too often passed over for the riotous color of bigger modern hybrids. Watch for the little crocus poking up through ice and snow. Search out the blue grape hyacinth, hardly more than a tuft of grass but bearing unique flowers. When you find them, it is cause for celebration, for there is life in the ground that proves that the forces of nature and life shall never be denied.

species tulips

When you find a tulip described as genus and species, it is not a fancy hybrid but one very close to its original state when first discovered aeons ago. Species or botanical tulips tend to be very rugged plants, not as tall and showy as the hybrids but perfect for naturalizing. Exotic *Tulipa turkestanica*, pink *Tulipa bakeri*, red *Tulipa wilsoniana*, and *Tulipa humilis* are some of those little glimmering gems that are strewn before us in spring. When we discover their true carefree beauty, they become clear visions of those mystical powers that manifest so dramatically at the close of winter.

february 10

All flesh is grass, and all its beauty is like the flower of the field: The grass withers, the flower fades, when the breath of the Lord blows upon it; surely the people is grass. The grass withers, the flower fades; but the word of our God will stand forever.

—Isaiah 40:6–8

This is perhaps the most beautiful passage in the Bible, and it has been borrowed by authors and poets for centuries. "All flesh is grass" and all living things are upon the earth but for a short span of time. Thus the earth and its Creator exist infinitely, and it is in them we may place our faith, not in people or other short-lived things. It is like the constructed parts of the garden, the paving or walls that remain long after the plants have died out. God is the stone and concrete, the earth our soil, and we are the flowers that flesh out the garden, coming and going like the grass. But although all flesh lives for just a short time, our faith in God merits the rewards of eternity.

Acts and Affirmations

If you live in the countryside, take a weekend to visit old cemeteries. It was common in the nineteenth century to plant grave sites with daffodil, jonquil, and narcissus bulbs because they could be counted on to survive marauding gophers and absence of care. As the originals multiplied, they spread into great patches that, when illuminated by the early spring sun, appear as though the souls of the deceased have risen to hover in golden clouds above their graves.

february 11

Feast of Our Lady of Lourdes

O ever Immaculate Virgin, Mother of mercy, health of the sick, refuge of sinners, comforter of the afflicted, you know my wants, my troubles, my sufferings; look with mercy upon me. By appearing in the Grotto of Lourdes, you were pleased to make it a privileged sanctuary, whence you dispense your favors; and already many sufferers have obtained the cure of their infirmities, both spiritual and corporal.

—Prayer of Our Lady of Lourdes

The famous Grotto of Lourdes has become the world's most often visited place of miraculous healing. It became the place where the Virgin appeared to a poor young girl, Bernadette, and later a spring began to flow with water that heals the body. Lourdes is a more recent, twentieth-century example of healing waters that were originally sacred to the nature spirits, then earth goddesses, and finally the Virgin Mary. This holy water is sent around the world and is treasured by those seeking both physical and emotional healing.

Acts and Affirmations

The water of Lourdes may never be sold—it may only be given away. (see the address in Resources). The healing properties of the water are released with faith, and many people regularly anoint themselves as proof of their trust in the Virgin. Many who may not have found the body healed by the water have greatly benefited from its effect on the soul and the ability to cope with daily infirmity.

february 12

The Psalmist compares a godly man to a tree that is planted by rivers of water, whose leaf shall not wither,—seeing in the stateliness and beauty of such a tree an emblem of the noble virtues of the human heart.

—Wilson Flagg, *A Year Among the Trees*, 1890

These days, we do not talk much of virtues, because all things have become negotiable. But when society neglects virtues such as charity, love, fidelity, and faith, the community disintegrates into chaos. Though we may reject these values as outdated, over time the consequences of such negligence will present themselves in ugly ways. It is the same in the garden: the virtues of growing plants are the horticultural rules that guide our work. We know that failure to adhere to these will cause plants to decline or die. Let us never be blinded to the fact that human survival—and that of gardens—is based on laws, and if these are ignored, ill fortune inevitably follows.

Acts and Affirmations

No matter what your religious affiliation, you will find the Book of Psalms in the Bible inspiring because of the abundance of natural references. The often quoted twenty-third Psalm states, "In green pastures you let me graze, to safe waters you lead me . . . ," illustrating how green, natural places are so deeply restorative. If you have never read the Psalms, start each day with a single psalm and discover how these songlike poems are enriched with nature-based spirituality.

february 13

There is a divine urge in all of us, the urge to want to create something ourselves, and poor indeed is the person who has lost it, who takes no heed of it. The old fable puts it correctly: If you want the power (the joy), do the thing yourself! You must work in your garden a bit to get the most out of it. You must put something of yourself into it, or it will never truly be yours! The law is absolute. And the joy you take in a garden is usually in proportion to the amount of yourself you have invested in it!

—Edith Knapp Bhermann

Our gardens become an intimate reflection of who we are. The flowers we choose are a sign of our natures, whether romantic or more practical. Our trees are a subconscious symbol of immortality. The formality of the landscape may indicate our need to control, and a dozen other human qualities are reflected there. Thus the garden is so personal a place that, like human beings, no two are exactly alike. In fact, no two gardens are even somewhat alike, as each site, its solar exposure, soil, and gardener are extraordinarily unique.

Acts and Affirmations

I will invest more of my personal nature into my garden this year. I will grow plants that appeal to me, not to impress others. I will consider each hour spent during these early spring days an investment that will yield much fruit later on. For my unique, personal vision will become tangible as trees leaf out, shrubs blossom, and the grass turns green with the warming days to come.

february 14

Valentine's Day

Perhaps the old monks were right when they tried to root love out; perhaps the poets are right when they try to water it. It is a blood-red flower, with the colour of sin; but there is always the scent of a god about it.
—Olive Schreiner, *The Story of an African Farm*, 1883

Valentine's Day does not have much to do with love. The true root of this romantic day dates to the Middle Ages, when the feast of St. Valentine was first recognized. It marked the day birds began to choose their mates. It was also recognized as the beginning of spring. This is a good example of how the feast days of saints were integrated into agricultural seasons. As the birds found mates, farmers began mating livestock for spring births. Taking our cue from the animals, let us celebrate Valentine's Day as the time of sexual coming together of all living things on earth.

Acts and Affirmations

Instead of offering a bouquet of a dozen red roses to your lover, try the old Roman idea of using the petals rather than the whole flower. Buy the most fragrant hothouse roses you can find in any color. Carefully pluck the whole petals off the stems. Then strip your bed down to the bottom sheet and sprinkle the petals over its whole surface. Replace the top sheet and blanket to capture the scent, and when the time comes to make love on Valentine's Day, you will do so in a fragrant bed of roses.

february 15

A garden, whether formal or natural, must be cared for, and even those natural plantings are not so easy to maintain as they look. The weeds that Jesus spoke about, the weeds of worldly desires and cares and frustrations, must all be pulled out. Of course, no gardener would expect his flower beds to weed themselves, but God does expect it of us because we have both hearts and minds.

—Marcia Hollis, *Down to Earth*, 1971

Stress causes damage to both the mind and the physical body. The process of spiritual growth is an effort to transcend these negative influences through a higher state of consciousness. A discipline of the mind keeps us from bouncing off every negative force until we are bruised and battered. A good spiritual practice is to recognize sources of stress and negative thoughts as soon as they germinate and to consciously refuse to tend them, like a gardener pulls out weeds. This practice makes room for beautiful flowers to grow.

Acts and Affirmations

Stresses are the weeds of our spiritual life. As you pull these tough weeds from the garden, save a few pieces and put them in special places around the house. Put one in your wallet, one taped to the bathroom mirror, one over the kitchen sink, and on your desk at work. They are little reminders to rise above the stress and remember that the most important part of life is to allow your higher self to emerge.

february 16

She is the mother of all, for contained in her are the seeds of all. The earth of mankind contains all moistness, all verdancy, all germinating power.
—HILDEGARD VON BINGEN, *Meditations*, twelfth century

The writings of Hildegard, the great medieval abbess who wrote extensively about God, the earth, and plants, still speak to us. She wrote often about "verdancy" or the greenness of the botanical world. Her vision was that the earth as the ultimate mother gave birth to all through her dark and fertile soils. Hildegard wrote about the intense spiritual energy of spring, which fueled the quickening or greening of the year. More important, she wrote of an energy so pervasive it influenced humanity in terms of health and the condition of the soul. Not until many centuries later were these same ideas rediscovered by contemporary ecospiritualists such as John Muir, Ralph Waldo Emerson, Rachael Carson, and Aldo Leopold (Thoreau).

Acts and Affirmations

Hildegard believed that plants were valuable to the health of the body and the spirit. She recommended herbal leaf and root tonics, which contain important vitamins that were often lacking in the winter diet of peasants and farmers. From this, the old-fashioned spring tonic was born—a rich liquid of simmered leaves and roots that fortified the system and stimulated the organs. There are dozens of recipes for spring tonic, but here is a simple one: Gather a handful of fresh dandelion leaves and simmer gently in two cups of water for fifteen minutes. Strain off the liquid and drink while still warm. Nobody said it tastes good! Add honey if desired.

february 17

It was the act of a lofty spirit to examine the hidden places of the nature of things, and not content with their exterior to look into, and descent into, the deep things of God.

—Lucius Annaeus Seneca, first century A.D.

Some people are content to merely look at a forest or gaze on a garden. Though visually inspired by the beauty, they lack the desire to look closer at the hidden places where far greater mysteries reside. A botanist does not just know the plants; he or she understands the unique order that defines what plants grow together, how they help one another, and the subtle distinctions among them. As the deeper gardeners gaze into the mystical world of plants, the more they realize that a palpable force, perhaps God, does indeed dwell there. For few humans on earth can make such a discovery and fail to believe that something quite powerful with supreme logic has designed these perfect and complex botanical miracles.

Acts and Affirmations

Looks are deceiving, and just as the physical beauty of a person does not reflect who they truly are inside, the looks of a landscape or plant do not tell its story, either. Strive to become a better observer of every landscape to experience its true nature. Don't just go to the brightest masses of color; learn to recognize the subtle pastels, the rich greens and browns. Single out the trees and shrubs with an eye for the texture of their bark. Next time you remove a dead plant, take a moment to study the nuances of its remarkable roots.

february 18

The branches of the Tuba tree, the tongue reciting the Koran, the roses there in Paradise, their fragrance is Allah, Allah . . .

—Yunus Emre, Anatolia mystic, 1240

The poetry of the Arab world is wrought with symbols of plants and gardens. Plants define the image of heavenly paradise, which is central to their religious conciousness. All of creation stems from the archetypal garden of Paradise, filled with beautiful flowers and rivers, with trees loaded in fruit and shade from spreading palms. To people in virtually every culture, the garden became the most appropriate metaphor for life. This is because, until recently, plants provided virtually everything essential to survival: shelter, food, medicine, and clothing. Therefore gardens speak to us on a more subconscious level, serving as a universal link that binds our species on this single horticultural plane.

Acts and Affirmations

Beautiful ceramic tiles were often integrated into Persian gardens to provide bright colors during the long, dry season when few plants bloomed. This idea is as beautiful in a modern office as in a Persian garden. Seek out an exceptional multicolored tile to keep at your desk to set a coffee mug on or to use as a paperweight.

february 19

But my garden is nearer, and my good hoe as it bites the ground revenges my wrongs & I have less lust to bite my enemies. I confess I work at first with a little venom, lay to a little unnecessary strength. But by smoothing the rough hillocks, I smooth my temper; by extracting the long roots of the piper grass, I draw out my own splinters; & in a short time I can hear the Bobalink's song & see the blessed deluge of light & colour that rolls around me.

—Ralph Waldo Emerson, journal, 1839

There is no better place to work out anger and frustration than in gardens. The harder the physical work, the better it soothes the furious heart. Not only do we release our aggressions, but the beautiful surroundings remind us what a futile thing the temper can be. It is as though all the fury travels down the rake or the shovel like lightning to bury itself in the good earth, leaving us free to return to living refreshed and renewed.

Acts and Affirmations

Avoid internalizing your anger. Medical research shows that quiet anger can be far more damaging than explosive temper tantrums. If you internalize your anger, use the garden as therapy by going out to hack at the stubborn grasses and yank on the deep-rooted weeds. Cultivate your garden vigorously with hoe or spading fork. In the process, you will find your anger has given way to spiritual calm.

february 20

> *It was our Indian rule to keep our fields very sacred. We did not like to quarrel about our garden lands. One's title to a field once set up, no one ever thought of disputing it; for if one were selfish and quarrelsome, and tried to seize land belonging to another, we thought some evil would come upon him, as that some of his family would die.*
>
> —BUFFALO BIRD WOMAN, as told to Gilbert L. Wilson, 1917

It was an enormous amount of work to clear land with nothing but fire-hardened sticks, antlers, and bone hoes. Such effort meant that a garden was highly valued among the Hidatsa and other farming tribal peoples. It was not that the people owned the land, they simply staked their claim to garden upon it. For them there was a spirituality about the field, for their whole ceremonial year was centered around the activities of the field. We too may find deeper meaning in our own gardens if we considered them simply rented from the Great Spirit. And if we structure our year around the seasons and activities in our gardens, we not only find meaning but live it close to the Native American way.

ACTS AND AFFIRMATIONS

Tobacco was used as a sacred offering in the Americas. When not smoked by shamans or used in sealing treaties, it was ignited and held up to the winds as a sacrifice to the spirits. If you grow native tobacco, or use the commercial Burley types, this simple ceremony of burning evokes the ancient spirituality of the indigenous peoples. They recognized the power of its smoke in sanctifying sacred places, homes, and gardens. To make a pipe offering of your own, simply arrange a small amount of tobacco in your garden in a ceramic dish and light it. Then stand so the dish faces north, then south, east, and west, as the smoke rises on the wind.

(*Nicotiana rustica*)

santo domingo ceremonial tobacco

The very potent annual tobacco called Santo Domingo was a sacred plant cultivated by the Pueblo tribes. It is very similar to the tobacco grown by Plains tribes of the upper Midwest, where it was smoked during important ceremonies in long-stemmed pipes. It was used as both a ritual and a medicinal plant. Among the Hidatsa, this crop was unique, for while all others grown for food were cultivated by women, tobacco was strictly a man's plant. This very ancient plant is enjoyed for its spiritual beauty and night-blooming flower. Find seeds through heirloom and Native American seed sources, and grow it like any warm-season annual.

february 21

Yew trees live to a great age, the timber is hard, the leaves are poisonous, and the berries are red. So the yew was a protective, offensively defensive tree, one of the best to plant by your house, and the very best to make into bows. The yew beside the house, near to the gables and the chimneys, not only protected but looked comforting. It tied the house to the landscape.
—Geoffrey Grigson, *The Englishman's Flora*, 1955

In many English churchyards are two things: a yew tree and a standing stone. The stones date back to the Bronze Age, and the great old yews were planted before the Norman Conquest in 1066. The yew is a tree of Hecate, goddess of death and witchcraft, probably due to the fact that few plants grow under a yew and the effects of its highly poisonous foliage. The yew reminds us that what we plant may have ties to ancient civilizations. Who is to say their myths and magic are not still powerful? Perhaps it is our beliefs that make the magic. To grow such plants is a sign of faith in the old ways, of protection and defense, of comfort and wisdom.

Acts and Affirmations

Since pre-Christian times, the English yew, *Taxus baccata*, was considered protective around the house as well as the churchyard. Its stiff upright growth was resistant to wind damage, which allowed it to live to a great age. To protect your house in this ancient European way, plant a yew in the garden. If you grow it by the front porch, as women often did, the goddess Hecate will dwell there to head off any practical magic that might accidentally slip inside.

february 22

George Washington's Birthday

I know of no pursuit in which more real and important services can be rendered to any country than by improving its agriculture, its breed of useful animals, and other branches of a husbandman's cares.
—George Washington, letter, July 1794

The early settlers of the American colonies were farmers seeking religious freedom. They took on the awesome task of carving a life out of the New World wilderness. That began a great American tradition that links spirituality to the earth—one that continues to this day on a smaller scale in our gardens. The story of George Washington and the cherry tree illustrates how much the Americans fleeing the treachery of the English monarchy valued truthfulness and straightforwardness. This is our heritage—one composed of the freedom to follow any spiritual path through cultivation of the soul to the truth that inevitably follows.

Acts and Affirmations

The legend of George Washington and the cherry tree has made this species a symbol of truth in American culture. Yet in recent years the division between truth and untruth has eroded. Let the spring cherry blossoms remind us that we can never be wholly spiritual if we are unable or unwilling to distinguish a lie from the truth. It is only through clear and unquestionable truth that the soul can evolve into a state of spiritual peace.

february 23

ROMAN FEAST OF TERMINALIA

And so we ask for peace for the gods of our fathers, for the gods of our native land. It is reasonable that whatever each of us worships is really to be considered one and the same. We gaze up at the same stars, the sky covers us all, the same universe compasses us. What does it matter what practical systems we adopt in our search for the truth. Not by one avenue only can we arrive at so tremendous a secret.

—ROMAN SENATOR QUINTUS AURELIUS SYMMACHUS, fourth century

Terminalia, the last festival of the Roman year, honored the god Terminus, protector of all land boundaries. Property lines were marked with special hewn stones to assert ownership, and it was at these stones that the spirits of the land resided. On this festival the spirits were offered sacrifices of wine and honey to encourage their protection of the family and its gardens. Our garden is like that Roman landscape, and the corners of our plots are as important to our sense of place as they were to the Romans nearly two millennia ago. For within their protection the landscape changes from the chaotic, untended wilderness to the ordered creation of our labors.

ACTS AND AFFIRMATIONS

Celebrate Terminalia in your own garden this day, while life is still dormant. Before you prepare to turn the soil, toast the land with a good Italian red wine, aged cheese, and a freshly baked baguette. Share it with someone special, and then pour a few drops of wine at each corner of your garden and bury a crust of bread there to protect what lies within.

february 24

MARDI GRAS (FAT TUESDAY)

Carnival is a butterfly of winter whose last real flight of Mardi Gras forever ends its glory. Another season is the season of another butterfly, and the tattered, scattered, fragments of rainbow wings are in turn the record of his day.

—PERRY YOUNG, *The Mistick Krewe*

The advent of spring is steeped in pagan fertility rites of the Old World. The season of Lent is a unique example of how pagans, Romans, and finally Catholics celebrated their rites of purification that marked the end of winter. During the forty days of Lent that begin on Ash Wednesday and continue until the lunar resurrection festival of Easter, Catholics are expected to abstain from all fats. Fat Tuesday is the last day before the period of denial. The faithful "pigged out" with a festival of debauchery that became "butter week" and finally Fat Tuesday (Mardi Gras). Although Mardi Gras is now a party celebrated by Catholics and non-Catholics alike, it is a day rooted deeply in faith.

ACTS AND AFFIRMATIONS

The official colors of Fat Tuesday are purple for justice, green for faith, and gold for power. Decorate your home or garden altar with beads in these colors or candy coins, which are also traditional gifts of this last great day before the symbolic winter of Lent.

february 25

ASH WEDNESDAY (VARIES)

To everything there is a season, and a time to every purpose under the heaven:
a time to be born and a time to die; a time to plant, and a time to uproot . . .
—ECCLESIASTES 3:1–8

It is traditional on this first day of Lent to be anointed with ashes of burned palm fronds from the Palm Sunday mass the year before. A dark smudge on the forehead is a sign of seasonal completion, the ashes representing the death of winter and the spiritual death that results from sin. Whether our sin is as benign as a little gossip or as real as adultery, sin destroys our life piece by piece. But our lives may be rekindled from the darkness, just as the earth is reborn in the spring. When we celebrate the seasons and rituals, we learn a pattern of living—one that invites us to introspection and contemplation of our sins followed by a fresh start each spring.

ACTS AND AFFIRMATIONS

Ashes contain potash, one of the three most important nutrients to plants. It has long been traditional to scatter fireplace or woodstove ashes around the base of fruit trees or into the soil of a kitchen garden. This is a perfect day to clean out your fireplace and spread the ashes atop the winter soil. Let it be your symbolic act to celebrate the death of dark winter and the preparation for the new sun-filled life of spring.

february 26

I am a bird of God's garden, I do not belong to this dusty world.
For a day or two they have locked me up in the cage of my body.
I did not come here of myself, how should I return of myself? He who brought me must take me back again to my own country.

—Jalal-Ud-Din Rumi, *The Masnawi*, thirteenth century

If the soul is immortal, then we come to this life but for a short time. We were created in God's garden, and it is natural to want to re-create that same holy place for ourselves here on Earth. If we are reincarnated, perhaps those of us who have lived and gardened before return with an irresistible compulsion to make ever greater landscapes. Each life and garden contributes to our body of understanding over the span of many living voyages to Earth. The wisdom and experience of former lives become manifest as our hands fashion earthly versions of God's garden. And with each rebirth, our gardens become closer to the perfection that is Paradise.

Acts and Affirmations

If we are all reincarnated to attain perfection over many lifetimes, imagine how many times Vita Sackville-West must have lived before she could conjure a garden such as Sissinghurst? If we are to live again and again, let us spend more time learning about gardens and tending them. Perhaps if we gain enough wisdom, our cumulative time on Earth will leave behind a single great garden for the world to enjoy long after we have returned to God's garden in a final state of perfection.

february 27

Nature, in its ministry to man, is not only the material, but is also the process and the result. All the parts incessantly work into each other's hands for the profit of man. The wind sows the seed; the sun evaporates the sea; the wind blows the vapor to the field; the ice, on the other side of the planet, condenses rain on this; the rain feeds the plant; the plant feeds the animal; and thus the endless circulations of the divine charity nourish man.

—Ralph Waldo Emerson, *Commodity*, 1844

What may appear to be merely the simple act of growing a plant is far more than we realize. Emerson illustrates the long progression of natural processes that helps our efforts. Though we water the plant with the garden hose, this water can be traced back to its source—evaporation from the sea that condenses and then falls as rain. The water then runs off into rivers and flows back to the sea once again. Remember this each time you water the garden, because this endless circulation is divine charity that quenches our thirst, nourishes our lands, and replenishes our well of spiritually.

Acts and Affirmations

February is the month of false spring, when rare warm days bring us out into the sunshine. Make a point of going out on sunny days this month, and let the rays soak into your bare skin to enliven the cells with solar energy. Intense sunlight this time of year is truly a divine gift to help you get through the dreariness of the end of winter.

february 28

Yet save me, Lares of my fathers! Ye too did rear me when I ran, a little child before your feet. And feel it not a shame that ye are made of but an ancient tree-stock. Then faith was better kept, when a wooden god stood poorly garbed in a narrow shrine. His favor was won when a man had offered a bunch of grapes as first fruits, or laid the spiky garland on the holy hair.
—Caius Catullus, first century

Sacred places exist around the world on both large and small scales. They include the monumental standing stones henges of Britain, the earth at the ruins of the great temple at Jerusalem, and the stones of Mecca—ordinary places made hallowed by different faiths. The courtyard altars of Roman houses were considered equally as sacred, though much smaller altars ensconced the household gods honored on special occasions. We lack places of meaning in our homes today but may reclaim this ancient tradition by dedicating a special part of household or garden to things relevant to our personal spiritual paths. With a bit of careful thought and the use of meaningful symbols, colors, and choice surroundings, we may pause there each day to rekindle a deeper awareness of spiritual belonging just as the Romans did two millennia ago.

Acts and Affirmations

We have much to learn about the sanctity with which Roman families treated their *lares*. When Vesuvius erupted, the citizens of Pompeii fled with their sacred statues rescued from courtyard altars. This devotion illustrates a personal relationship with the gods. It was a common tribute on holy days to leave flowers and offerings on these altar tables. Our garden shrines can be equally as personal, so that when we celebrate or grieve, we do so intimately before our own *lares* that protect us.

march

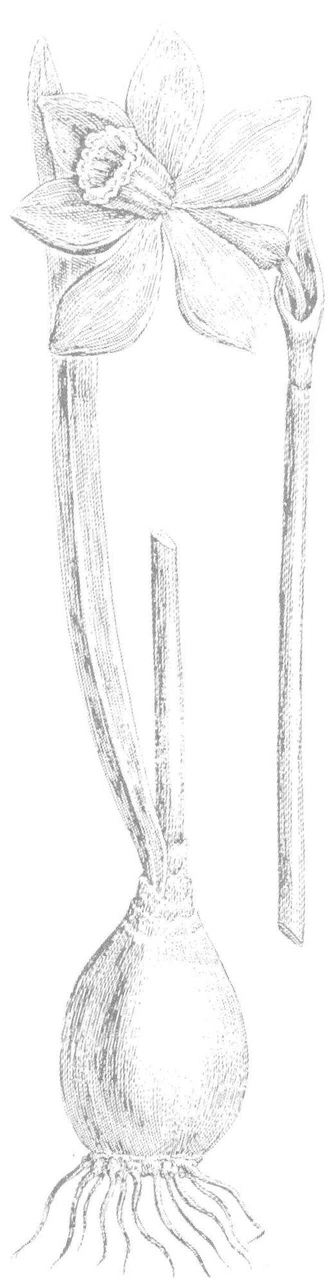

Until the eighteenth century, March, not January, was considered the beginning of the year because it is the start of the traditional agricultural year. Most cultures shared the belief that March would be an unpredictable weather month.

In England it rains in February, and farmers prayed for the winds of March to dry the fields enough for them to sow and plant.

In fact, the expression "A dry March never begs for bread" refers to the sowing of wheat on time, for if the sowing is delayed, the crop may not have time to fully ripen before the early frost of autumn.

The flowers of this month are daffodils, which includes the daffodil itself and its cousins, jonquil and narcissus. Their bulbs bloom from midwinter to early spring. These flowers found their way from the Mediterranean to China, where the tazetta species became the sacred Lily of China and a treasured emblem of spring.

CHEROKEE
STRAWBERRY MOON

march 1

St. David's Day,
Patron of the Welsh

Some people still follow, no matter how unthinkingly, lessons they first learned hundreds of years ago, and just as bears coming out of their winter sleep will eat mightily of certain leaves and berries to awaken themselves for the time of frolicking and love, so country people instinctively eat such things as dandelions in the spring . . .
—M. F. K. Fisher, *A Cordial Water*, 1961

The coming of March is a doorway into spring, although it is notorious for its winds and fickle weather. Until the twentieth century it was a time when edible greens were scarce, and after a long winter the poor of the countryside went searching for the first few leaves of spring. We cannot appreciate how welcome the greens were for those with a limited diet, for by now the stored apples and potatoes were running out or rotted. It is no wonder that many wayside pot greens were under the patronage of a variety of saints, gods, and goddesses who ensured they were plentiful in this difficult and lean time of year.

Acts and Affirmations
Greens are God's medicine chest, and they belong in our gardens. Leaf crops can be surprisingly resistant to cold, sprouting from seed despite cooler temperatures. Rather than spend money on vitamins, plant natural vitamin-rich greens such as spinach, kale, and chard and spend time at home tending them in these cool days of spring.

(*TARAXACUM OFFICINALE*)

dandelion

The common dandelion is easily identified by yellow flowers that turn into a ball of feathery seeds beloved by children. They may be considered stubborn weeds by lawn owners, but to European peasants and winter-weary American pioneers, dandelion leaves offered a much-needed edible green and "spring tonic." During abnormally cold winters, when crops failed or drought struck, it was this common wayside weed that saved whole villages. Now when you look into those bright daisy flowers, you may see the very soul of this misunderstood little plant.

march 2

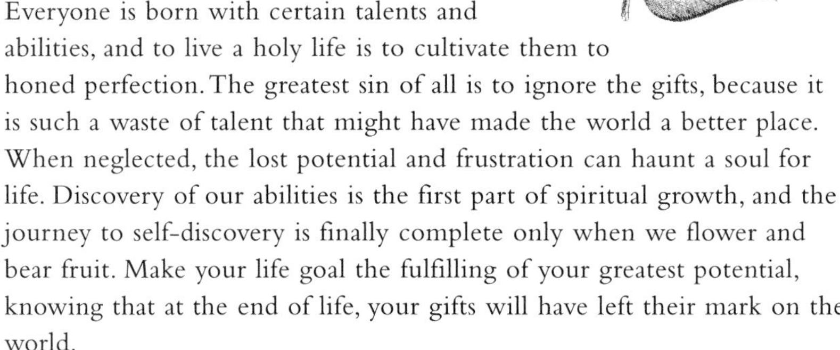

The pale flowers of the dogwood outside this window are saints. The little yellow flowers that nobody notices on the edge of that road are saints looking up into the face of God. This leaf has its own texture and its own pattern of veins and its own holy shape, and the bass and trout hiding in the deep pools of the river are canonized by their beauty and their strength.

—Thomas Merton, *Seeds of Contemplation*, 1949

Everyone is born with certain talents and abilities, and to live a holy life is to cultivate them to honed perfection. The greatest sin of all is to ignore the gifts, because it is such a waste of talent that might have made the world a better place. When neglected, the lost potential and frustration can haunt a soul for life. Discovery of our abilities is the first part of spiritual growth, and the journey to self-discovery is finally complete only when we flower and bear fruit. Make your life goal the fulfilling of your greatest potential, knowing that at the end of life, your gifts will have left their mark on the world.

Acts and Affirmations

A dogwood tree does not try to live up to the potential of an oak. I, too, shall never set my own potential by the standards of others. My God-given talents and abilities are mine alone, and I will strive to recognize and cultivate them. Just as a tree must be cared for many years before it reaches perfection, so my spiritual life requires nurturing as I travel ever closer to the light of fulfilled potential.

march 3

But was there ever such a spring? Did orchards ever before praise God with such choral colors? The whole landscape is aglow with orchard radiance. The hillsides, the valleys, the fields, are full of blossoming trees.
—HENRY WARD BEECHER, *The Month of Apple Blossoms*

Spring is never exactly the same from one year to the next. Our winter dreams of the nature of the spring are often filled with expectations that may be fulfilled by warm temperatures and just the right amount of rain to make plants grow and bloom perfectly. But years come that are cold into summer, when the rain never seems to stop, when the plants rot and flowers flop over in the mud. In both the garden and in life, great expectations can lead to equally great disappointments. Perhaps it is best to look toward spring humbly, so that if it is dismal, we may take the delay in stride. But if it is glorious, we rejoice at its unexpected wonders.

ACTS AND AFFIRMATIONS

If you live close to orchard country, take a drive to see the blossoming of the trees. The beauty of a single flowering tree in your yard is nothing compared to a whole field of them, with the air scented and the place humming with the sound of bees. It is an important experience for children, who often lack a tangible link between the supermarket fruit and the majestic parade of trees and buds and flowers that must come before.

march 4

Man without God is a seed upon the wind: driven this way and that, and finding no place of lodgement and germination.
—T. S. Eliot, *Complete Poems and Plays*, 1952

We as humans are all seekers. We long to find the right direction, the path that leads to contentment. For many, the path is strewn with things of the world, such as wealth, beauty, indolence, and sex, but rarely do any of these satisfy. They always seem more attractive while one longs for them, but once we get them, we feel a lingering emptiness that drives us to search still further. The only true path to contentment is that of the spirit. It doesn't matter whether we seek it in a church or in nature: what truly matters is that we stick to our spiritual path so that the winds of the world do not blow us away and our seeds can germinate with roots pressed deeply into the fertile soil of the soul.

Acts and Affirmations

The seed of the cottonwood tree, like many plant species, relies on its lighter-than-air fibers to help it travel. These seeds seek the right environment, usually one of adequate moisture, where they are likely to sprout. Moisture saturates the fibers, making them heavy and limp, preventing the seed from traveling farther. This spring, take note of the fibrous seeds all around you, and when they travel through the air, let them remind you of your spiritual life. Every aspect of that seed and its fluff is expressly created to find fertile, moist ground, just as every person is born with a desire to find spiritually fertile ground to nourish the soul.

march 5

But to plant, you have to dig. And in digging, you get muddy. There was mud on my shoes, and my face, and my hands, and I thought what a mess it was and what a chore it would be to get all cleaned up. My foot sank into the mud around the newly planted tree and I remembered the innocent joy of getting dirty.

—Marcia Hollis, *Down to Earth*, 1971

It is bare-root season in the garden when winter thaws and the sap begins to move. This is a special time of year when young dormant trees are dug out of the ground to be sold bare root—without any earth around the roots at all. What appear to be dead sticks contain incredible life force, and we plant them believing in their ability to grow as the weather warms. Some swear that trees planted bare root develop better root systems than a container-grown plant of the same age. To seize this growing edge, we bundle up to go out into the mud to plant during the dormant season. Perhaps the bare-root tree is the most perfect plant to represent our spiritual life. Seeds of spirituality sown deep early in life before maturity improve the quality of day-to-day living. These slow to mature roots of faith will sustain us better in the long run and provide the strength needed to stand up to the inevitable challenges of the future.

Acts and Affirmations

Plant a bare-root tree as a symbolic act of faith. Bare roots may seem to be dead, but they are full of life and grow vigorously once established. In no other plant does the miracle of life seem so dramatic. Our spiritual life is barren, too, when we first venture down the path of the soul. But when we summon faith, conscious growth follows, and we too will bear verdant green leaves and plentiful fruit.

march 6

JAPAN'S DAY
INSECTS AWAKEN

Nineteen centuries ago, when Pliny the Elder was writing his natural history in Rome, men believed that insects were creatures without blood, that butterfly eggs were drops of solidified dew, that echoes killed honey bees, and that gold was mined in the mountains north of India by a giant ant "the color of a cat and as large as an Egyptian wolf."
—EDWIN WAY TEALE, *Oddities of the Insect World*, 1952

Of all God's creatures, insects are at once the most beautiful and the most loathed and feared. Their numbers alone are inspiring, with an estimated two and a half million different species on earth. Although the actual worldwide population of each species is incalculable, insects are vital to the hidden processes of every ecosystem. Yet some of our most important species are under siege. Though echoes do not kill honeybees, pressures from Africanized bees and newly introduced diseases are threatening their numbers every day. Through such practices as organic gardening and leust-toxic pest control, gardeners can play a role in protecting insects. When we garden with them in mind, we can become vital to their very survival.

ACTS AND AFFIRMATIONS

Invasive and exotic species of plants threaten every region of the United States. It takes money and labor to control hydrilla weed in waterways, Japanese honeysuckle in the upper midwestern forests, and Australian melaleuca trees in the marshes of the Southeast. Express your support for environmental conservation by joining a group dedicated to preserving native plant communities. These protected wild places will become the last of native America in a rapidly changing world.

march 7

To live in right relation with his natural conditions is one of the first lessons that a wise farmer or any other wise man learns.
—Liberty Hyde Bailey, *The Holy Earth*, 1915

The "right relation" is the appropriateness of our gardens relative to the land and environment. Too often we impose some preconceived garden on the land that is not suitable to the environment. These gardens require extraordinary resources to make them thrive. Would you attempt to grow a verdant English garden with the limited water resources of the desert West, or grow desert plants in rainy England? The same applies to our own lives: when we force our lives in a direction that is not in right relation with our natural self, the inevitable struggle can become our undoing.

Acts and Affirmations

If you have found that your garden is demanding more and more of your time, perhaps it is because the landscape is not in "right relation with natural conditions." Many people are discovering that if they gradually replace high-demand plants with better adapted species, both native and exotic, they not only reduce maintenance but are able to limit the need for large amounts of water and chemicals as well. Begin this path toward making your garden better suited to local conditions.

march 8

Everybody needs beauty as well as bread, places to play and pray in, where Nature may heal and cheer and give strength to body and soul alike.

—John Muir, *Our National Parks*, 1901

We exist in an increasingly cold, technological world that threatens to consume our souls one tiny byte at a time. The separation from nature is so subtle that we rarely notice these rapid changes. Natural beauty offers a therapeutic effect on humanity, for we were created for that world, not the man-made one. We cannot measure nor define these effects, but John Muir recognized them nevertheless. It is not difficult, then, to conclude that we are meant to dwell in nature, but when we cannot venture into the wild due to our worldly obligations, we may at least spend some time in the microcosm of nature that is our garden. And when even this is impossible, we may simply contemplate a houseplant in the window.

Acts and Affirmations

God: Keep me ever mindful that it is more than bread that gives us life. You have surrounded me with places rich in natural beauty as another form of sustenance—that food vital to my spiritual well being. When I become too closely focused on my physical needs, remind me that my soul is equally as important to a whole and balanced life.

march 9

As the leaves of trees are said to absorb all noxious qualities of the air, and to breathe forth a purer atmosphere, so it seems to me as if they drew from us all sordid and angry passions, and breathed forth peace and philanthropy.
—WASHINGTON IRVING, *Sketch Book*, 1820

Many of the great naturalists of our time such as Henry David Thoreau, John Muir, and Theodore Roosevelt believed that the forests were sacred places that beneficially influenced the soul of man. Irving, too, pondered the ability of trees to change or improve our state of mind. Why do trees have such a calming effect on us? Perhaps it is because they are such magnificent living things. Maybe it is because they so powerfully change the whole environment that surrounds them. Or perhaps it is from childhood that we are taught to value trees because they cannot be quickly replaced. Just as trees are the perfect filters for polluted air, it is conceivable that they may also become our spiritual filters, sifting out the detritus of our chaotic lives to allow love and beauty to pass directly into our souls.

ACTS AND AFFIRMATIONS

Trees planted along parkways or sidewalks are the responsibility of the city, but as residents we enjoy them every day. If you are fortunate enough to have a parkway tree, take care of it as if it was your dear friend. Dress its wounds when careless drivers gouge it with car doors. Clip away the suckers at the base of the trunk and give it extra water in the dry season. It will return the favor by providing welcome shade, beauty, and cleaner, more oxygen-rich air. Remember, it takes a very short time to kill a tree but decades to grow a new one.

march 10

> *There are thoughts which are prayers. There are moments when, whatever the posture of the body, the soul is on its knees.*
>
> —Victor Hugo, *Les Misérables*, 1862

When you are down on your knees in the mud setting bulbs, pulling weeds, or planting flowers, your posture is one of great humility. It seems as though the getting down upon Mother Earth is in itself a physical form of prayer, for we rarely encounter the earth so intimately. Even when we are not sprawled out upon her, the thoughts of how we shall clothe and feed her can be construed as prayers. Therefore, whenever you kneel on the earth, think of it as a prayerful stance when your soul is closest to Mother Earth, the source of life.

Acts and Affirmations

An old Scottish prayer was said often during the spring primrose season (the English hybrid is called polyanthus). When you are on your knees in the mud of the early cold days of spring, remember this prayer, which thanks God for the beauty of these romantic little flowers: "Oh Lord, who painteth the petal of the polyanthus purple—shine down in all thy power."

march 11

Then with the sickle of the Truth of Karmic laws, the reaping of the Noble Life is practiced. The fruits, which are of truths sublime, are stored within the granary to which no concepts can apply. The gods engage in roasting and grinding this most precious food, which then sustains my poor humble self while I for truth am seeking.

—Life and Hymns of Milarepa, *A Buddhist Bible*, eleventh century

To live nobly, to mine each day for its spiritual fruit, is like cultivating an enormous garden for harvest over the coming year. The fruits and vegetables of spiritual food are put up in the root cellar of our soul to provision for the inevitable hard times to come. Though we may carve out a good life, there is always some rain that falls: deaths of loved ones, illness, or disappointments. When it comes, a full larder will make us strong enough to cope and eventually triumph rather than crumbling under heavy burdens.

Acts and Affirmations

When we practice the art of living spiritually through contemplation, meditation, scholarship, and prayer, we grow stronger through experience. To pray daily means prayer will come most naturally when we are in real need. To find the still center of our being while everything around us is in chaos can be difficult. But if we practice this process as we create and tend our gardens during the year, we reap a dual harvest: food for the home and for the soul.

march 12

It pushes aside the branches, fondles with its breath the olive tree that quivers with a silver smile, polishes the glossy grass, rouses the corollas that were not asleep, recalls the birds that had never fled, encourages the bees that were workers without ceasing; and then, seeing, like God, that all is well in spotless Eden, it rests for a moment on the ledger of a terrace which the orange-tree crowns with regular flowers and with fruits of light, and, before leaving, casts a last look over its labor of joy and entrusts it to the sun.

—Maurice Maeterlinck, *News of Spring*, 1898

Plants maintain a very unique relationship with the sun and are green because they contain chlorophyll, which reacts to sunlight. The many ways that plants relate to the sun parallel those of human spirituality. The plant always grows toward sunlight, and we grow spiritually when we are oriented down a clear path to God. Some flowers open with the sunrise and close at sunset, just as we are more healthy when we live by the sun. And plants feed themselves by photosynthesis, a process requiring energy from sunlight, just as we are energized by exposing ourselves to what is inspiring to the soul.

Acts and Affirmations

My spirit grows toward the light. It is drawn by the great powers of the universe to grow ever closer to the divine source of all energy. I may be drawn by the sun or by something vastly larger than the sun. But no matter what the origin of the energy, I will always strive to grow toward enlightenment every day of my life.

march 13

Dig a hole in your garden of thoughts. Into it put all your disillusions, disappointments, regrets, worries, troubles, doubts and fears and—forget. Cover well with the earth of fruitfulness, water it from the well of contentment. Sow on top again the seeds of hope, courage, strength, patience and love. Then, when the time of gathering comes, may your harvest be a rich and plentiful one.
—Anonymous

The expression "you get out of life what you put into it" is illustrated in this beautiful recipe for happiness. It does not say you win the lottery and run off into a blissful eternity, for that is not the true recipe for a fulfilling life. This garden recipe is a series of acts or ingredients that allow you to release negativity. Into the resulting void we pour fertile earth in which all good things grow. For nothing will thrive in a starved soil or a life weakened by inactivity and unwillingness to contribute. For only when we perform all these vital acts does the time of gathering come, and the harvest transforms life into a garden of plenty.

Acts and Affirmations

When you are sick or housebound, it can be difficult to bear the separation from the living plants outdoors, particularly during the cold winter months when even the view outside is colorless. To brighten the life of a housebound friend, acquaintance, neighbor, or relative, send them an amaryllis bulb, which you can order from a mail-order gardening catalog or full-service nursery. Better yet, visit them and bring one along all potted up. You have no idea how much the gradual flowering of an amaryllis can add a sense of expectation to the everyday act of waking up in the morning.

march 14

The Supreme Being does not build up nature around us, but puts it forth through us, as the life of the tree puts forth new branches and leaves through the pores of the old. As a plant upon the earth, so a man rests upon the bosom of God; he is nourished by unfailing fountains, and draws, at his need, inexhaustible power.

—Ralph Waldo Emerson, *Nature*, 1836

We tend to experience spring as outsiders looking in, but Emerson shows that spring occurs through us and that primal quickening during these warming months is something we cannot ignore. What is it that awakens the drive to turn the dark earth and to insert a tiny lifeless seed? Could it be a taste of the power of the Creator? Could it be something that we in our educated, technologically advanced culture have failed to recognize as one of the most elemental acts of humanity?

Acts and Affirmations

Grace is the blessings of God, the invisible energy gained from pleasing the Creator with our thoughtful, conscious actions. Let us fully respond to the call of spring by gardening, not merely as a compulsive response to spring, but as a conscious act of earning grace and thereby growing closer to the Creator and all that has been created.

march 15

IDES OF MARCH

I wish to preach, not the doctrine of ignoble ease, but the doctrine of the strenuous life.

—THEODORE ROOSEVELT, speech, 1899

Our bodies, the temples in which we dwell, are happiest when we are using all our faculties, both mental and physical. To garden, and to do it well, means we break a sweat now and then, we lift heavy things, pry recalcitrant plants from the soil, and execute our full range of movement while accomplishing a variety of tasks. Perhaps gardening lifts our spirits because the physical exertion releases the endorphins in our brain, or because physical labor is so absent from modern life that our bodies welcome it as a most natural act. Let no one tell you that spiritual happiness is found in luxury or the easy life because there is powerful yet intangible benefits to our entire being when we go out and labor upon the land.

ACTS AND AFFIRMATIONS

Theodore Roosevelt created our national park system because he felt the natural beauty of the United States is its greatest asset. Each park offers a different view of our diverse landscape, from the dark redwood glades of the Pacific Coast to the geysers of Yellowstone and the great swamps of Florida. Vow to visit as many as you can in the coming years while you are still young enough to hike through them. There you will find a deeper personal relationship with God through these breathtaking natural wonders.

march 16

By the transformation of Yang and its union with Yin, the five agents arise: water, fire, wood, metal and earth. When these five forces are distributed in harmonious order, the four seasons run their course. The five agents constitute the system of Yin and Yang, and Yin and Yang constitute one Great Ultimate.

—Chou Tun-Yi, eleventh century

When we garden, we come into a direct relationship with the fundamental elements of the universe. These same elements are recognized in whole or part by virtually every culture on earth. All agree water is critical to life. They identify the earth, or soil, as the sacred terrestrial realm. Fire is the destroyer and purifying element. Air, or ether, is the invisible spirit. The fifth element varies most often, based on the culture's values. To the Chinese it was metal; to the Hopi, corn. When we work intimately with these elements, we share something far more ancient than mere gardening. We touch that intangible link to the fundamental harmonies of the universe.

Acts and Affirmations

Contemplate the five elements of the natural world. What tree would be the fifth element in your area? In New England, it may be the maple tree. In Louisiana, the bald cypress. The process of identifying your fifth element will help you gain a greater understanding of how we identify with native plants, and how they sculpt our perception of the universe.

(*Phyllostachys aurea*)

bamboo

In the cultures of Asia, bamboo is among the most common plant to be included in the five elements. This is because bamboo, an enormous grass, fills many different needs. Timber bamboo is a strong and long-lasting building material for shelters. Smaller bamboos are used for virtually everything else, from kitchen implements to fencing. Bamboo grows quickly on marginal soils, producing a reliable and renewable fuel source. Even the sprouting clums are used as a common ingredient in Asian cuisine. No wonder it is the fifth element: it would be difficult to imagine life in these cultures without it.

march 17

FEAST OF ST. PATRICK

God is seen God
In the star, in the stone, in the flesh, in the soul and the clod.
—ROBERT BROWNING, *Saul*, 1855

St. Patrick was the fifth-century saint who converted the Irish to Christianity. He has had such a great influence because he understood that the Druids of northern Britain shared a reverence for nature. Their pagan religion recognized spirits in all things—the most powerful of which resided in ancient trees and the waters of holy wells. Once when he was preaching about the Holy Trinity to a group of Druid priests, they asked, "How can one be three?" Patrick reached down to pluck a clover to illustrate how a single leaf was divided into three sections. This small woodland plant has remained his hallmark ever since, linking contemporary Christianity to its predecessors in a beautiful blending of earth, botany, and spirit.

ACTS AND AFFIRMATIONS

Celebrate this festive Irish holiday with an ancient practice. Pick your clover leaf in the morning and wear it pinned to your clothing. Then at the end of the day, drop it into your last glass of drink—then toast to the health of all and pick it out again and toss over your left shoulder. St. Patrick's Day is also the traditional feast day on which peas are planted in Britain. As long as the soil is not frozen, you, too, should plant peas in the cool weather.

shamrocks galore

There is much confusion over exactly which clover is the original shamrock of St. Patrick. Two candidates are members of the pea family. Black medick, or *Medicago lupulina*, is a large annual clover. The other, white clover, *Trifolium repens*, is a perennial. A third plant considered the closest to the true shamrock is wood sorrel, *Oxalis acetosella*, which belongs to an entirely different family. Though it is quite similar to the other two, its flowers are tubular. No matter which clover you use on this day, when you wear the green in honor of the saint, remember how it symbolizes the Holy Trinity.

march 18

PALM SUNDAY (VARIES)

The next day the great crowd that had come for the Feast heard that Jesus was on his way to Jerusalem. They took palm branches and went out to meet him shouting, "Hosanna! Blessed is he who comes in the name of the Lord!"
—JOHN 12:13

Palm Sunday, which falls a week before Easter, celebrates Jesus' triumphant return to Jerusalem. The people waved palm fronds and laid them in front of him to pass over—a very old practice in Israel dating back to Old Testament times and the Feast of Tabernacles. The palm was prevalent at desert oases in the Middle East, and it came to signify life-giving water. It continues to this day to be an important symbol in Judeo-Christian rituals. Jews and Catholics integrate living palms into their celebrations, a rare example of ancient plant-related practices still practiced in contemporary religious ritual.

ACTS AND AFFIRMATIONS

If you can obtain a piece of palm blessed in Catholic mass this day, place it on your home altar or in a sacred space as a symbol of life for the coming year. To complete the devotion, burn the palm next year on Ash Wednesday and spread those ashes into the hallowed ground of your garden. This is a very ancient devotion that brings the ancient religions of the Holy Land into your house or garden.

march 19

Think not of God, my children, as a great tyrant sitting away up there in Heaven removed from you. Why, look down! There is a flower, and a blade of grass, and a stream, and a grain of sand—and that is God too! He is there! He is everywhere!

—Baal Shem Tov, *Discourses*, eighteenth century

Baal Shem Tov, the great leader of Hasidic Jews in Eastern Europe, stressed a joyous, enthusiastic worship of God, not just the mechanical following of ritual law. He taught his followers to find God everywhere—that all Creation was imbued with the sacred presence. Rather than seek out the hidden esoteric world, he inspires us to realize the presence of God in everyday things, whether a simple grain of sand or the most complex and beautiful flower in the garden. Such attention, which needs no great temple or endless texts to evoke God, is truly the source of well-rooted spirituality.

Acts and Affirmations

There are many programs devoted to helping Israel plant trees to improve the barren and eroded soils of their country. Plant a tree in the name of a loved one in the soil of the Holy Land by contributing to the Jewish National Fund (see Resources for address). Although you may never have a chance to make a pilgrimage to Jerusalem, purchase a legacy that will become a living monument for your family, friends, and loved ones.

march 20

Every morning the day is reborn among the newly blossomed flowers with the same message retold and the same assurance renewed that death eternally dies, that the waves of turmoil are on the surface, and the sea of tranquility is fathomless.

—Rabindranath Tagore, *Sadhana*, 1916

Rabindranath Tagore was a Nobel laureate who sought through stories and poems to reconcile the philosophies of the East and West. His work addressed the strife so prevalent in India during the colonial period, suggesting that through nature and the spirit the people could find peace. He reminds us that although the world may be chaotic and ugly on the surface, tranquillity still exists if we look for it. There is no better place to begin searching than in the garden each morning, where the day is reborn in peace, and in the heart of our newly blossomed flowers.

Acts and Affirmations

God: Make my garden a sea of tranquillity. Each morning remind me to greet the sun there so I will feel renewed and energized to meet the challenges of the new day.

march 21

VERNAL EQUINOX (VARIES)

If there is joy in meditation upon the sun and moon, the planets and fixed stars are the magic creation of the sun and moon; make thyself like unto the sun and moon thyselves.

—MILAREPA, *The Message of Miolarpina*, eleventh century

The art of meditation as shown by the Tibetan holy man Milarepa involves losing the self to the universe. And on this celestially auspicious occasion, when day and night lie in perfect balance, to meditate on the sun or moon becomes an exercise in harmony. In the garden world, it is the time when new growth quickens, when the light becomes stronger than the dark, and all things in nature feel the changes. As gardeners, we may share the promise that darkness has lost its strength and become wholly identified with the sun in its last quarter of rising into the summer solstice.

ACTS AND AFFIRMATIONS

Do not let the vernal equinox pass without a celebration. Toast the equilibrium of day and night with a good wine or beer and with a muffin made of whole wheat, sunflower seeds, and citrus fruit—all foods that symbolize the sun.

march 22

DEATH AND RESURRECTION OF ATTIS, ANCIENT ROME

If we lived in olden times among young mythologies, we should say that pines held the imprisoned spirits of naiads and water-nymphs, and that their sounds were of the water for whose lucid depths they always sighed.

—HENRY WARD BEECHER, *A Discourse on Trees*, 1870

Attis, son of the Roman goddess Cybele, was resurrected each year on this date with processions through Rome. Attis, often seen as the embodiment of all vegetation, was first identified with the pine tree and later oversaw all green and growing things. His priests were tattooed with ivy vines, and on this day they carried a freshly cut pine tree through the streets, its trunk swathed in woolen bands of cloth and the whole decked with wreaths and garlands of violets. An old statue of Attis in Rome depicts him carrying sheaves of wheat, fruit, pinecones, and pomegranates, all symbols of fertility. On this day all Romans celebrated, for it meant that Attis had risen again in the fields to turn the whole world green with spring.

ACTS AND AFFIRMATIONS

It is said that violets sprung from the blood of Attis, so it is appropriate to give these little flowers to friends on this and many other spring fertility feast days. It is also appropriate to give little bags of grain such as barley as a symbol of faith in an abundant future crop. We don't treasure fertility as people once did, but gardeners still look for a heavy crop, be it of flowers, grains, or tomatoes.

march 23

THE ANNUNCIATION
(LADY DAY)

O Mary, Mother, we pray to you; your life today with fruit was blessed. Give us the happy promise, too, that our harvest will be of the best. If you protect and bless the field, a hundredfold each grain must yield.
—CENTRAL EUROPEAN BLESSING OF THE GRAIN SEED

The Annunciation was the angel Gabriel's visit to the Virgin Mary informing her that she would conceive and bear a son. This date became deeply integrated into the agricultural year, for seed about to be sown in the fields would be blessed with the above rhyme and given to the Virgin's care. In Russia the priests also blessed wafers of bread to be shared by the family and workers—the remaining crumbs were deemed "Annunciation bread." These were sown into the soil to protect the new seedlings from blight, hail, frost, and drought. This holy day became many things to many people—an equinox celebration of the pagan Mother Nature, the dedication of spring wheat to the Virgin, and the incarnation of Christ.

ACTS AND AFFIRMATIONS

The angel Gabriel's role in the Annunciation earned him a place in agricultural folklore. Rhymes show how he was connected with the end of the coldest weather and the return of migratory birds. "When Gabriel does the message bring—return the swallows, comes the spring." Keep your eyes open for the first swallows of the season.

march 24

In the land of the living we ought to have a root. Let our root be there. That root is out of sight; its fruits may be seen, the root cannot be seen. Our root is our charity; our fruits are our works. It is needful that thy works proceed from charity; then is thy root in the land of the living.

—St. Augustine of Hippo, fourth and fifth centuries

The roots of our spirituality grow deeply, spreading unseen into each day of life. They should be fed through every aspect of living so that even our most mundane actions are supportive of our spiritual core. The three basic ways in which spirituality yields fruit are through faith, hope, and love. By maintaining our trust in God we live out our faith. By refusing to yield to despair, negativity, and evil, we turn our face toward hope in the future. And when we shower generous acts of love on those around us, we bear the fruit that makes the world a better place.

Acts and Affirmations

Strive to remain always in the land of the living by planting a good-size patch of strawberries. Each original will produce many daughter plants, just as each person who acts out their spiritual philosophies will spread their energy into the lives of others. Teach others that they, too, may enrich the world by potting up your strawberry daughter plants and giving them to friends. They in turn may spread their own daughter plants like a living chain letter that will bear fruit farther and more abundantly than you ever imagined.

march 25

The state of the crop in the surrounding farms alters the expression of the earth from week to week. The succession of native plants in the pastures and roadsides, which makes the silent clock by which time tells the summer hours, will make even the divisions of the day sensible to a keen observer. The tribes of birds and insects, like the plants punctual to their time, follow each other, and the year has room for all.

—RALPH WALDO EMERSON, *Nature*, 1836

Many old-time gardeners can tell the date by the kinds of plants that are in bloom. What Emerson means is that there is a perfect clock within nature, and each organism responds accordingly. A mosquito may not fly until dusk, when the birds are roosting. On a larger scale, flowers will not blossom before their time, either; the crocus, for example, is a child of the early spring, followed by tulips and lilacs. At the other end of the growing season blossom the asters and chrysanthemums, which no sunny day can coax to open before their time. To discover these nuances of season and time, of day, week, month, and quarter is to share in a divine schedule that is always miraculously accurate.

ACTS AND AFFIRMATIONS

To gain a deeper sense of the timing of things in and around your garden, keep a journal. Use a daybook to record the circumstances in which your flowers or native plants blossom or turn color in the fall. You may also note when insects appear and go away, which will tell you so much about their relationships with various plants. You will finish the season with a revelation of how ordered and logical nature's calendar is, and how much you had overlooked with each seasonal change.

march 26

Mata Syra Zemlja,
Slavic Day of the "Moist Earth Mother"

Earth, divine goddess, Mother Nature who generatest all things and bringest forth anew the sun which thou hast given to the nations; guardian of the sky and sea and of all gods and powers and through thy power all nature falls silent and then sinks in sleep.
—twelfth-century herbal guide

In Eastern Europe, it was forbidden to plow the earth before March 26 because the soil or "Moist Earth Mother" was not prepared for disturbance. Tilling soil too early in the season may actually damage the soil structure if it is cold and wet. Plowing cannot be forced, it must occur when the soil is dry enough and the days warm and ready to evaporate the moisture. As with all in life, we can work hard toward accomplishments, but we cannot force them if the time is not right. We must practice patience and look forward to the signs that it is time to pursue our goals.

Acts and Affirmations

When you till your kitchen garden, you must reconcile the days you have free to do the task and the date when the soil is ready for the spading fork or rototiller. Watch the weather closely and venture out to dig a test hole. While doing so, you may ask the Mother if she is ready to begin the birthing process with you, serving as both lover and midwife.

march 27

Easter (varies)

But Mary stayed outside the tomb weeping. And as she wept, she bent over into the tomb and saw two angels in white sitting there, one at the head and one at the feet where the body of Jesus had been. And they said to her, "Woman, why are you weeping?"

She said to them, "They have taken my Lord, and I don't know where they laid him." When she had said this, she turned around and saw Jesus there, but did not know it was Jesus.

"Woman, why are you weeping? Whom are you looking for?"

She thought it was the gardener and said to him, "Sir, if you carried him away, tell me where you laid him, and I will take him."

Jesus said to her, "Mary!"

—John 20:11–16

Mary Magdalene was granted the privilege of being the first human to see the risen Christ. But what is more fascinating is that she mistakes him for a gardener! This resurrection is the most holy day of Christendom; it proves that Jesus triumphed over death. No wonder the church placed this date when nature is resurrected from the cold death of winter to the warm light of spring. And Mary Magdalene becomes the personification of earth, which is given special value as the divine feminine in this intimate account.

Acts and Affirmations

It's tragic how many beautiful potted white lilies, *Lilium longiflorum*, go to waste after Easter. Make a point of resurrecting them from friends and family. Place plants in the sun either in their pots or planted out in the garden, where soil is well drained. Feed and water without saturating the soil so they may recover from the ordeal of forcing and bloom again for you the following spring.

march 28

Ostara, Anglo-Saxon
Goddess of Spring (varies)

Eostar, the name remains mysterious. The song breathes the pleasure and worship of ancient tillers of the soil in the labours of the earth and in the goods the mother gave. It has grown, it seems, out of the breast of earth herself; earth is here the Mother of Men.
—Grimm's Fairy Tales

Ostara is the Celtic goddess of the dawn and the fertility of spring in her many aspects. Here she rises out of the earth in her maiden form, bursting with new life. All symbols of fertility are associated with her: seeds, eggs, and rabbits—still a part of our contemporary Easter rites. These things came far earlier than Christ, yet they have lingered in a world that lies beneath the biblical religion. Her signs also include the budding of the trees, the very first flowers, and the greening of the hills with vivid slips of grass. She is truly the great goddess of the garden.

Acts and Affirmations

The hot-cross bun is a legacy of the Celtic wheel of the year with the cross on top representing the four quarters, or four seasons. On this day the buns were baked and eaten as a new year celebration. Celebrate the old pagan festival by baking sugar cookies with crosses, and color each quarter appropriately. Spring may be green for the earth mother, summer gold or blue to represent the sun or sky, autumn orange or red for fire, and winter white for snow.

march 29

PASSOVER (VARIES)

For the Lord your God is bringing you into a good land, a land with streams and springs and fountains issuing from plain and hill; a land of wheat and barley, of vines, figs and pomegranates, a land of olive trees and honey; a land where you may eat food without stint, where you will lack nothing; a land whose rocks are iron and from whose hills you can mine copper. When you have eaten your fill, give thanks to the Lord your God for the good land which was given to you.
—DEUTERONOMY 8:7–10

Passover is the most well known of all the Jewish festivals and marks the start of the grain harvest. Like Ostara and Easter, it is observed on a date set by the first full moon after the spring equinox. At the traditional Passover meal, called a Seder, unleavened bread and bitter herbs are eaten to recall the difficult times of the Israelites enslaved by the Pharaoh. When they were finally freed, they reached the promised land—a vision of a land of plenty that may be manifest in our gardens. When some of the food, or perhaps just the parsley and horseradish for the Seder, is grown in our home garden, the act of cultivating it becomes a link to the ancient days of the Torah and the promises of God in the land of Israel.

ACTS AND AFFIRMATIONS
We are blessed to own a small patch of earth for our garden. Jews in Europe were often barred from land ownership, which separated them from the earth for many centuries. It was rare to find a Jew who farmed or kept livestock, and this estrangement from things of the soil was healed by the sense of permanence found in modern Israel. Let us all learn from the forced wandering of Jews that every inch of our garden is a gift, and it is our sacred duty to cultivate this ground that God has provided to seal our covenant with the land.

march 30

I go into my library, and all history unrolls before me. I breathe the morning air of the world while the scent of Eden's roses yet lingered in it, while it vibrated only to the world's first brood of nightingales, and to the laugh of Eve. I see the pyramids building; I hear the shoutings of the armies of Alexander.

—Alexander Smith, *Dreamthorp*, 1863

Gardens are ancient places. They have existed in nearly every culture since the dawn of agriculture. Each civilization was defined by its crops, and the cultivation of fields ordered the seasonal calendar. Plants can tell the history of people and their links to a pantheon of gods, goddesses, and dieties that oversaw food creation. They held sway over the whims of weather and could spell plenty or famine and death. As gardeners, the more we learn about the ancient people who grew the same trees, vegetables, and flowers we do, the more profound the age-old act will seem.

Acts and Affirmations

Strive to become more intimate with the history of the plants you grow. The best place to start is to identify the correct botanical name according to genus (akin to a person's last name) and species (akin to a person's first name). Plants that share the same genera are closely related. Then take a more broad look at its family, which it shares with other plants that are closely related not by growth habit but by flower shape. Those with flowers typical of the pea family are members of *Leguminosae*, which includes huge trees as well as bush beans. Daisy flowers belong to the family *Compositae*. Look up the place of origin for your plant. That tells you what climate it prefers and points to the people who first brought it into cultivation. If you accomplish these things you will become intimate with both the plant and the botany that surrounds it.

march 31

Look at beauty as you look at beautiful clouds, and your mortal passions will be milder; listen to the song of lutes as you listen to the flowering water, what harm is there.

—Confucian proverb

We have marveled at the beauty and harmony of the universe since the earliest days. The construction of our gardens is an exercise in re-creating natural harmony through creative arrangement of space and plants. No one can create a harmonious garden without tasting what it must be like to be divine. Are we all harboring a secret passion for divinity, or is it divinity that guides our secret passions? Only the contemplative gardener knows for sure.

Acts and Affirmations

God: Help me to see the architecture of life as clearly as I see that of buildings or gardens. Let me know a strong spiritual foundation, a soaring ceiling of inspiration, and the windows of enlightenment that make life unfold like the thousand petals of the lotus flower.

Spring is the season of the quickening of new life. The tiny seeds lying dormant in the cold soil respond to warming temperatures, and the days grow slightly longer with each sunrise. We, too, recognize the change and are charged with the irresistible compulsion to plant, to get out and work the earth into a living creation of leaf and flower and fruit. Spring is the awakening, the resurrection, the birth of all living things. Every culture fills this season with its own rites of fertility, hoping that its revelry will appease the gods that make the plants grow bigger and more abundant.

Spring

The Time to Plant

Spring is the time of our greatest spiritual inspiration, for there is no miracle quite like that of a seed coming to life, the countryside greening with billions of fresh grass shoots, and the barren branches of the fruit trees budding out into glorious clouds of flowers.

april

The month of April was sacred to Venus, the Roman goddess of love and fertility. Some believe the name was a corruption of the name Aphrodite, the Greek aspect of Venus. The Latin word *aperire* means "to open," which refers to the buds of trees and flowers that are so active in spring. In the Christian emperor Charlemagne's calendar, it was called grass-month. In ancient art the manifestation of April is a young girl dressed in green and holding garlands of hawthorn and myrtle in one hand and violets and roses in the other. The official flowers of April are sweet pea and the English daisy (*Bellis perennis*). The name Bellis is derived from Belides, the Greek name for dryads, or tree spirits.

APACHE MOON OF THE BIG LEAVES

april 1

Roman Feast of Fortuna Virilis (Birth of Venus, Goddess of Fertility)

All-bounteous Venus, parent of Rome, joy of men and gods, who under the starry girdle of the heaven makest the ship-bearing sea and fruitful earth to teem with living creatures, to thee all owe their birth, and springing forth enjoy the enlivening light of day; the winds are hushed and the clouds of heaven disperse at thy approach; the earth with various art puts forth her scented flowers to welcome thee . . .

—Lucretius, first century B.C.

As the Roman goddess of fertility, Venus was the embodiment of spring, with its bursting forth of new life. The Romans believed she touched everything, from earth to flower and sky, imposing a decidedly feminine aspect to the natural world. At this time of year we can observe in our gardens the coming forth of new life and the resurrection of plants that have slept through winter. This magical transformation is as predictable as the dawn.

Acts and Affirmations

It was a common tradition for bridesmaids to plant a myrtle tree at the doorway to the home of a new bride. As wedding season approaches, buy very young myrtle shrubs and pot them in decorative containers. Clip them into charming topiary forms and decorate them if you wish. Have them on hand for evocative wedding and shower gifts dedicated to Venus, the ancient goddess of love.

(*Myrtus communis*)

common myrtle

Myrtle is an aromatic Mediterranean evergreen shrub sacred to Venus. Her earliest temples were built amid groves of old myrtle trees. Murals depicting myrtle have been found in the ruins of Pompeii, surrounding courtyards where the household goddess Venus of the garden was honored. This ancient classical legacy lives on: myrtle sprigs are still combined with roses in wedding bouquets throughout Europe. With its evergreen beauty and glossy foliage which, when crushed, releases pungent aromatic oils, the myrtle is still an integral part of the American landscape.

april 2

The face of the water, in time, became a wonderful book—a book that was a dead language to the uneducated passenger, but which told its mind to me without reserve, delivering its most cherished secrets as clearly as if it uttered them with a voice. And it was not a book to be read once and thrown aside, for it had a new story to tell every day.

—Mark Twain, *Life on the Mississippi*, 1883

Water speaks to us. It tells us of the natural flow of things, the universal truths such as its unwillingness to flow up hill, that it will always follow the path of least resistance. Yet, gradually, over a very long time water can erode mountains and sculpt solid rock. Tenacity, whether it is that of water wearing away stone or a human being struggling to overcome an obstacle, is often the key to success. We learn from water that it is not always the most talented who enjoy success, but through waterlike tenacity the less able may also achieve. Water has many lessons to teach us if we are simply willing to take the time to observe and then learn its secrets.

Acts and Affirmations

It was an old Native American custom to use a fresh willow whip to represent a prayer or request. The next time you have a special concern or need, cut a thin whip or wand from any kind of willow tree. Stand in the garden and tie a single knot in the willow and present your petition. Then store away the whip until such time as the request is answered, then in thanks to the spirit of the wood, untie the knot.

april 3

The joy of sound sleep, the relish of a sufficient meal of plain and wholesome food, the desire to do a good day's work and the recompense when at night we are tired from the doing of it, the exhilaration of fresh air, the exercise of the natural powers, the mastery of a situation or a problem—these and many others like them are fundamental satisfactions, beyond all pampering and all toys, and they are of the essence of goodness.

—Liberty Hyde Bailey, *The Holy Earth*, 1915

Some people live their whole lives without ever manually laboring in the soil. They spend decades without the primal experience of digging and planting the earth. For those who have experienced physical weariness after a terrestrial day in the garden, it is deeply satisfying to watch the sun set over the place we have labored. No one has defined exactly why this is so beneficial to the human psyche, although it is likely a mixture of brain endorphins from the exercise coupled with the performance of a most primal act that dates back to the very dawn of humanity. Is this goodness, and have we found in the garden the most satisfying of therapies? Many believe so and have given up their material toys to gain more of this mysterious earthy goodness that is without rival in our modern world.

Acts and Affirmations

It is hard to remain grounded while at work each day. Keep a small bottle of earth in the office to keep you close to the garden. Choose a small but beautiful bottle and gently fill it with garden soil you've freshly turned over. Cork it or seal the top. Place it where you'll see it during the day as a reminder that, though you spend so many hours in a man-made environment, you are never wholly separated from the soil.

april 4

I, the highest and fiery power, have kindled every living spark and I have breathed out of nothing that can die . . . I flame above the beauty of the fields, I shine in the waters; in the sun, the moon and the stars, I burn . . . All living things take their radiance from me; and I am the life which remains the same through eternity having neither beginning nor end.
—Hildegard von Bingen, *Meditations,* twelfth century

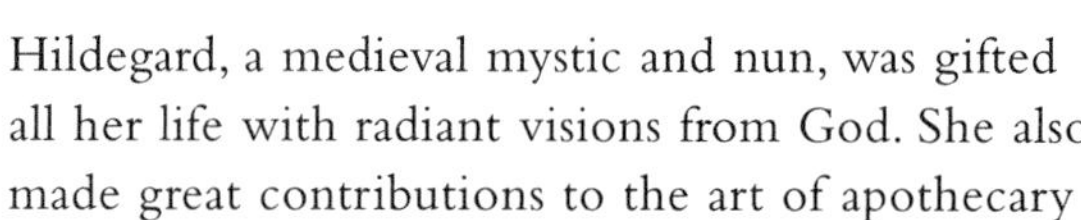

Hildegard, a medieval mystic and nun, was gifted all her life with radiant visions from God. She also made great contributions to the art of apothecary after being taught by monks from a nearby monastery about healing plants. Here she refers to the sun, with its predictable rising and setting each day, and its vital contribution to life. Today we tend to take it for granted, for it's not the powerful enigma it was a thousand years ago. Yet the position of the sun in equinox or solstice was the only calendar of the ancient farmer. As tenders of plants, we need to honor months, the position of the sun as it moves in that great arch from low in the southern sky of winter to directly overhead at the summer solstice, and then back again.

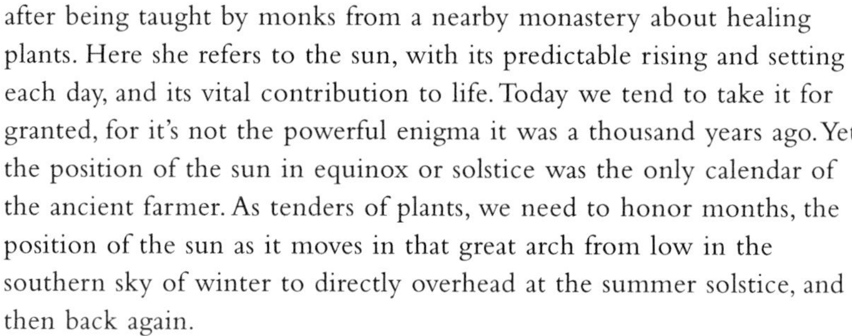

Acts and Affirmations

To honor the sun, grow at least one daisy or flowering plant in yellow or orange this year. At the height of the summer, pluck the petals from a few flowers and dry them on paper plates in the shade. Then bring them out for the winter solstice salad, which heralds the ancient rebirth of the sun on December 21.

april 5

The garden must be prepared in the soul first or else it will not flourish. Tickle it with a hoe, and it will laugh into a harvest.
—Old English proverb

In winter, gardeners spend their days dreaming of what they will do in the spring. Their minds explore the reasons why a plant or parts of their garden did well or failed in the previous year. Similarly, we reflect on our successes and failures in life. No human is perfect, just as no garden is perfect, yet we continue to identify our weaknesses and try to over come them. Each time we work hard to correct our faults, whether it is using the hoe more vigorously on the weeds or pushing ourselves to be more attentive to the needs of others, we and they will be happier.

Acts and Affirmations

Purslane is a common garden weed in both Europe and America that's closely related to the flower known as *moss rose* or *portulaca*. It's easily identified from other weeds by its low, ground-hugging habit and fleshy succulent leaves. Purslane is quite edible; Thoreau wrote in *Walden*, "I have made a satisfactory dinner on several accounts, simply off a dish of Purslane which I gathered in my cornfield, boiled and salted." If the plant is growing in the wild nearby, you can add it freshly chopped to salads or stew it with other greens. Should it crop up in your garden, don't pull it as an unwanted plant, but join Thoreau in the celebration of nature's unexpected abundance by harvesting its nutritious stems and leaves.

april 6

Flowers seem to have retained more of the fragrance of a world which dwelt around the gates of the terrestrial Paradise than anything else in creation. To be in contact with them is purifying, refining, ennobling; their simple gentle life soothes and softens the mind.

—Alfred E. P. Raymund Dowling, *The Flora of the Sacred Nativity*, 1900

Flower scents are more than just pleasing fragrances. They are believed to be a messenger to the body that turns on chemical switches in the brain that promote well-being and healing. Aromatherapy is a technique that utilizes the essential oil of certain plants and flowers to turn on specific chemical switches through a scented environment. The scent of lavender promotes relaxation. Jasmine stimulates the brain and improves mental awareness. Orange blossom fragrance is believed an effective anti-depressant. Perhaps a garden of fragrant flowers does far more than just please the eye, and the scents actually interact with our subconscious to make us feel better.

Acts and Affirmations

Scents based on the aromatic oils in plants are believed to effect a certain degree of healing when inhaled or absorbed through the skin. To experiment with these olfactory connections, cut herbs such as rosemary or lavender and breathe in the aromas from the freshly wounded stems and leaves. Then sit back and quietly feel whether it has resulted in a sense or refreshment or stimulation or evoked creative thought.

(*Lathyrus odoratus*)

sweet pea

Sweet peas, the official flower of the month of April, have long been cherished for their spring flowers and sweet scent—rare so early in the season. The sweet pea is a wildflower native to Sicily, where it blossomed in purple and sky blue. It was brought under cultivation in 1650, and the garden experiments of a devout monk, Francis Cupini, yielded wider color strains. These plants were sent to Holland and Britain, from whence came over 300 new varieties. Sweet peas are grown by sowing seed in the fall or very early spring. They require a fine net trellis on which to climb, and they will begin to decline with the onset of summer heat.

april 7

Fondness for the ground comes back to a man after he has run the round of pleasure and business, eaten dirt, and sown wild oats, drifted about the world, and taken the wind of all its moods. The love of digging in the ground, (or of looking on while he pays another dig) is as sure to come back to him, as he is sure, at last, to go under the ground, and stay there. To own a bit of ground, to scratch it with a hoe, to plant seeds, and watch their renewal of life—this is the commonest delight of the race, the most satisfactory thing a man can do.

—CHARLES DUDLEY WARNER, *My Summer in a Garden*, 1870

Have you ever looked for something in a cupboard but failed to find it, then gone back to discover it was right in front of you all the time? Sometimes things that should be obvious are overlooked as we focus on points farther afield. Today we seek ever more unusual hobbies or hunt for an elusive object that we think will satisfy our current cravings. Perhaps the real solution is right in front of us, an act so simple that we fail to recognize it. Our own backyard lies waiting for us to till, plant, and transform it from an empty or overgrown space into a satisfying realm. Best of all it is not necessarily the final garden that satisfies but the process of getting there that is so deeply fulfilling.

ACTS AND AFFIRMATIONS

Many people suffer most toward the end of winter with seasonally affected depression. Use the vivid hues of English primroses as an anti-depressant by generously planting many different colored flowers in your garden, window box, or pots. The flowers will gladden your heart, and you may cut them into little bouquets and give them to friends and relatives who are suffering from depression or grief. When you do, be sure to tell them "it worked for Queen Victoria and it will work for you."

(*Primula auriculata*)

english primrose

The English primrose is one of the most vivid of all early spring flowers. It grows in the forest in partially shaded areas. The primrose was a favorite blossom for raising spirits after a long, dreary winter. Queen Victoria's prime minister, Benjamin Disraeli, said that the primrose was his favorite flower, and to cheer up the newly widowed queen, he brought her freshly picked wild primroses in the spring. Long after both their deaths, an English society known as the Primrose League was created to continue this sentimental exchange of these little woodland flowers as a tribute to the queen and a celebration of winter's end. It is said that "England displays a rose on the royal coat of arms, but she carries a primrose in her heart."

april 8

Quid enim aliud est natura, quam Deus, et divina ratio, toti mundo et partibus ejus inserta?
What else is nature but God, and divine reason residing in the whole world and its parts?
—Lucius Annaeus Seneca, *De Benef*, first century A.D.

Seneca, the wise tutor of the Roman emperor Nero, points out the great logic in the natural world. What may appear to be a dense confusion of plants in forest or countryside is actually an ordered composition. Each plant dwells in its assigned position: trees overshadowing, brush standing tall, the grasses spreading out beneath with wildflowers of every kind. Such orderly perfection is the most tangible proof of a divine intelligence, and it shows us that chaos does not reign supreme. Even though our lives may seem to be equally as confused, we are reminded by the natural order of the garden that there is an overseer. Amid the plants, we find the elusive, whispering hand of the divine as it dictates where plants will grow and how each is perfectly adapted to its place on Earth.

Acts and Affirmations

Lady's slippers are highly specialized orchids. Visit an orchid florist to see flowers of two genera: *Paphiopedilum* and *Cypripedium*. Notice their coloring, the shape of their flowers, and the size of their pouches, designed to entice certain bugs. Vow to never again pass by such unique flowers without pausing to remember that they exist in a very narrow window of the environment and are manifest in the divine but often fragile order of the natural world.

april 9

There is a certain consideration, and a general duty of humanity, that binds us not only to the animals, which have life and feeling, but even to the trees and plants. We owe justice to men, and a kindness and benevolence to all other creatures who may be susceptible of it. There is some intercourse between them and us, and some mutual obligation.

—Michel de Montaigne, *Essays*, sixteenth century

As creatures of the earth, we share a bond with all living things. When we show respect and kindness to other human beings and animals, they respond to our presence, voice, or touch. But plants are not so animated, and we often overlook their subtle but important responses. If a growing tip wilts, it is the visual language of the plant begging for water. When we provide it, the tip stands up once again, happy and turgid in its own quiet thanksgiving. The wisdom of great gardeners is the accumulation of knowledge of recognizable plant signs and the ability to respond to them correctly.

Acts and Affirmations

Create your own dictionary of silent messages from the plant kingdom. Add them to your gardener's journal, or create a special booklet of signs and wonders as you gather plant wisdom. Each entry should include a sketch or description of the feature, and then a short translation. Begin by finding a plant that twines corkscrew-style like the jasmine, and press a leaf or stem as a visual example in the pages. Then begin to explore other signs in plants as your dialogue with green and growing things evolves.

april 10

My corn is green with red tassels; I am praying to the lightning to ripen my corn, I am praying to the thunder which carries the lightning. Corn is sweet where lightning has fallen. I pray to the six-colored clouds.

—Amy Lowell, *Songs of the Pueblo Indians*, 1920

For the Pueblo peoples of the desert Southwest, corn meant the difference between life and death. In a land of diminishing rainfall, they grew their thirsty crop on the floodplains of the Colorado River and prayed for violent thunderheads that produce summer rainfall. It is scientifically proven that lightning indeed adds nitrogen to the soil, which highlights this wisdom that corn does grow better where "lightning has fallen." Their words even today remain poetic. They illustrate how a plant, even one as ubiquitous as corn, can be revered. Perhaps there is sanctity in every plant, rooted in the relationships of people the world over and the plants that sustain them.

Acts and Affirmations

This year, grow a small stand of heirloom corn from the desert Southwest. Cultivate it in your garden the Native American way: not in rows, but in clumps. (Planting in rows was the result of plows, but to cultivate by hand this technique proved far more efficient.) Create an area about thirty inches in diameter with a berm around the edge so you can flood it with water. Plant three to five seeds in each one and keep them well watered. Listen to the corn as it grows, watch for the tassles that sprout on top, and wait for the magic of this ancient plant to fill your garden with the universal songs of the Pueblo.

april 11

Why scurry about looking for the truth?
. . . Can you be still and see it in the mountain? the pine tree? yourself?
—LAO-TZU, Chinese philosopher, sixth century B.C.

Truth is an often elusive thing, yet in the natural world, in our gardens, it is undeniably clear. That a pine tree grows or a mountain is forced up by power of tectonic plates is truth beyond dispute. In a world where everything seems negotiable, all things are relative, and the guideposts of our childhood are vanishing with ever-quickening changes, there are few pure truths left. When you feel pulled apart, dismembered by the myriad powers that exist in your life, return to your garden to find the great nonnegotiable realities. Know that plants grow with sun, water, and soil, guided by the unchanging hand of Mother Earth . . . now and forever.

ACTS AND AFFIRMATIONS

Leave the world behind and discover your inner peace through a pine-scented bath. Pine needles are filled with aromatic oils that are released by heat. Gather them fresh from any kind of pine tree, and create a bundle about one inch in diameter. Bind them tightly with a thick rubber band. Snip the tips off both ends of the bundle to let the oil flow out, then drop it on hot bathwater. As you relax in the pine-scented bath, close your eyes and visualize yourself flying over endless mountain forests of majestic pines.

april 12

ROMAN FESTIVAL OF CERALIA

When rust is falling on the herbs, then Beritius in his husbandry instructions willeth . . . to make a great smoke forthwith round about the garden.

—THOMAS HYLL, *Art Garden*, 1593

This begins the eight-day ancient Roman festival honoring the goddess Ceres, who was thought to secure the health of the grain crops, a vital staple food of Europe. Wet winters left the fields riddled with fungus such as "rust" and in rye, the more insidious ergot. Though the Romans—and 1,500 years later, Thomas Hyll—knew that outbreaks of St. Anthony's Fire (ergot poisoning), caused by invisibly infected rye grain, usually followed wet years. Ergot fungus poisoned anyone who consumed it. Since early times, the health of plants meant the health of humanity, and goddesses in many forms were invoked to protect both.

ACTS AND AFFIRMATIONS

Honor the goddess Ceres by sowing a small patch of wheat or rye in a pot or in the garden. Let it be a microcosm of the fields that cloaked Europe in millennia past. You will find whole cereal seed or "berries" at the health food store that you can plant just like grass. When the grain flowers and matures with seed, cut the grain and save it as a decorative sheaf for autumn decorating. Then sow it again in next year's garden.

april 13

[The labyrinth] represents the path to Heaven. We have choices of right and wrong all through our lives. But if we choose our way through life wisely, keep going on or turn back to the right way even though we find ourselves sidetracked temporarily by alluring temptations, we shall at last happily find our goal.

—Rosetta E. Clarkson, *Magic Gardens*, 1939

The old European tradition of laying out mazelike patterns on turf, in paving, or as living hedges has returned as a contemporary path of contemplation. The maze has many ways through, but the labyrinth has a single path. During the Crusades, the Pope decreed that anyone who made a pilgrimage to the Holy Land would receive powerful spiritual benefits. Since so few could make the journey, the church developed a secondary devotion using the labyrinth as a symbolic pilgrimage. These patterns were set into the floor of the cathedral at Chartres and other churches built around that time. People would walk the complex pattern while praying. Today walking the labyrinth is growing popular again as a contemplative exercise. Labyrinths can be found with growing frequency in American churches, retreat houses, and in garden settings.

Acts and Affirmations

Create a miniature formal garden that represents the labyrinth. Purchase four or more rectangular terra-cotta French herb troughs and a bunch of gallon-size boxwoods (*Buxus microphyllus japonica 'Compacta'*). Plant them tightly to make portable hedges. Arrange them in different ways as the seasons pass, knowing that this act is a symbolic journey, not to a sacred place far away, but to the sacred land that lies deep within your own soul.

april 14

Yet it [the garden] must perform its primary function of being a garden in the true sense of providing trees and flowers; fruits and vegetables; a place where man can recapture his affinity with the soil, if only on Saturday afternoons. It must be a green oasis where memories of his bumper-to-bumper ride from work will be erased.

—Thomas D. Church, *Gardens Are for People*, 1955

There are more different shades of green than any other color in the spectrum, from bright yellow-green to a cool blue teal and deepest emerald. Green is the color of the plant kingdom, which God imbued with such incredible variety that we are never bored with forest, fen, or field. It is also the color most soothing to the eye.

Acts and Affirmations

Teach your eye to be more sensitive to the nuances of green in the landscape. Try to see it the way an artist sees it. Wander about and pick one leaf off each plant you see. Arrange them on a lovely white plate from the lightest to the darkest green. This simple act teaches both your eye and your heart to be more aware of the subtleties of nature, which enrich and diversify our everyday lives.

april 15

"Mr. Brown, I very earnestly desire that I may die before you."
"Why so?"
"Because I should like to see heaven before you have improved it."
—Anonymous, told of the famous eighteenth-century gardener, "Capability" Brown

Lanceolate "Capability" Brown was famous for improving on nature by remodeling the countryside using all sorts of trees, both native and exotic, on an enormous scale. The changing of wild places for our own aesthetic tastes is viewed as sacrilege by some, for it alters the natural arrangement of plants and their relationships to one another. We must learn that the natural landscape is always best when planted with native species that preserve these arrangements and relationships rather than forcing exotic plants, as Brown did, into this idealized vision of nature. Remodeling cannot improve on the natural world any more than it can heaven.

Acts and Affirmations

In ancient Europe people had a tradition of carving dates, names, and statements of great importance into the bark of beech trees. (Some believe the words *beech* and *book* share the same common origin.) Remember a birth, death, or marriage by carving the names and dates into a piece of found wood. Then ceremoniously hang it from a tree in your garden for posterity.

april 16

In the beginning were the waters. Matter readied itself. The sun glowed. And a lotus slowly opened, holding the universe in its golden pericarp.
—East Indian creation myth

The lotus is a universal symbol for personal growth through various states of consciousness, as it rises out of the mud to grow and eventually produce flowers of perfection. The round leaves represent the circular motion of the intellect. The lotus's springing up out of the mud with large leaves and blooms of pure white flowers symbolizes the dominance of divine wisdom. The lotus is an important plant in many other faiths worldwide, primarily because of its remarkable ability for resurrecting itself in the ebb and flow of floodwaters. It may become our own personal symbol for spiritual rebirth as we heal after periods of grief or adversity.

Acts and Affirmations

The lotus seed can lie in river mud for up to a thousand years and still sprout when conditions are right. This makes the seed a very auspicious gift to give at a birth or marriage, or to celebrate one's embarking on a new path in life. You will find the marble-size lotus seeds inside the dried pods sold by florists or craft supply stores. Break open the pod, extract the seeds, and package them in a beautiful container for a special gift or talisman that promises resurrection and rebirth.

Let the farmer forevermore be honored in his calling; for they who labor in the earth are the chosen people of God.
—Thomas Jefferson

To be a farmer, particularly a small organic farmer, is a deeply rewarding lifestyle. Organic farmers more closely resemble their early nineteenth-century predecessors, before the introduction of advanced machinery and chemicals, than they do contemporary corporate agriculture. Organic gardening is a more holistic view of the earth, plants, and the role of the farmer. It forces you to be aware of soil microorganisms, insects that crawl and fly, and the larger animals that eat the plants. You learn what natural materials such as homemade compost can be used to fortify the soil. You take advantage of companion planting to help the plants protect one another. You even learn what bugs protect your garden by preying on those that would eat it. Organic gardening is indeed the best way to live more naturally, and it helps us cultivate greater appreciation for the countless miracles of life that occur every day within our garden.

Acts and Affirmations

Make a pledge to yourself and the environment to learn to grow organically. Commemorate your pledge by setting up a compost heap in the yard to remind you that all things that come from the earth should be returned there. Vow to feed the heap instead of putting valuable organic matter down the garbage disposal and use the finished compost to anoint your garden soil. It will return the favor by producing larger, more prolific plants.

april 18

But the greatest mystery in the bursting forth of plants is that it is done when growth is at its tenderest age; when the shoot is tender and brittle it has power to push through everything that binds it down.
—HENRY N. ELLACOMBE, *A Glouchestershire Garden*, 1895

The miracle of the seed is not the life sequestered inside that small capsule but the bursting forth of a tiny shoot that is capable of forcing itself through rock-hard soil. This insistence is a remarkable example of the strength that lies in small, young things, the drive to survive the most inhospitable of circumstances. Children who have suffered disease, injustices, and abuse rarely give up as adults do but face each day with stalwart hope and an unceasing drive. We learn from the seedling and the child that we, too, can better abide the difficulties of life by always stretching ourselves toward the sun and filling each day with childlike hope of a better tomorrow.

ACTS AND AFFIRMATIONS

Unleash the mysterious power of your seeds this year by helping them get started more quickly. Large seeds such as corn, beans, peas, and morning glory must absorb a lot of moisture from the soil to rehydrate before they germinate. Give them a hand by presoaking them in warm water for a couple of hours before you plant. This act places you in a midwifelike role, helping Mother Earth more efficiently resurrect the dormant life in these small but powerful packages.

april 19

Those of our time do use the flowers [of borage] in salads, to exhilarate and make the mind glad. There be also many things made of them, used everywhere for the comfort of the heart, for the driving away of sorrow, and increasing the joy of the mind.

—JOHN GERARD, *Gerard's Herbal*, 1597

The famous herbalist John Gerard was inspired by a much older work by the Roman herbalist Pliny the Elder, who first recorded the folk saying "I borage give thee courage, and gladden a heavy heart." As long as human beings have walked this earth, they have suffered with bouts of heavy heart. Known as melancholy in earlier times, it is now diagnosed as depression. Long ago people turned to garden plants for strength to face fear or depression. Borage was such a universal symbol of courage that medieval knights drank a tea of it before every jousting match. Borage was actually used to flavor wine, and the question remains, Was it the herb or the wine itself that "gladdened the heavy heart"?

ACTS AND AFFIRMATIONS

Create a beverage of liquid courage with borage flowers, which begin blooming this month. Gather a few flowers from the garden or from a spot where the plant has naturalized in the countryside. Create the ancient drink of the warrior by combining some borage blossoms in white wine to share with someone who is struggling to recover from grief or winter doldrums. Either bottle it up in a creative container as a gift to send, or pay them a visit and sip your borage wine together—either way it's bound to cheer anyone's heart.

april 20

The healer: well versed in herbs, who knows through experience the roots, the trees, the stones. She is experienced, tests her remedies, examines, keeps her secrets, her traditions.
—*Florentine Codex* (translated from Aztec by Charles E. Dibble)

In Mexico the Indians believe there are two types of healing. They will see a medical doctor to treat the body, but they also pay a visit to their local *curandera*, the wise woman who practices the old ways of healing the spirit. Modern medicine is just beginning to recognize this second aspect of healing, and today herbal healers and the religious are resurrecting these spiritual arts. As gardeners, we too may know some healing roots and herbs from our own experience. Cultivate these plants to offer as a healing tea for the spirit when friends or relatives suffer colds, flu, or more serious ills of the body.

Acts and Affirmations

Artemisia, the American cousin of wormwood—(*Artemisia mexicanum*), is so aromatic it has been used to produce a strong purification incense by native peoples of the Americas. Bundle green wands of artemisia into cigar-shaped smudge sticks and tie them with colorful embroidery floss. Allow them to dry and then light one end to purify a home or garden with the smoke. It's also great to toss sprigs of artemisia onto the coals in your barbecue when grilling chile peppers or meats for the subtle flavoring of old Mexico.

april 21

Near the beginning of time, Kakh, Brother Crow, brought to the people seeds of all sorts, especially corn, to nourish and replenish them. And the people cultivated their gardens so that when game was scarce they did not go hungry. Because Sister Corn gives of herself that they might live, the people return thanks to her in songs and ceremonies at planting time and harvest.

—Yuma legend, Carol Buchanan, *Brother Crow, Sister Corn*, 1997

The Yuma tribe lived in the arid deserts of Arizona where living is difficult due to heat, lack of water, and sparse vegetation. They, like so many other Native Americans, shared creation myths that explained the beginnings of humankind, animals, and plants, both wild and cultivated. The growing of the corn crop was punctuated by ceremonies at each step of the way to honor spirits of nature and the garden. They rejoiced in the planting, the green sprouts, the emerging of silk and tassels, and the milk stage—the stage at which we eat corn today. But the crop was not harvested until the stalk dried and the corn was picked and shucked. Today we take the flowering of the squash or the forming of tassels for granted, yet it is really a beautiful thing that offers us a great excuse to celebrate the vegetable garden throughout the growing season.

Acts and Affirmations

Join the Native Americans who celebrated the first fresh food of the garden year. Cook up some of your first winter and summer squash blossoms for a unique dish. Heat two teaspoons of olive oil in a large frying pan. Saute two cloves of garlic until brown, then add about fifteen fresh squash blossoms with the stems removed. Cook slowly and turn frequently for around five minutes, then serve piping hot. Season with a pinch of oregano, salt, and pepper.

april 22

EARTH DAY

So bountiful hath been the earth and so securely have we drawn from it our substance, that we have taken it all for granted as if it were only a gift, and with little care or conscious thought of the consequences of our use of it; nor have we very much considered the essential relation that we bear to it as living parts in the vast creation.

—LIBERTY HYDE BAILEY, *The Holy Earth*, 1915

Liberty Hyde Bailey, America's most famous horticulturist, grew up in the world of nineteenth-century American farming, when planters turned the sod and felled trees to create fields. By the time he reached middle age in 1915, he had seen the devastation caused by these indiscriminate practices and wrote the first great work on sustainable organic agriculture. He warns us not to take our earth for granted—a good message for Earth Day. Let us vow to always remain conscious of the consequences of our actions for the Earth.

ACTS AND AFFIRMATIONS

Help reestablish native grasses in America beginning with your own backyard. Plant an experimental patch of blue grama grass (*Bouteloua gracilis*), or replace your water-greedy turf grass lawn with it to conserve resources. Now is the time to sow seed, or plant it with rooted plugs you can buy at the nursery. Native grass lawns restore part of the natural habitat that was destroyed when the prairies were plowed under a hundred years ago.

april 23

But the rose is older than Eden, older than any civilization known to history. Scholars have told us that the rose is one of the oldest of the vegetable forms. Millions of years ago, this same delicate plant impressed its charming outline against the Oligocene slime where it may still be seen preserved in stone: leaf, stock and flower.

—JOSEPHINE CRAVEN CHANDLER, *The Romance of the Rose*, 1949

Few plants have been bred into such a wide variety of colors and forms as the rose. It is a genus that shows the infinite genetic potential that exists in every single living thing. From simple red or pink, roses have been bred in virtually every hue except blue or black (breeders are still trying to produce a blue one). It shows that deep inside that Oligocene rose there lay genes that would enchant the world with its beauty, fragrance, and medicinal properties. Such potential is clear in every species, from the giant redwood to the tiny crocus.

ACTS AND AFFIRMATIONS

This year, plant an ancient rose species. Although modern breeds dazzle with their intense colors, older varieties are richly fragrant and do not need to be sprayed or hoed. They are a reminder that the greatest things in life are not always the boldest or most attractive but lie hidden in the small and humble.

Flowers . . . that are so pathetic in their beauty, frail as the clouds, and in their colouring as gorgeous as the heavens, had through thousands of years been the heritage of children—honoured as the jewelry of God only by them.
—Thomas De Quincey, *Confessions of an English Opium-Eater*, 1822

Flowers, with their bright gemlike coloring, are the jewelry of God. Some flowers live only for a day, others for a week or more, but every one will die in a relatively short time. Perhaps this fleeting beauty is what makes them so enchanting. Flowers remind us that all life is short and we must live each moment of each day with great intensity.

Acts and Affirmations

Live in the moment with poppies because these flowers wither instantly after cutting. Sow a great blooming patch of them early in spring with seed from your local health food store. Buy refrigerated because their seed is viable only for a short time at room temperature. Long before other flowers come into their own, your florist's poppies will blossom, and with each opening flower you may relish its brief existence out in the garden.

april 25

St. Mark's Gwok (Return of the Birds)

Spring at last is at hand. Birds, then, are harbingers of spring; they return to us early each year with the message that spring is on the way, thereby adding to our happiness.

—Alvin M. Peterson, *The ABC of Attracting Birds*, 1937

The gwok is a common British name for the cuckoo bird, the first migratory species to return to the isles in spring. It most often appears around April 25, the feast of St. Mark. The art of living in tune with one's piece of earth and garden is the acknowledgment of signs that were far more apparent to farmers of old. Just as the famous swallows return to California's Mission San Juan Capistrano every March 19, each region has its early arrivals that are our living, singing harbingers of spring. Conscious living means we come to know the signs and celebrate their occurrence with the turning of every season.

Acts and Affirmations

For all nature offers, we should return in kind. This spring, reward the birds that help the gardener by feeding on unwanted insects. As they return to the meager food supply of winter's end before bugs hatch, offer them high-quality seed. Regular birdseed often requires more energy of the bird to crack and eat than its grain offers. Make your offering power-packed with raw shelled sunflower seeds (available in bulk from the market or health food store). Continue to offer seed until the insect populations grow to feed the gardener's best friend through the rest of the year.

april 26

I never had any other desire so strong, and so like Covetousness as that one which I have had always, that I might be master at last of a small house and a large garden, with very moderate conveniences joyned to them, and there dedicate the remainder of my life only to the culture of them and study of Nature.

—PREFATORY LETTER TO JOHN EVELYN'S *Kalendarium Hortense*, 1664

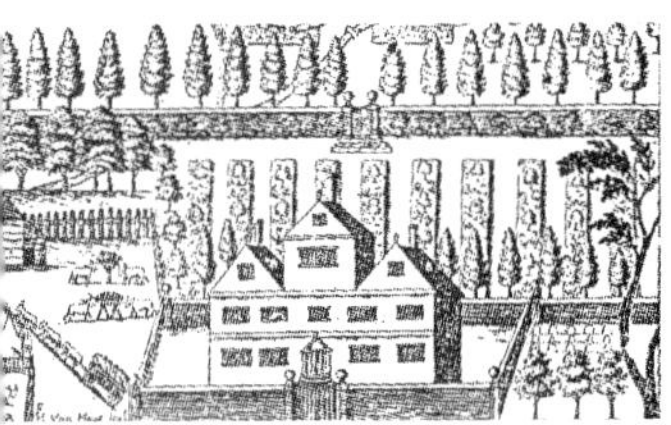

A small house and a large garden—Evelyn's covetousness is no sin. Today we tend to wish for the opposite: large house, too often surrounded by a small garden, or sometimes no garden at all. This ratio of house to garden is one that reminds us that the garden lives and houses are inanimate. As living things ourselves, it seems far more appropriate to dwell in the land of living things and to while away our days not with paint and wallpaper but with vines and flowers.

ACTS AND AFFIRMATIONS

Make every letter you write or card you send an expression of your love of the garden and of the recipient. This spring, begin pressing a few of every flower in the garden between the pages of books. This practice is also a good way to get to know flowers more intimately, for you must spread out their petals and stems just so to produce a fine pressed specimen.

It is an odd, but very real thing—the nostalgia of the gum trees . . .
I never smell the pungent, aromatic scent, which for twenty-two years was the breath of my nostrils, without being carried back to the old, vivid world of untrodden pastures and lonely forests, without falling again under the grim spell of the bush.

—Rosa Campbell Praed, *My Australian Girlhood*, 1902

We are linked to our roots by the plants that define home in our heart. When there is a dominant species with distinguishable aromas, such as pine of the mountains, sagebrush of the West, or eucalyptus that blankets Australia, they are inextricably linked to who we are. While buildings come and go, civilizations rise and fall, and even whole cultures blossom and then melt away with time, the trees that existed there live on. This is the timeless aspect of wild places so vital to inner peace, and when we plant these species in our gardens, we may rekindle that same sense of calm sanctuary we felt in nature in our childhood.

Acts and Affirmations

Let the scent of familiar aromatic plants make our work experiences more pleasant by hanging fresh boughs nearby. Plants familiar to us from childhood or happy times past create a mind-set that is subliminally positive. Trees rich in essential oils, such as eucalyptus or conifers, can subtly transform everyday work tasks from drudgery to peace. And as you scrub the pots and pans, your boughs will rekindle visions of grandmother's farm, or memories of the scent of aromatic Italian cypress that made the honeymoon trip to Italy so magical.

april 28

FEAST OF FLORA

I enjoy perpetual spring. To me the year is always most beauteous; the tree always bears its foliage, the earth its herbage. A fruitful garden in the fields of my dowry is mine. The breeze cherishes it; it is irrigated by a spring of trickling water. This my husband has filled with flowers of the choicest kinds; and he says, 'Do thou, Goddess, rule the empire of the flowers.'

—PRAYER OF GODDESS FLORA, from Ovid's *The Fasti*

Flora, goddess of the spring and flowers, was celebrated over five consecutive days in Greco-Roman culture. She was not only its overseer but the creator, dispersing seeds of plants over all the earth and claiming that before her influence the "earth was of but one tint." Flora represents diversity in the vegetation, and a fruitful garden is the equivalent of a rich dowry. Her statues often stood in the courtyard gardens of Roman homes, where her feast was celebrated with offerings of fresh-cut flowers and seeds.

ACTS AND AFFIRMATIONS

Celebrate springtime with the goddess by gathering the flowers of the Romans to offer her a bouquet or weave into a crown to wear in her honor. They were known to weave garlands and chaplets of roses, anemone, morning glory, cyclamen, hyacinth, iris, lily, narcissus, violets, and, of course, oleander. And all of them could be found on her altars throughout the Roman Empire at the end of April.

april 29

Pagan Tree Day

That I may each day walk continuously on the banks of my water,
that my soul may repose on the branches of the trees that I have planted,
that I may refresh myself under the shadow of my sycamore.

—Inscription on the tomb of Serrufer, an Egyptian royal gardener of ancient Thebes

Modern city life can be very similar to that of the parched Egyptian desert. Concrete sidewalks and buildings are like the endless sand and rocky outcrops of Saharan Africa that reflect heat and drive temperatures higher. It is an inhospitable environment for living things, but along the thin banks of the Nile this forbidding desert becomes green and verdant. Trees grow and the air becomes moist and life flourishes. We have come to realize that the addition of trees to our cities is not merely an aesthetic benefit but may also make conditions more comfortable during the hot summer, just as they did in the Egyptian gardens. Trees are a gift to humanity and our most valuable tools to modify climate and transform hard city streets into beautiful, shaded avenues.

Acts and Affirmations

The tree exists in virtually every city in America. Get to know it in a most tactile way by feeling its unique trunk and bark. Close your eyes and run your fingers down its surface and imagine it as a living, breathing organism that is a precious source of life-giving shade. Then visualize your soul up there, perched on the branches amid the leaves, just one step from heaven.

april 30

Walpurgis Night

The fire was done in this way. Nine men would turn their pockets inside out, and see that every piece of money and all metals were off their persons. Then the men went into the nearest woods, and collected sticks of nine different kinds of trees. These were carried to the spot where the fire had to be built. There a circle was cut in the sod, and the sticks were set crosswise. One of the men would then take two bits of oak, and rub them together until a flame was kindled. Each person was compelled to leap three times over the flames to be sure of a plentiful harvest.

—Sir James Frazer, *The Golden Bough*, 1922

For days before May Day, the rural people of Medieval Europe sought to chase the last of the dark spirits of winter out of their homes and farms. Over time the spirits became witches, and Walpurgis Night became the ritual date of cleansing the witches by fire. To smoke them out, villagers burned bundles of hemlock, rosemary, or juniper in every room of their homes, barns, and outbuildings, then banged pots and rang bells to chase the spirits out. This opens the annual Beltane fire festival, when bonfires are kindled so people can leap over them, thus cleansing their bodies and garments with smoke.

Acts and Affirmations

The day before May Day is the traditional date for spring cleaning. Put your house in order, then fill it with the delightful smoke of pine incense to spiritually cleanse it as well. Then hang sprigs of herbs such as angelica, lamb's ear, rosemary, mugwort, and vervain over the doorways to ensure a bountiful harvest from the summer garden in the season to come.

(*Sorbus aucuparia*)

the rowan tree

The native European rowan tree is the most powerful "witch bane" known to the ancients. Commonly called European mountain ash, it was also known as witchwood, quickbane, wicken tree, and witchen. It is imbued with the power to ward off witches because it was believed that should they touch a leaf they would be sent back to the devil to suffer punishments. Many medieval ship masts were made of rowan to protect the ship, and sprigs of it were often hung over doors to prevent a witch from entering a house or barn. Today it is a good landscape tree. Bearing bright red berries attractive to birds, the rowan is good for landscaping and for incorporating into magical gardens. There are now many cultivars with more varied shapes and berry colors than the original species.

may

May was the month given by the Romans to their great god Apollo. The name was derived from that of the goddess Maia, who oversaw all growth and increase in nature and agriculture. Most cultures have held great festivals in May, such as the weaving of a maypole, a phallic symbol of the fecundity of the earth. This month also marks the festival of the goddess Flora, patron of all flowers. The good goddess of the earth Bona Dea was honored by the women of Rome. To celebrate the consummation of the marriage between the earth mother and the sun god, on the sabbat of Beltane, Druids built bonfires on hilltops and leaped through the flames in an ancient rite of purification. It was a common custom for people to bathe their faces in the dew from the morning grass, which was thought to enhance beauty. The official flowers of May are lily of the valley and blossoms of the hawthorn tree.

Algonquin
Moon of
"When the Women
Weed Corn"

May 1

Beltane

And thus it passed on from Candlemas until after Easter, that the month of May was come, when every lusty heart beginneth to blossom, and to bring forth fruit; for like as herbs and trees bring forth fruit and flourish in May, in likewise every lusty heart that is any manner a lover, springeth and flourisheth in lusty deeds.

—Sir Thomas Malory, *Le Morte D'Arthur*, 1470

Beltane, the Celtic May Day, is the ancient celebration of fertility that paired the earth goddess Maia with the spirit of the vegetation, known as the "green man." It is truly a sexual event, evidenced by the phallic shape of the maypole. This is the time of pollination for all species of plants and animals. To go "a-maying" was to venture into the woods and return with flowers and tree branches to decorate the home. All this activity was believed crucial to stave off the ever-present threat of famine by honoring the earth and plants to ensure their fertility.

Acts and Affirmations

Celebrate May with your own maypole in the lawn or garden. Choose a broom handle–size staff and plant it solidly in the ground. Tie multi-colored ribbons to the top and weave them around in a beautiful pattern to about halfway down, and let the tails of the ribbons hang to a few inches above the ground. When the breeze blows, the ribbons will flutter and reflect the sunlight. Crown the pole with flowers or greens, and let it stand for many days as a symbol of the union of the green man and Mother Earth.

(*Convallaria majalis*)

lily of the valley

Lily of the valley is a lovely little woodland flower that is native to Europe. It became the symbol of the many goddesses of spring: it was the flower of the Celtic Ostara, of the Norse goddess of the dawn, and later, Mary. The dainty blossoms were a common ingredient in medieval love potions and wedding bouquets. They naturalize well in shade gardens and are among the few plants to grow under canopies of large trees. Though their small size has made them less popular these days, they are so simple to grow that everyone should have a few to honor the goddesses—or to enjoy the charming fragrant flowers.

may 2

The Green Man is the guardian and revealer of mysteries. He speaks of the mysteries of creation in time, of the hidden sources of inspiration, and of the dark nothingness out of which we come and to which we return. As the fruit of vegetation, he signifies the mystery of law and intelligence in natural forms and expresses our own instinctive desire to anthropomorphize everything that is beautiful, touching or powerful in the world around us.

—William Anderson, *Green Man*, 1990

The green man is a half-human, half-tree mythical figure. He combines the animal with the vegetable in an ancient, all-knowing entity. Ancient celebrations of the green man in Europe marked the leafing out of the deciduous plants, an event vital to rural life. And he becomes the universal male paired with the verdant feminine earth to produce the crops. His image is found carved into the stone decorations of medieval churches, illustrating that these pagan traditions continued even after the advent of Christianity. To modern-day pagans he represents a "father earth," a symbol for rekindling the spirit of the old earth-based religions.

Acts and Affirmations

It was an old practice in early of May for couples to venture into the "greenwood" to make love in a "lovers bower." The bower was created by cutting evergreen boughs and piling them into a resilient cushion on which a blanket was laid. Whether your greenwood is a backyard or a true woodland sanctuary, arrange a romantic tryst to celebrate this ancient rite of the green man and his lover, Mother Earth.

may 3

There is so much in nature which can fill us, day and night, through plants, animals and flowers, with the eternal in life.
—C. G. Jung, *Collected Works*, 1959

The plants and animals that comprise the natural world around us are perhaps our richest source of enjoyment. The natural beauty touches our more primal emotions, while the divine order of it all appeals to our sense of logic. Perhaps the eternal that Jung speaks of is the very existence of this life force that is manifest all around us in nature and garden. Though we are alive but for a short time, nature in one form or another will exist forever.

Acts and Affirmations

Share in the timelessness that is the garden by enjoying violas, as they did a millennia ago in old Europe. In King Arthur's time, salads of "violas and onions" were relished after a long winter without fresh vegetables. Add pretty viola petals to your salad tonight as a way to reach back in time.

may 4

> *My garden is an honest place. Every tree and every vine are incapable of concealment, and tell after two or three months exactly what sort of treatment they have had. The sower may mistake and sow his peas crookedly: the peas make no mistake, but come up and show his line.*
>
> —Ralph Waldo Emerson, journal, 1840

As you sow, so shall you reap, the old saying goes. It is as true in the garden as it is in other aspects of life. We have the ability to influence our own future by doing the right things at the right time to ensure a desired outcome. Before we plant seed, it is essential to soften hard ground by adding organic matter followed by deep cultivation. Failure to do so will reduce the number of seeds that sprout, and those that do will suffer abnormally small root systems in dense soil. No matter how much water and fertilizer you pour on, this fundamental error cannot be corrected, and the plants will never flourish and show their true beauty. In all things we should strive to make the same preparations before we perform the task at hand with care and attention, knowing that only then will our efforts be rewarded by success.

Acts and Affirmations

We tend to speed through the process of sowing seed because it is tedious, and there are so many other things to do in the garden. But sowing perfect rows at the ideal spacing is a study in self-control, and the smaller the seed, the more control required. As you sow your beans and radishes and carrots, strive for perfection and make it an act of self-discipline that will sharpen your awareness of exactly how much space every plant deserves. Well-spaced plants grow better and yield more with far less chance of disease.

may 5

They [orchids] are offered by the devotee at the shrine of his favorite saint, by the lover at the feet of his mistress, and by the sorrowing survivor at the grave of his friend; whether, in short, on fast days or feast days, on occasions of rejoicing or in moments of distress, these flowers are sought for with an avidity which would seem to say that there was no sympathy like theirs.
—J. Bateman, *Orchidaceae of Mexico and Guatemala*, 1880

Each culture has its favorite flowers, and in the tropical rain forests of Latin America, the orchid is the universal symbol of sentiment. This family of exotic flowers is a language unto itself, speaking with color and petal what words cannot describe. Their transient life is so limited that each one, once picked, is a sacrifice of beauty for a few brief moments of personal pleasure.

Acts and Affirmations

An artist thrives by evolving with his or her work, and it is crucial to the creative process to grow spiritually. As gardeners, we, too, should be forever evolving, and the best way is to grow a new plant this year. This simple step pushes us out of the cocoon of familiarity and opens the door to miracles. Even if the plant dies through our ignorance or neglect, it is a death that teaches us a lesson from its shortened life, and it is thus elevated to more than a mere flower. It has lived so that we may grow.

may 6

When our learning exceeds our deeds we are like trees whose branches are many but whose roots are few: the wind comes and uproots them . . . But when our deeds exceed our learning we are like trees whose branches are few but whose roots are many, so that even if all the winds of the world were to come and blow against them, they would be unable to move them.
—Oral Torah

The very wealthy can literally buy a garden—hire the best landscape architects, import tons of fertile loam, and hire a staff of gardeners. But these gardens are like trees with great branches and no roots. A humble patch of ground in the backyard, if turned and fertilized, sowed, and tended by a single hand, is like a tree with deep roots.

Acts and Affirmations

One of the practices of the Jewish festival Purim is *Misloach manot*, the sending of food to a friend, which fulfills the *mitzvah* obligation. The traditional offering is a poppy seed pastry created in the shape of a triangle. The gift is always more meaningful if it is something you have grown or made in your kitchen. The beauty of this act is in how you prepare it, with visually pleasing wrapping and containers and a personal note that says how much you care.

May 7

The beauty of the garden must be so devised that one is not consciously aware of it. It must simply be there, fulfilling the heart, without producing any notion of its own existence. The harmony of the whole layout must be such as to cause the heart to resonate in sympathy.

—Horst Hammitzsch, *Zen in the Art of the Tea Ceremony*, 1980

The tea garden is designed to be a microcosm of nature. With discipline that is rare in the West, the designer takes care to control every element, from plant to stone to water. Every view and every step are carefully manipulated so that, from the moment a visitor enters the main gate of a tea garden, he or she will have the most beautiful and harmonious experience. The experience releases the viewer from effort and opens the way for pure thought.

Acts and Affirmations

Tea drinking in Japan began as medicine, so it is not surprising that recently green tea has been shown to discourage tumors. Celebrate the tea tradition by taking tea in a leisurely manner in your garden. Brew green tea in a teapot and pour it into porcelain cups. Serve it with a plate of Chinese almond cookies to nibble on. Sit on traditional woven reed beach mats or a blanket spread out on the lawn, as the Japanese did who were not fortunate enough to have their own teahouse.

(RHODODENDRON)

azalea

The azalea is one of the few sources of flower color in the Japanese tea garden. There are literally hundreds of different hybrids, some hardy and deciduous, others tender and evergreen. Such diversity allows people to enjoy azaleas in all but the coldest climate zones. In the Japanese garden, azaleas are carefully manicured to produce an abundance of blooms on very fine branching structures. They are not grouped with other shrubs but planted as individuals around rocks and mosses, just as they occur in the wild.

may 8

Dead bones in their grave lie Mary and Elizabeth, queens, and dead dust of death is all they did; but the flowers, they grew in their gardens still continue giving comfort and delight perpetually, down through the continuing generations.
—Reginald Farrer, *The English Garden*, 1932

Human life is so fleeting that after the famous are dead and gone most are forgotten with time. But those who created gardens, or collected plants around their homes or castles, live on through their botanical legacy. Author Vita Sackville-West lives through her garden at Sissinghurst, and Gertrude Jekyll is immortalized in the flowers of Munstead House. And every American pioneer who ventured across the midwestern plains left a trail of plantain and thistle and a thousand other seeds to populate the new lands.

Acts and Affirmations

If feverfew (*Chrysanthemum parthenium*) doesn't already grow in your garden, plant it this month in honor of the millions of women who relied on it to control fever before modern medicine. This herb, once called "the housewife's aspirin," was brought with the Pilgrims from England to the New World. Enjoy its charming daisies, and join the ancient Romans, those health-conscious vegetarians, by adding a medicinal dose of fresh chopped leaves to your morning scrambled eggs.

So extravagant is Nature with her choicest treasures, spending plant beauty as she spends sunshine, pouring it forth into land and sea, garden and desert. And so the beauty of lilies falls on angels and men, bears and squirrels, wolves and sheep, birds and bees, but as far as I have seen, man alone, and the animals he tames, destroy these gardens.

—John Muir, *My First Summer in the Sierra*, 1911

The famous turn-of-the-century naturalist John Muir traveled in the summer of 1869 through the rugged High Sierras with a Basque shepherd and his flocks. In his eloquent prose, Muir writes that livestock are a threat to nature's most fragile plants and flowers. This illustrates one of the great dilemmas facing ecologists: that of grazing in wild areas. Domestic animals not only introduce exotic seeds into native ecosystems but they also gobble up the most tender seedlings and flowers of treasured species before the plants have a chance to reproduce.

Acts and Affirmations

Become proactive in the effort to preserve the native plants of your region. Join the nearest native plant society and volunteer at a botanical gardens that seeks to grow indigenous species. Only by a concerted effort can we protect nature's greatest gifts, which are threatened by incompatible land uses and dangerously invasive exotic plants.

may 10

Gardens are not made by sitting in the shade.
—Rudyard Kipling

When we break sweat on the forehead, it is something akin to a badge of courage, for only when we put our back into it will a beautiful garden result. To garden is to don one's mud boots, roll up one's sleeves, and take into one's hands the hoe, shovel, rake, and spading fork. As the days warm into summer, the gardening zealot abhors the shade, reveling in it only for a noon respite, and stopping during that glorious hour at sunset to admire the fruit of one's labor.

Acts and Affirmations

When forced to do something they hated, Catholics used to "offer it up" as a sacrifice of self-denial. As you move into the heat of summer and want to rest in the shade, when sweat drips off your nose and you hear the chaise lounge calling, vow to spend an extra thirty minutes with your plants. The discipline will make you a physically and spiritually stronger person.

may 11

Every great locality has its own pure daimon [spirit], and is conveyed at last into perfected life. Every great locality expresses itself perfectly, in its own flowers, its own birds and beasts, lastly its own men, with their perfected works.
—D. H. LAWRENCE, "The Spirit of Place," *Studies in Classic American Literature,* 1923

If you consider all the beautiful places in the natural world, you will realize that the single most important defining element is plant life. Except for geological wonders such as the Grand Canyon, the native plants of a continent or region dictate its character or spirit. Towering forests with their dark, fern-covered recesses are the hallmark of the Pacific Northwest. The sun-filled, tall grass prairie is the signature of the endless midwestern plains. Fiery maples draw visitors to New England in autumn year after year. Thus, it is the plants that we respond to when we find a place beautiful and inviting. When we spend time in a place, there we not only learn the qualities of its defining plants but we become intimate with the diversity of wildlife that is an integral part of its holistic pure spirit.

ACTS AND AFFIRMATIONS

Each garden, no matter how small, is a universe unto itself. The art of knowing a garden is to feel its sense of place and experience the miraculous vision of the Creator. Make a point of visiting a great garden this year. Take the time to sit awhile and notice what contributes to its sense of place. Often it is the trees or flowers. This helps you learn how to view a garden conceptually, as the original designer did when it was little more than a few small lines on a piece of paper.

Great-flowered Magnolia M. grand-iflora
Duval Co. Fla. J.R.C. coll.

Buffalo-nut Pyrularia pubera

Fruit & flower of Small Magnolia M. virginiana

Island Heights Barnegat Bay N.J. J.R.C. coll.

may 12

Let your prayers for a good crop be short, and your hoeing be long.
—EARLY AMERICAN PROVERB

Many people who depend on their single annual crop for life itself charge the act of farming with all kinds of mystical religious observances. These practices, from offering sacrifices to singing to the plants, are a beautiful reflection of the belief in a separate being that governs all plants and their growth. Prayer may satisfy the fickle gods of nature, but frequent and thorough hoeing is a far more reliable way of ensuring an abundant crop and gorgeous garden.

ACTS AND AFFIRMATIONS
At dawn or dusk, after all the hoeing is done, say this short East African prayer over your garden:

Seed we bring . . . Lord, to thee, wilt thou bless them, O Lord!
Gardens we bring . . . Lord, to thee, wilt thou bless them, O Lord!
Hoes we bring . . . Lord, to thee, wilt thou bless them, O Lord!

may 13

FEAST OF
OUR LADY OF FATIMA

Then, just a few yards away, at the very top of a small holm-oak tree, their attention was attracted by another, unearthly light, which enveloped or sprang from the figure of a lovely young lady, beautiful beyond anything they had ever seen or imagined.
—ALPHONSE CAPPA, *Fatima: Cove of Wonders*, 1979

The appearance of the "Shining Lady" to three children in Portugal in 1917 was believed by some to have not only spiritual but political significance. The vision of Our Lady of Fatima appeared standing on a holm oak—the same species that the pagans believed the most sacred in the forest. Her presence on it suggested to some that through her the Communist empire of the Soviet Union would someday be overthrown through prayer and devotion. Such predictions came to fruition in our lifetime, led by Pope John Paul II and the faith-filled people of Poland, who comprised the first country to throw off the yoke of Soviet Communism. It was not long after that all of Eastern Europe became free.

ACTS AND AFFIRMATIONS

The Shining Lady could be seen only by three young children, which reminds us that the innocence of childhood is the fertile earth where we sow the seeds of humanity's future. Let us vow to garden more patiently with children and to show them through planting seeds that the seeds of peace must be sowed by every one of us and tended well if the world is to become a better place.

(*Quercus ilex*)

holm oak

The holm oak is indigenous to southern Europe and is one of the few evergreen species of this large genus. It was considered sacred around many temple grounds of both the Greeks and Romans. Because oaks are proven to be struck more often by lightning than any other tree, they became the abode of the thunder gods Zeus and Apollo. Holm oaks make fine landscape and street trees, and their drought-resistant qualities make them even more popular in Mediterranean-inspired gardens.

may 14

It's great, and there is no other greatness—to make one nook of God's creation more fruitful, better, more worthy of God; to make some human heart a little wiser, manlier, happier—more blessed, less accursed.

—THOMAS CARLYLE, nineteenth-century essayist

Many of us are gifted with a tiny nook of God's creation. It is our choice to leave it as is or to render it more fruitful by planting foliage and flowers. In a sense that "the whole is greater than the sum of its parts," so a garden created has far more potential to bless the human heart than a mere collection of plants. Such is the nature of free will, which allows us to fill each day with the beauty of lush, Eden-like gardens that will feed, decorate, and enhance our common existence.

ACTS AND AFFIRMATIONS

Many infirm or elderly people live in dreary apartments and rarely have the opportunity to encounter living flowers. To make their lives more fruitful and blessed this year, buy some flats of blooming pansies or primroses, and plant them densely in small red clay pots that fit on a windowsill. Then take them to the housebound or nursing home seniors in your neighborhood, and make "some human heart" a little brighter.

may 15

Feast of St. Isidore the Farmer

Lord of the harvest, you placed the gifts of creation in our hands and called us to till the earth and make it fruitful. We ask your blessing as we prepare to place these seeds in the earth. May the care we show these seeds remind us of your tender love for your people.

—Blessing of Seeds at Planting Time, *Book of Blessings*, 1989

Today in Latin America and Spain, the crops are still blessed the traditional way at planting time. The blessings usually include a flower-decorated statue of St. Isidore, patron of farmers and farmworkers. The figure is carried in procession through each field in the community to shed St. Isidore's blessing on the young seedlings. This saint, once a Spanish farmer who lived at the end of the first millennium, was famous for feeding the poor even though he himself was almost as poor. Like the biblical loaves and fishes, St. Isidore's small supply of homegrown vegetables seemed to multiply miraculously as a reward for his generosity.

Acts and Affirmations

As a statue of St. Isidore is carried through the newly planted fields, the priest or spiritual leader sprinkles holy water by dipping a sprig of hyssop or palm frond into a bucket. These water blessings exist in many other cultures and faiths, particularly in dry climates, where scant rainfall is invoked by the casting of droplets onto the earth. Bless your new garden this year with water drawn from a natural source such as a river, lake, or spring. Ask God, nature, or St. Isidore to imbue the seedlings with fertility and the skies with abundant rainfall.

may 16

The garden is the poor man's apothecary.

—German proverb

The ancient Doctrine of Signatures was a belief that the shape and color of a plant was a sign from God indicating what ailments that plant was capable of curing in human beings. This belief persisted until the nineteenth century, and even today in parts of rural Europe, herbal folk remedies based on this approach are still used. The belief in herbal healing in conjunction with divine providence illustrates that healing the body and healing the mind go hand in hand. Although it is unlikely that many herbs carry a signature, many people are rediscovering that God offers us, free of charge, an entire apothecary garden to cure or comfort those who suffer illness.

Acts and Affirmations

Take advantage of the free gifts of God and nature by enjoying an ancient beauty treatment for dark hair. Harvest a quantity of rosemary leaves and chop them finely. Boil a saucepan of water, then remove from heat and add the rosemary. Allow it to steep for a day or more, then use a strainer to pour off the fragrant water. Use this rinse on freshly shampooed hair to discover nature's own free gift of lustrous, shiny, and naturally fragrant tresses.

may 17

I remember gazing with interest at the swamps about those days and wondering if I could ever attain to such familiarity with plants that I should know the species of every twig and leaf in them, that I should be acquainted with every plant (excepting grasses and cryptogamous ones), summer and winter, that I saw.

—Henry David Thoreau, *Journal*, 1906

There are three steps to identifying a plant, and once accomplished that plant will be a friend for life. Step one is to become familiar with its size, shape, color, growth habit, flower, and fruit. That way you will be able to identify it in a nursery container or its natural habitat. The second step is to hear its botanical name spoken and learn to pronounce it yourself so you get an ear for the lyrical sound of its genus and species. Third is to write its name down so that you recognize the plant in the printed word. These qualities are just the beginning of the friendship, though, for to *know* a plant you must be concerned with its personal preferences concerning soil, exposure, temperature, and water requirements. Plants can be as complex as people, and it takes time and patience to understand them and to develop deep, lifelong friendships with them.

Acts and Affirmations

If you cannot name all the plants in your garden, make a point to do so using the three steps outlined above. It may require a little detective work to identify them, so take some samples to your local nursery for assistance and ask for the correct pronunciation of their Latin names. Strive to learn them all so that your garden is transformed from a collection of plants to a close-knit group of familiar friends.

may 18

What is life? It is the flash of a firefly in the night. It is the breath of a buffalo in the wintertime. It is the little shadow which runs across the grass and loses itself in the sunset.

—Eagle Chief Letakos-Lesa, Pawnee tribe

How long has it been since you've watched a shadow move across the grass? There always seems to be pressing things to do. In life as in the garden, while we are busying ourselves with cleanup and watering and weeding, we forget to take the time to observe and enjoy. In doing so, we miss out on the nuances that define the very heart and soul of the garden.

Acts and Affirmations

Challenge yourself to rebel against the need to stay busy. Choose a time in the morning or evening when your garden is most beautiful. Find a comfortable lounge chair and spend at least thirty minutes doing *nothing*. Don't pull weeds or clean up, don't think about work, don't plan, don't worry about anything. Just observe each leaf, every flower, the busy movement of honeybees. You will find this much harder than you think, but like meditation, it will develop a gift of sharpened observation that brings harmony and peace to body and soul.

may 19

Well Dressing Day

The sacred wells became "Holy" wells, the goddesses who had presided over them became nymphs and guardians of wells, or saints to whom the wells were dedicated. Some have survived against all odds, hidden away in the depths of the countryside and still able to evoke feelings of veneration for the Earth Mother, as symbolized by a mysterious pool of life-giving water.

—J. Bord, *Earth Rites*, 1978

The goddesses often dwelled in the springs and wells of pre-Christian Europe. The Arthurian Lady of the Lake is but one example of the feminine quality attributed to springs. On special days, the Druid priests of the Celts made sacrifices to the spirits of the water, and the springs were decorated to further please the incumbent spirits. Well Dressing Day is still observed in parts of Britain. The banks of springs, now dedicated to saints, are decorated with massive floral displays.

Acts and Affirmations

If you have a birdbath or a basin in your garden, use it to honor the spirits of the water today. (Basins are growing in popularity as a more natural-looking way to lure wildlife than a traditional birdbath.) Choose different colored flowers from your garden or florist and pull the petals off. Then scatter them on the still water, where they will float for hours. You'll enjoy a new face on the water as the petals swirl into ever-changing patterns.

may 20

There are certain things, often very little things, like the little peanut, the little piece of clay, the little flower that cause you to look within—and then it is that you see into the soul of things.

—George Washington Carver, *The Man Who Talked with Flowers*, 1939

George Washington Carver, born a slave, became the greatest American botanist in history. Yet despite his great work and fame, he remained a humble man who still saw the enormous value in small things. His work proved that even the most common, lowly creations such as the peanut contained the ability to rescue whole populations of people suffering from illness and malnutrition. How often have we overlooked the potential of commonly found things in favor of the glamour of shining things that have no soul?

Acts and Affirmations

To live off the land, get to know useful and edible plants. Those who can survive on wild plants will never be burdened by the fear of starvation. Start in your own backyard by gathering a "bunch" of fresh dandelion leaves and either stew them gently and salt to taste, or add to a salad of other greens.

may 21

I do not know what human sentiment the principal division of my garden was intended to reflect; and there is none to tell me. Those by whom it was made passed away long generations ago, in the eternal transmigration of souls. But as a poem of nature it requires no interpreter.

—Lafcadio Hearn, *Glimpses of Unfamiliar Japan*, 1894

Japanese gardens can live for centuries relatively unchanged because each tree and shrub is skillfully pruned to a precise form and scale. Though Lafcadio Hearn, a Westerner, had no idea of the incredible effort and planning required to create his garden, or of the Buddhist messages it conveys, he is still in awe of its beauty. The garden speaks in a single silent language understood by all people. And for those who wish to learn more of its endless depths, there is a lifetime of knowledge to be gleaned.

Acts and Affirmations

Create your own expression of nature by planting Japanese garden juniper (*Juniperus procumbens 'Nana'*) as a potted bonsai. Choose a large, deep bonsai pot and a very small juniper, found at most nurseries. Prune the roots only enough to fit into the pot, and let the long branches cascade over the edges. Then use a small pair of clippers or scissors to carefully sculpt the juniper over many weeks or months. The key to survival of any bonsai tree is to keep the small root system evenly moist, which may require watering it every day.

may 22

The clouds are our water carriers,—and do you see that hand-breath of greener grass where the cattle have dropped dung? That was the first lecturer on Agriculture.
—Ralph Waldo Emerson, journal, 1835

Observation is our most vital tool for learning about gardening. The ability to observe keenly allows us to see the subtle changes in plants or to discern the effects of this task or that material on individual species. Observation is a skill that serves us in other aspects of life as well. It is vital in the art of interpersonal communication because so much of what people don't say is reflected in the subtle language of their bodies. To observe is to learn, to learn is to grow, and to grow throughout your whole life means that every day brings a new discovery.

Acts and Affirmations
God: Help me to be more observant every day. Grant me the eyes of an artist, tuned to the slightest detail. May I pick out the subtle differences in colors and light and the contrasting textures that make a garden so dynamic. Most of all, let me better observe people to hear the silent messages they convey when words do not suffice.

may 23

Rosalia: Roman Feast of Roses (varies)

Let them leap in a great bow or fall in a creamy cataract to a foaming pool of flowers. In the midst of the garden set a statue of Venus with a great bloom trained to her hand, or of Flora, her cornucopia overflowing with white roses, or a tiny basin where leaden amorini *seated on the margin are fishing with trailing buds.*

—Sir George Sitwell, nineteenth century

Romans loved the rose more than any other flower, and they dedicated a whole festival to them. Goddesses Flora and Venus were invoked during this festival, known as Rosalia, by decorating homes with fresh flowers. Romans loved the rose's wonderful scent, which they used to scent their homes and banquet halls. Citizens of the empire wore garlands of them at every religious celebration. This practice was inherited by Catholic priests, who wore flowers on feast days until the Reformation.

Acts and Affirmations

Romans were known to drench pigeons in rose water and release them over the heads of Rosalia festivalgoers for a rain of scented droplets as the birds flew away. Create your own rose water for sprinkling around your home and garden by simply adding a few drops of rose oil (available from drugstore perfume counters or health food stores) to a spray bottle of water. Turn the nozzle to mist and scent everything in sight (including yourself, your family, and your friends) to honor this queen of flowers on her special day.

(*Rosa Damascena*)

Damask rose

The damask rose was first discovered by the Romans in the Middle East near the city of Damascus, hence the botanical name. They were so enchanted by the flower because, unlike all other roses, it bloomed not just in spring but again more modestly in the fall. Romans discovered that it did so only in warm winter climates, so their gardeners went to great lengths to produce fresh blossoms out of season using greenhouses and artificial heat. Cultivars of the damask rose are still fine garden plants that require little work and let you experience firsthand the fragrance so coveted by the ancients.

may 24

While the aristocracy, wealthy and even religious stumbled and fell into their gardens, God continued to tend the "wild" flowers of the countryside. The pleasant, small householder, or gardening monk, too, tended his field or his modest garden. As garden worker he understood how utterly dependent he was on God's providence for his daily bread and how his loving stewardship for God's creatures, seeds, plants, blooms, fruits, was an integral part of the providential ordering of nature.

—JOHN S. STOKES, JR., *Man in God's Garden*, 1953

Monks have tended gardens for millennia. A knowledge of plants and horticulture is traditional in these religious communities, be they Tibetan Buddhists or Franciscan monks. Monastic communities are often self-sufficient, living a vow of poverty and sustained by what foods they can grow. St. Francis called this way of life true freedom. If we strive to free ourselves from outside dependencies by turning to our garden for healing, gifts, decoration, and spiritual inspiration, we may gain a glimpse of how deeply the roots of horticulture grow into the fertile ground of monastic life.

ACTS AND AFFIRMATIONS

Inks used by monks to write illuminated manuscripts were derived from plants in their gardens. Elderberries and mulberries were used for blue ink. Follow their example by writing a special note to someone using berry ink on parchment. Try either a fine paintbrush, a calligraphy pen, or—if you're ambitious—a quill. Blackberries from the garden or growing wild are ideal for this purpose, but if none are available, use frozen blackberries or blueberries. Simply crush the berries and strain off the juice—then choose your words carefully.

may 25

The Tree of Eternity has its roots in heaven above and its branches reach down to earth. It is Brahman, pure Spirit, who in truth is called Immortal. All the worlds rest on that Spirit and beyond him no one can go.

—The Upanishads, 600–300 B.C.

Many cultures and faiths recognize a tree of life or a source tree of their people. Why a tree? Because trees have two distinct yet equal parts: the canopy, with its many branches and leaves, exists in the heavens, while the root system, often of a similar scale, rests in the earth. The trunk unites these two realms.

Acts and Affirmations

In India, women honor the fig tree as a powerful bridge between heaven and earth. They pour flavored drinks onto the ground at the base of the trunk, then utter the prayers of fertility as they tie a red or yellow string around the trunk. Choose a tree of your own to symbolize this bridge. Share a glass of wine or fruit juice with the tree by pouring half onto the ground. Then claim it as your own by tying brightly colored strings around its trunk.

may 26

Stones, plants, animals, the earth, the sky, the stars, the elements, in fact everything in the universe reveals to us the knowledge, power and the will of its Originator.

—Abu Hamid Muhammad Al-Ghazzali, eleventh century

Were the Earth and its creatures created by God or by a chaotic cataclysm? Many great writers from the ancients to moderns continually reflect on the same idea. Certainly there is order to the natural world. There is order to the way plants grow in our gardens. There is order to the way plants arrange themselves naturally on the land. It is difficult to believe that this is a random factor when all the clues point to some kind of larger plan. Whether it is God or a divine intelligence we may never know, but by gardening we are forever reminded of the order and, thus, are forever urged to ponder its mysterious genesis.

Acts and Affirmations

The ancient Egyptians, the court of King Solomon, and the Persian Moguls all created cooling drinks out of the juice of pomegranate seeds. To enjoy this refreshing, astringent drink as temperatures warm up, buy or pick ripe pomegranates, extract the hundreds of seeds, then press them against the sides of a bowl and pour off the juice. Add the juice to carbonated water and add sugar to taste.

may 27

Lying in the sunshine among the buttercups and dandelions of May, scarcely higher in intelligence than the minute tenants of that mimic wilderness, our earliest recollections are of grass; and when the fitful fever is ended, and the foolish wrangle of the market and forum is closed, grass heals over the scar which our descent into the bosom of the earth has made, and the carpet of the infant becomes the blanket of the dead.

—Kansas senator John James Ingalls, *In Praise of Blue Grass*, 1872

From cradle to grave, the grass that spreads out beneath us is a living carpet that cushions our feet, protects the soil, and fills the landscape with a great swath of emerald beauty. Grass can be thought to embody forgiveness, for no matter how we scar the earth, wild grass seeds flying on the breeze put down roots to quickly heal that open wound.

Acts and Affirmations

Practice a personal act of forgiveness in your garden. Think about something someone did that offended or hurt you. Then choose a flower, a bundle of herbs, or even some ripe strawberries from the garden. Wrap them in bright tissue paper, and bury them in a special place in your garden. This ritual will help you shed your resentments. Over time, you will be better able to ask forgiveness of others as well.

may 28

In the woods we return to reason and faith. There I feel that nothing can befall me in life,—no disgrace, no calamity which nature cannot repair.
—Ralph Waldo Emerson, *Nature*, 1836

Into every life a little rain must fall, and for some it falls in torrents. We cannot expect our life to be without sorrow, but we can try to cope with it in constructive ways. Emerson knew, as the ancient authors did, that the best place to dull the pain is in a garden or the woods. Somehow the eternal nature of great trees, the transient yet serene faces of flowers, and the soft curling tresses of ferns seem to reach out to us in sympathy. Though they utter no words, we are assured that they will always be there to offer their silent solace.

Acts and Affirmations

The bleeding heart (*Dicentra spectabilis*) is a woodland perennial with very flat, pendulous, heart-shaped flowers that have long made them a favorite choice for pressing in books. As they bloom this year, press some flowers carefully in a big book until fully dry. Then add them to sympathy cards for friends and relatives on the inevitable sad occasions that are part of every human life.

may 29

When the Pope alights in a new country his first gesture is to kneel down and kiss the ground. This is a sign of his intense respect and devotion to that part of the earth—a feeling which most of us have at some time or another, particularly about our own land.

The Pope re-enacts what may be a very ancient religious rite, for the mystical bonding of mankind to earth found its expression in the Divine Mother who was herself the earth.

—Anne Bancroft, *Origins of the Sacred*, 1987

In the modern world, we are losing the ancient rites that gave our lives spiritual meaning. Rituals are not only grand religious experiences but small acts that connect us with antiquity. When the Pope kisses the ground, he is reenacting a remnant of the old religions of Europe, which held the earth in great reverence. This simple act says more in just seconds than orators or authors can conceive in a lifetime. Let us not reject rituals because of their connections to certain dogmas but rather embrace them as vital experiences that enrich our lives with a unique form of spiritual expression.

Acts and Affirmations

All of earth is sacred, but certain places are more hallowed than others. Religious pilgrims have long fulfilled their obligation to visit such holy places as Mecca, Rome, and Santiago de Compostela. If you have the opportunity to travel to some of the sacred places of the world, consider bringing back your own pinch of earth. Whether it originates at the Egyptian temples, the Black Hills medicine circles of the Dakotas, or at the sites of martyrdom of Tibetan monks, bring home some earth (sealed in a glass bottle) and store in a beautiful box or bottle.

may 30

We have nothing to fear and a great deal to learn from trees, that vigorous and pacific tribe which without stint produces strengthening essences for us, soothing balms, and in whose gracious company we spend so many cool, silent and intimate hours.

—Marcel Proust, *Pleasures and Regrets*, 1948

There is little doubt that trees large and small have a great influence on our environment. It is no wonder that ancient people saw trees as the abodes of spirits, for when humans were still in daub-and-wattle huts, they knew nothing larger in their world. As the days warm into summer, let us remain fully aware of the beauty of every tree in the street, park, or garden. These trees shield us from the elements, oxygenate our air, and enhance the environment by their presence.

Acts and Affirmations

Is there a perfect tree? Is there one with a perfect trunk, well-distributed branches, or a totally balanced canopy? Some artists look for it every day of their lives as a sort of personal observation exercise. When commuting, traveling, or simply wandering around your neighborhood, look for that perfect one—and teach your children to do so, too. The reward is not in the finding of the perfect tree but in the looking—for it sharpens our consciousness of this "vigorous and pacific tribe."

may 31

The way of cultivation is not easy.
He who plants a garden plants happiness.
—Chinese proverb

The way of cultivation is living the consciousness of a farmer who is governed by the natural cycle of the seasons, which orders tasks from quarter to quarter. Each season presents its own character, from labor-intensive spring planting to resting by the fire during winter. It is natural to live by the schedule dictated by sun and temperature rather than by those artificially imposed on us by a technological society. It is living had in hand with the earth that returns us to the fundamental relationships with plant and soil, and as we plant each year's new garden we invariably sow happiness.

Acts and Affirmations

The way of cultivation includes deep respect for the finite existence of all wild plants. Never gather plants from the wild to transplant into your garden or use for other purposes. There may appear to be a great supply of wild plants, but with so many people wild-crafting medicinal plants, many species are threatened.

june

June is the month of the summer solstice, a time that was celebrated as the day of longest light. But along with the festivities, there was the sad realization that from this time onward, the days would only grow shorter—leading some to call it the "bittersweet" solstice. This month is likely named after the Roman goddess Juno, patron of marriage and childbirth.

She is the reason we consider June the best month for weddings. The Celts also considered it the best month for pasture, and the name "Woed-monath" (weed month) describes the food that their cattle grazed. June is the month of roses. It is also the month of honeysuckle, or woodbine—a plant whose flowers were used in perfume, as a medicine, and as a protection against evil spirits.

MOHAWK MOON OF RIPENING TIME

CELTIC WOED-MONATH, OR WEED MONTH

june 1

You are privileged to create new varieties of roses, new shapes, new colors. To you it is granted to improve the garden of the Lord.
—Pope Pius XII, 1955

In 1955 Pope Pius XII, a supporter of emerging twentieth-century science, addressed an international gathering of rosarians in Rome. His words evoke the great mystery and magic of plant breeding, the art of coaxing out recessive genes through selective breeding. We take plant propagation for granted, but, when you consider that the thousands of roses we know today originated from a handful of wild species, there is little doubt that humanity has indeed improved on the garden the Lord has created.

Acts and Affirmations

The flower of the month of June is the rose, so celebrate by making rose petal sugar for topping fresh fruits or sweetening iced tea. Choose a few small, highly fragrant, flawless roses and bury them whole in a quart of white sugar. Seal the container and let it stand in the sun for three or four weeks as the rose fragrance penetrates the sugar. Remove and discard the roses—then enjoy this simple yet decadent sweetening throughout the summer.

(ROSA GALLICA OFFICINALIS)

the apothecary rose

The ancient medicinal rose of Europe, *Rosa gallica officinalis*, could be found in virtually every apothecary garden since ancient Rome. It is the species so often depicted in the stained-glass "rose windows" of medieval cathedrals. Treasured by Romans and kings throughout Europe and later carried by the Moors into northern Africa, this beautiful plant and its progeny are still widely favored today for their rich magenta flowers, heavy scent, and large, round hips. Spanish missionaries in the eighteenth century brought the apothecary rose to the New World colonies of Latin America, from which it traveled northward to the California missions. By the end of the nineteenth century, *Rosa gallica* claimed a place in the ancestry of most contemporary rose varieties.

june 2

But I am now come to speak of the pleasures of a country life, with which I am infinitely delighted. To these old age never is an obstruction. It is the life of nature, and appears to me the precise course which a wise man ought to follow.

—CICERO, first century B.C.

Cicero no doubt suffered from the oppressive summer heat and crowded living conditions in Rome. In his great wisdom, he believed that the country was a better place to live. And he also knew that, though we grow old, we will always be able to enjoy the pleasures of farm and garden, if only to recline amid the plants and flowers. As old age approaches, let us find consolation in the knowledge that we can spend our waning days living a natural life.

ACTS AND AFFIRMATIONS

Roman chamomile, *Anthemis nobilis*, is in bloom now and should be harvested while in flower. Use a pair of scissors to snip off the buds, which are the part used in medicinal tea. Lay out the flowers in a single layer on a brown paper bag or flat basket. Dry them in a place out of direct sun and away from moisture. When dried, store in an airtight jar for making tea. Chamomile flower tea is the most widely used medicinal for upset stomach.

june 3

A soul that is not close to nature is far away from what is called spirituality. In order to be spiritual one must communicate, and especially one must communicate with nature; one must feel nature.
—HAZRAT INAYAT KHAN, master Sufi musician

We gaze on nature and work amid her in the garden, but it is another thing entirely to feel her. This intuitive experience is one that involves our whole consciousness and all five senses. Touch the leaves to discover their textures. Smell the perfume of flowers. Listen to the rustling of leaf and branch, a sound that spoke to the ancient Druids. Look at plants on a microscopic level to appreciate their minute parts. All of these things combine to allow your mind, body, and spirit to actually feel nature in all her infinite manifestations.

ACTS AND AFFIRMATIONS

Open new lines of communication with your garden by really listening to its subtle sounds. You must close your eyes to block out the visual sense, which makes your hearing more acute. Listen to how the breeze rustles noisily through the treetops or ruffles the tall grasses. Open your ears to the birds busy nesting and feeding their young at this time of year. This new dimension will bring you a much deeper sense of belonging any time of day and in every season.

june 4

The rose is the flower of Venus: in order that her sweet thefts might be concealed, Love dedicated to Hippocrates, the God of Silence this gift of his mother. Hence the host hangs over his friendly table a rose, that the guests underneath it may know how to keep silence as to what is said.
—COLUMELLA, *De Re Rustica*, first century A.D.

In the days of the ancient Roman Empire, the rose became a symbol of secrets kept so that what was discussed or said under a rose was never to be repeated. The phrase "Sub-Rosa" meant "under the rose." Actual roses hung over treaty signings well into the nineteenth century. This practice reminds us that gossip is a most damaging habit. When something is shared in confidence, it is our moral duty to keep it so.

ACTS AND AFFIRMATIONS

The Sybarites were an ancient people who took their love of luxury and pleasure to the extreme. Their celebration of Rosalia was no different: rose water flowed from their fountains, and they stuffed their beds with flowers. Get in touch with your own sybaritic side by drawing a warm bath and sprinkling a large quantity of fresh rose petals on top. Bathe in sybaritic splendor.

june 5

There grows no herb to heal a coward's heart.
—Ancient proverb

The ability to stick with a problem or challenge requires great courage. We tend to give up quickly after mild discouragement, yet it is an undeniable truth that nothing worth having comes easily. Be it mastering the cultivation of a favored flower or training a recalcitrant child, the eventual success is always made sweeter by the struggle.

Acts and Affirmations

Use the culinary rue (*Ruta graveolens*), also known as "herb of grace," to bless your garden. Use water drawn from a special place such as a sacred well or a beloved lake. If you are Christian, use holy water from Lourdes or water blessed at your church. Or create your own "holy" water by steeping a sacred object in spring water for a week, then sprinkle it at an auspicious moment.

june 6

What is the most rigorous law of our being? Growth. No smallest atom of our moral, mental, or physical structure can stand still a year. It grows—it must grow; nothing can prevent it.

—Mark Twain, *Complete Essays*, 1884

One law of plant life, what botanists collectively call "biomass," is that it is always on the increase. Trees grow steadily larger. Roots are forever seeking new ground, and seeds continue to sprout year after year. Perhaps this is one of the few things we can count on in life, for just as change is a constant, so is the growth of plants.

Acts and Affirmations

Biomass is always increasing, but the rain forests of South America are being cleared by commercial loggers and by poor farmers who use slash-and-burn agriculture to support their large families. We can help reduce logging or slash-and-burn clearing not by forcing the poor off their land but by donating generously to organizations that provide financial aid and education to poor farmers. In this way we can help protect the ecosystem while providing a compassionate alternative to this environmentally disastrous way of life.

No race can prosper till it learns there is as much dignity in tilling a field as in writing a poem.
—Booker T. Washington, Atlanta Exposition, 1895

We don't use the word *peasants* much these days, but in the past it was a term for people who lived off the land and farmed it but usually did not own it. Peasants were considered lowly, uneducated, uncultured people who had little to offer the world except the labor of their dirt-encrusted hands. Yet without the tilling of the fields, there cannot be any food, and without food there is no humanity, educated or not. Clearly, the writing of a poem, the design of a skyscraper, and the turning of the soil are all of equal value to the world. But the world can live without poems or skyscrapers—it cannot live without farmers.

Acts and Affirmations

In June many of the annual wildflowers are coming into bloom. We drive so quickly these days that we pass millions of them on the roadside every day and fail to see the amethyst and emerald, gold and ruby gems that peasants studied as they traveled by at horse-and-wagon speed. Make a point to begin watching the roadside for flowers. Take time to stop for a few minutes to see them up close, or pick a humble bouquet of charming flowering weeds.

june 8

> *You are reading when incense is burning and all your human obligations are fulfilled, while outside the screen the flower petals are dripping and the moon has come up to the top of the pine trees, and you suddenly hear the temple bell and push open the window and see the Milky Way—such a moment is superior to daytime.*
>
> —Confucian proverb

The enjoyment of singing insects such as crickets and cicadas dates back thousands of years in China. Farmers recognized the first singing of crickets as their signal to plow the fields. The Chinese also believed the key to success was to have many children, and these insects, which laid many hundreds of eggs at a time, became their symbol of prosperity both in the field and in the home. It became a popular custom to catch crickets in the fall and keep them in cages in the warm indoors to enjoy their singing through winter when the rest fell silent outdoors. We don't consider the songs of the crickets musical, but they are so loved in China that keeping caged crickets became a popular hobby that still continues today.

Acts and Affirmations

As you lie awake in the moonlight listening to the songs of the crickets grow louder through the summer, take a moment to appreciate their many voices. Discover that not all sing the same tune, nor share similar rhythms. As you relax after a frenzied day, let them lull you to sleep as peace comes, dropping low into the warm evening.

june 9

To sit in the shade on a fine day, and look upon verdure is the most perfect refreshment.

—Jane Austen, *Mansfield Park*, 1814

Having a garden is not all work and activity. As the afternoons warm, it comes time to sit in the shade and enjoy the verdure of your lawn, the fruits of your spring planting, and the results of countless hours of weeding. We tend to feel guilty when relaxing because there is always something that can be done, but *must* it be done? It's easy to confuse the two, which indicates a problem with setting priorities. Too many people suffer needlessly because of misplaced priorities. They would find their lives far more peaceful if they sat in the shade and thought about it for a very long while.

Acts and Affirmations

The hammock is a very ancient invention that is wonderfully adaptable. Hang one between two trees in your backyard for the perfect way to comfortably relax in the shade on a hot June day. An inexpensive, fine net hammock takes up very little room and is easily stowed up in the tree branches when not in use. This summer, invest in this ancient lounge chair and gently lie swinging in the shade.

june 10

Give me books, fruit, French wine and fine weather and a little music out of doors, played by someone I do not know. . . . I admire lolling on a lawn by a water-lilied pond to eat white currants and see goldfish: and go to the fair in the evening if I'm good.

—John Keats, letter, 1819

Keats writes of the infinite beauty of the water garden and the mesmerizing golden fish that haunt its depths. Water gardens, with their great lily pads floating on the surface, are forever changing, as their surroundings are mirrored in the glassy surface. Psychologists often have aquariums of tropical fish in their waiting rooms to help patients remain calm, and it is no secret that the fluid movements of koi or goldfish are equally effective in calming the noise in our heads. When the noise quiets, we, too, might glide through our environment without concern, even when we are surrounded by total chaos.

Acts and Affirmations

Create a tiny, contemplative water garden of your own using a large, glazed ceramic pot. Choose it with care: those of Asian origin with emerald green or other colorful glazing are the best. Purchase a few water hyacinths and a pot of reeds from a local nursery or water garden shop. Set the reed pot on the bottom and drop the hyacinths in, and begin to feel the magic of the water garden's ever-changing beauty.

june 11

We've got this gift of love, but love is like a precious plant. You can't just accept it and leave it in the cupboard or just think it's going to get on by itself. You've got to keep watering it. You've got to really look after it and nurture it.

—JOHN LENNON, *Man of the Decade* broadcast, 1969

With time, our relationships and marriages can become stale, like a root-bound plant with no place to spread into new ground. The daily routines of life—work, kids, housekeeping, and paying the bills—combine to push out the romantic notions we had in our youth. To cultivate a passionate relationship with another, try new things, whether it is travel and adventure or simply a new restaurant for a night on the town. Just as we try new plants in our gardens every year to see if they are beautiful and suited to us, overcome complacency by adding new, even risky, surprises into your relationships.

ACTS AND AFFIRMATIONS

Almonds have always been considered erotic food, and almond paste, or marzipan, is an ideal food to share with your lover. To make the paste, grind up two cups of slivered or sliced almonds in a food processor with two tablespoons of sugar. Then add one cup sugar, one-half cup water, half a teaspoon of vanilla extract, three tablespoons of corn syrup, and one-quarter teaspoon of almond extract, and process until smooth. On a cutting board dusted with powdered sugar, form the paste into beautiful, perhaps erotic, shapes, and allow them to dry for a few hours. Then choose a beautiful place in the evening garden to share wine and nibble marzipan by candlelight.

june 12

Shavuot: Hebrew Feast of First Fruits

On the day of the first fruits, your Feast of Weeks, then you bring an offering of new grain to the Lord, you shall observe a sacred occasion: you shall not work at your occupations.

—Numbers 28:26

The Jewish holiday of Shavuot is one of the most beautiful of all agricultural celebrations. In biblical times, insects, diseases, wind, rain, fire, and drought were ever-present threats, and the Hebrews were dependent on God to protect the crops against failure and famine. This holiday focused around the wheat harvest, which provided the flour to make bread, a most important staple. During this time of thanksgiving for the harvest, the Hebrews offered up their most perfect fruits and vegetables at the temple in sacrifice. They baked bread to commemorate those delicious first yeasty loaves after the many lean months before the harvest.

Acts and Affirmations

It is traditional to decorate Jewish synagogues with boughs of evergreens for the presentation of the first fruits. In ancient times, these were likely palm or cedar, as both were plentiful in the ancient Holy Land. Commemorate First Fruits by burning cedar incense, or make your own out of leftover pencils. Take a strong knife and shave off all the cedar without nicking the graphite in the center. Create a small pile of shavings in a bowl, anoint it with a few drops of olive oil or beeswax. Take a sniff, and you'll know what the inside of King Solomon's temple really smelled like.

(*Cedrus libani*)

cedar of lebanon

In biblical times, forests of cedar of Lebanon existed on the mountain slopes of the Holy Land. It was a highly valued tree because its wood is resistant to rot and repells insects. From these forests King Solomon cut the trees with which he built his great temple that contained the Ark of the Covenant. The destruction of the forests was widespread in ancient times, and today only a few of the statuesque old groves remain on Mount Sinai. The cedar of Lebanon is a truly sacred species in the Judeo-Christian tradition, for it is featured throughout the Bible as a symbol of Israel. It has also proven a top-quality evergreen landscape tree and is now planted throughout the United States on large homesites, on boulevards, and in parks.

june 13

ANCIENT GREEK FESTIVAL OF ZEUS

Mountains are to the rest of the body of the earth, what violent muscular action is to the body of man. The muscles and tendons of its anatomy are, in the mountain, brought out with force and convulsive energy, full of expression, passion, and strength.

—JOHN RUSKIN, *Modern Painters*, 1843–1860

It is no wonder that the Greeks considered the mountaintops the realm of the thunder god, Zeus. The omnipotent king of the gods not only governed thunder but was thought to embody the very thunder itself. How glorious lightning and thunder can be when a summer storm moves across the hot, humid land, striking the highest points with sparks and fire. Trees struck by lightning were to the Greeks proof that Zeus dwelled within. These lightning-burned trees were protected and set apart as Zeus's sacred haunt.

ACTS AND AFFIRMATIONS

When was the last time you stopped to watch the lightning? When we were young, we hid from it, and when we grew older, for many people it became little more than a nuisance that interrupts our busy schedule. Stop and enjoy the thunderheads this summer, wait patiently to see the chains of bright light and the ground-shaking boom that follows. These theatrics of nature sparked the imagination of the ancients and can continue to do so to the open mind.

june 14

You may read the history of half the earth in one of those green oval leaves—the things that the sun and the rivers have made out of dry ground . . . There is nothing so constantly noble as the pure leaf of the laurel.

—John Ruskin, *Prosperina*, 1881

The evergreen tree bay laurel is often associated with victory. In ancient Greece, it was used to crown victors in the Olympic Games and later became the crown of *bacca-laurate*, the bachelor's degree. The laurel represents nobility through deed rather than birthright. It is a symbol of wisdom and knowledge. Laurel shows us that the greatest plants are not always the showiest, and that the greatest people are rarely the most famous or wealthy. Let us always remember that plants and people are chosen for their true character and that leadership and wisdom are often hidden under many layers of humility.

Acts and Affirmations

Wreaths of bay laurel are symbols that reach back thousands of years to classical civilizations. For special holidays use it to crown your garden statues or hang over portraits. Use it as fresh-cut decorations at special gatherings to honor a friend or loved one's promotion or graduation or any other noteworthy accomplishment.

june 15

From Wakan-Tanka, the Great Mystery, comes all power. It is from Wakan-Tanka that the holy man has wisdom and the power to heal and make holy charms. Man knows that all healing plants are given by Wakan-Tanka, therefore they are holy. So too is the buffalo holy, because it is the gift of Wakan-Tanka.

—Sarah Winnemucca, *Life among the Paiutes*, 1883

The spirituality of Native Americans is a reflection of their reverence for nature. It is a belief that all things on earth, and the earth itself, are creations of a single omnipotent spirit. Though Native Americans killed animals for meat and hides, the acts were nearly always accompanied by prayers to thank the dead animal for offering its life to them. The gathering of plants was equally sacred, and the women were careful not to exhaust their resources through overharvesting. They respected plants and often chanted to the plants' spirits during harvest. For medicinal plants, in particular, a chant was thought to help retain their potency.

Acts and Affirmations

Next time you have guests for an outdoor barbecue, enjoy fresh piñon (pine) nuts—available from gourmet markets and health food stores—just like the Paiutes did by roasting them on your fire pit or barbecue grill. Simply add a few tablespoons of olive oil to a heavy frying pan, heat it, and then add enough nuts to cover about half the surface area in a single layer. Place pan on the grill over medium heat, and keep the nuts rolling continuously until they gently turn from white to golden brown. Pour onto paper towels to absorb excess oil—then salt to taste and enjoy the true flavor of the wilderness.

june 16

The earth laughs at him who calls a place his own.
—Hindustani proverb

Even though we may rent or own the land we plant our gardens on, it is never really ours. Our short span of time working the soil is but a blink of an eye. We are more like stewards: we care for our little plot of soil for a limited time, and if we do our job well, it will be more fertile for our having been there. Poor stewardship allows soil to be destroyed by invasive weeds, blown away during the dry season, or eroded during rains. On the other hand, good management practices, like reforestation and erosion control planting, will ensure that the earth stays healthy and productive. Let us all strive to tend our land well as long as we are here on earth.

Acts and Affirmations

Officially accept the responsibility of stewardship of your land with a symbolic gesture. Pull some strands of hair from your hairbrush or comb, knowing that each strand carries a complete and unique DNA profile of your body. Dig a little hole with your bare hands, set the strands inside, and cover. Then mark the point with a stone or plant a seedling on top. It will forever remind you that we do not own our gardens, we just dwell in them for a while.

A man who lives with nature is used to violence and is companionable with death. There is more violence in an English hedgerow than in the meanest streets of a great city.

—P. D. James, *Devices and Desires*, 1989

All of nature and gardens is not serenity but is in fact a continuous struggle for survival. The caterpillar eats our greens because it wishes to become a butterfly; the field mouse strips the corn so she and her young survive the winter. The hunter and the hunted are everywhere. Though we may abhor violence, we are forced to accept it in the realm of nature.

Acts and Affirmations

Predators such as hawks and coyotes are at the top of the food chain and feed on a variety of prey species. Both predator and prey fill an essential role in the balance of nature. Do not impose your own non-violent attitude on predator species, but celebrate their existence, for these are the most endangered (by farmers, ranchers, pollution) species of all. Protect their habitat and they will protect you and your garden by keeping quick-to-reproduce species like locusts and rabbits from overpopulating.

june 18

The best remedy for those who are afraid, lonely or unhappy is to go outside, somewhere where they can be quiet, alone with the heavens, nature and God. Because only then does one feel that all is as it should be and that God wishes to see people happy, amidst the simple beauty of nature. As long as this exists, and it certainly always will, I know that then there will always be comfort for every sorrow, whatever the circumstances may be. And I firmly believe that nature brings solace in all troubles.

—Anne Frank, *The Diary of a Young Girl*, 1944

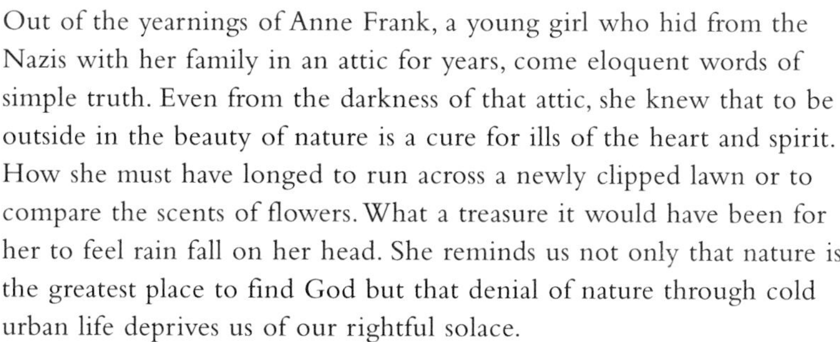

Out of the yearnings of Anne Frank, a young girl who hid from the Nazis with her family in an attic for years, come eloquent words of simple truth. Even from the darkness of that attic, she knew that to be outside in the beauty of nature is a cure for ills of the heart and spirit. How she must have longed to run across a newly clipped lawn or to compare the scents of flowers. What a treasure it would have been for her to feel rain fall on her head. She reminds us not only that nature is the greatest place to find God but that denial of nature through cold urban life deprives us of our rightful solace.

Acts and Affirmations

Most adults have not slept outdoors in the backyard since childhood, yet this is a marvelous experience to have—with or without your kids. To lie out on a summer night and fall asleep while gazing at a canopy of stars is infinitely satisfying. You don't need to go camping or spend time and money to partake in this very simple nocturnal experience all summer long.

june 19

The master's eye is the best fertilizer.

—Pliny the Elder, *Historia Naturalis*, 50 B.C.

While pinching and pruning, hand-watering and fertilizing, successful gardeners become familiar with each individual plant. This intimacy allows them to identify the signs that indicate a plant may need special care. Technology can be a great time-saver, but when a timer turns on your sprinklers automatically, you never get close enough to know your plants as individuals. If you use automatic sprinklers, make a point of inspecting your plants. In a similar vein, technology in our homes, such as e-mail, voice mail, and the telephone, can separate us from other human beings. To avoid a very subtle kind of loneliness that can result from technological separation, take extra time to get close—face to face—to the people you love.

Acts and Affirmations

The act of watering can be a very peaceful experience, particularly on a warm summer evening. Wait until the sun goes down and use the hose to gently wash the dust and grime off all your garden plants. (Don't do this in the sunshine because water can burn the foliage.) You will be surprised at their recovered beauty come morning.

From its hollowness arises the reality of the vessel; from its empty space arises the reality of the building.

—LAO-TZU, Chinese philosopher, sixth century B.C.

Above all, gardens offer human beings a beautiful place to spend time outdoors. Through the arrangement of plants, we can define the limits of the space, its visual appeal, and the way it makes us feel. We can even create separate areas, like rooms in a house, using trees and shrubs. Acts of spiritual significance—such as prayer, contemplation, and work—can also help define the nature of our sacred space, be it in the garden or hidden deep inside the secret realm of the soul.

Acts and Affirmations

The visual image of an empty vessel is a perfect analogy for an open mind. To symbolize this never-ending process of enlightenment and spiritual growth, choose a beautiful pot in a style that represents your sense of self. Dig a hole, set the pot in the hole on its side, then fill in the soil both inside and outside of the pot. Plant in and around it with mosses or low-growing plants as a symbolic reminder that we are all empty vessels and should remain open for nature, God, and life to fill us with wisdom and peace.

june 21

SUMMER SOLSTICE

Thou has grown by favor of the Sun, the Moon, and of the dew. I make this intercession, ye herb: I beseech thee to be of benefit to me and my Art, for thy virtues are unfailing. Thou art the dew of all the Gods, the eye of the Sun, the light of the Moon, the beauty and glory of the Sky, the mystery of the Earth. I purify thee so that whatsoever is wrought by me with thee may, in all its powers, have a good and speedy effect with good success. Be purified by my prayer and be powerful.

—WICCAN MAGICAL HERB-GATHERING INCANTATION

From this day forward the days grow shorter, and gradually the world darkens into winter. Although we cannot perceive it, the plant kingdom senses the change, and mechanisms begin to hasten the ripening of fruit and the setting of seed. If you watch, you will see the change in your vegetable garden over the next few weeks. This is a date for reflection on the reliability of the cycles of the seasons, all governed by the path of the sun as it travels across the heavens.

ACTS AND AFFIRMATIONS

Midsummer's day is the most powerful day of the year to harvest herbs, particularly vervain. If you wish to cut herbs for magical uses, it is best to harvest them under the light of the moon, preferably when it is waxing. Harvesting at night is also practical because cuttings are less likely to wilt as quickly. Many people believe it is best to cut herbs with a blade made of nonferrous metal or ceramic because iron will draw off the earth energy. You may choose to plant a bit of bread or honey to compensate the garden for your gleanings.

(*Verbena officinalis*)

herba sacra

Vervain is an Old World wayside weed that is not much to look at but is believed to be the most powerful of all herbs. This is best evidenced by its many common names, which include enchanter's plant, *herba sacra*, and holy herb. Vervain is traditionally gathered at midsummer solstice or on the rising of the Dog Star. Ancient Egyptians dedicated this wayside plant to their goddess Isis, and Romans revered it for use in purifying their temple altars. Vervain was linked closely with the goddess of love, Venus, and was included in almost every ancient love potion and philter. The crowning wreath of Druids was made of vervain. Christians claimed it was used to staunch the flow of blood from Christ's wounds. Though vervain is rarely found in gardens anymore, the herb that Pilgrims carried to the New World has naturalized across the continent. (Don't confuse it with garden varieties of flowering verbena or lemon verbena.)

june 22

The Sun, the hearth of affection and life, pours burning love on the delighted earth.

—ARTHUR RIMBAUD, *Soleil et Chair*, nineteenth century

Archaeologists have found in the hieroglyphics of ancient Egyptian tombs a wealth of poetic writings about the sun. In a barren land that had little relief from drought except along the flood plain of the Nile, the sun was clearly dominant and all-powerful. The discerning gardener will notice the power the sun has over the garden, as it moves across the sky through its positions in each season and each day. It is the energy source that drives photosynthesis in green plants. It casts shadows, dictating where plants can grow. It tells the plants when to shed their leaves and grow new ones, when to flower, and when the fruit must ripen. In fact, our frame of reference to the sun is linked to its influences on the plants of the field, as they change with the solar cycle from season to season.

ACTS AND AFFIRMATIONS

Witness the magical relationship between plant and sun by growing sunflowers. The single flower at the top of the ten- to fifteenth-foot-tall stalk will follow the sun across the sky each day like an enormous living sundial, turning gradually from east to west as the day progresses. Only when it opens does the flower become stationary. Plant your sunflowers outside an often-used window, and watch the heads follow the sun.

CHRYSANTH. PERVNIANVM.

june 23

Toil and pleasure, in their natures opposite, are yet linked together in a kind of necessary connection.

—Livius, *History of Rome*, first century A.D.

Philosophers say that when we love our work, be it writing or tending children or digging holes for plants, we have found the greatest source of happiness. This connection is nowhere better illustrated than in our garden. There is a unique satisfaction when the labor of weeding yields a deep taproot pulled out of the ground intact. An intangible reward follows carting and spreading mulch onto all the plants before the summer heat arrives. Something stirs in us when we succeed in the labor of nurturing a plant from seed packet to adult, or when we share in the pleasure of vivid flowers. These all involve toil, but the work is blended so thoroughly with pleasure in gardens that it can be impossible to know the difference.

Acts and Affirmations

When people find gardening to be too much toil and lacking in rewards, it is usually because their failures outweigh their successes. If you are a knowledgeable beginner or a more advanced gardener, share your skills with others as a personal gift. Your assistance shows newcomers how to make the toil easier and how to benefit from tips that ensure success. It is the little victories we take for granted that will sustain them: the first perfect flower, the basket of fresh-picked tomatoes, or a bunch of freshly cut Mexican sunflowers. Your act of sharing will in a short time change their minds and hearts from seeing their garden as a place of toil to a place of infinite potential.

june 24

FEAST OF
ST. JOHN THE BAPTIST

It was believed that since St. John instituted the Baptism as a sign of repentance, the dew which fell on the morning of this day was sacred. Flowers were, therefore, gathered before the sun rose, and if the eyes were washed with the dew, they would be preserved from harm through the year. If, however, flowers were picked after the sun rose, sickness would be inevitable.

—ADELMA GRENIER SIMMONS, *Saints in My Garden*, 1932

The feast of St. John the Baptist is the only saint's day in honor of birth, not death. The presence of this feast so close to the summer solstice allowed Catholic leaders to integrate their religious celebrations with pre-Christian solar rites. In the Gospel of Matthew, John is described as a wild man dressed in animal fur and wandering in the desert living off the land. And so he has become connected with shamans and hermits—all unconventional holy people who live in the wilderness. John shows us that living alone amid the wild plants is a sacred existence and that our striving for solitude in the garden will bear great spiritual fruit.

ACTS AND AFFIRMATIONS

Take a stroll in the early morning, and drag your hands across the dew-covered flowers of your garden. Then spread the dew over your arms and legs, face, and belly to gain the grace of St. John. This is a fun tradition for children, who will enjoy spreading the water all over you and each other. If you have Saint-Johns wort in the garden, pick bundles of it today to hang by windows and doors for protection against storms, thunder, ghosts, and evil spirits.

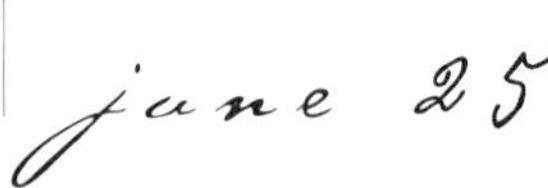

If you accept art, it must be part of your daily lives, and the daily life of every man. It will be with us wherever we go, in the ancient city full of traditions of past time, in the newly cleared farm in America.
—William Morris, *The Decorative Arts*, 1861

Art is a stimulator of consciousness. When we bring art into our daily lives, it helps us rise above our mundane existence to experience visions—both our own and those inspired in others. Gardens, too, are works of art. Every garden is a masterpiece, whether it is a tiny window box of flowers or the great garden at Versailles. To live in a garden and to tend one is to exist with a perpetual work in progress because no landscape is ever truly complete, and none is ever static.

Acts and Affirmations

Add art to your garden. Choose a piece that is meaningful to you, then create a fitting environment for it in a special spot. Inscribed stones, plaques, and statues in earthy hues are most beautiful amid natural greenery. Try evocative images such as a statue of St. Francis of Assisi, patron saint of ecology; symbols of religious meaning; or statues of gods, goddesses, or animals.

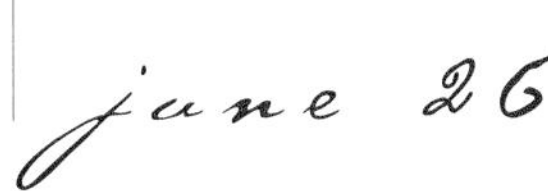

God ended His work, and He rested, and He made a bond of love between His soul and the soul of all things. And the ONE *became one with the one, and the two, and the three, and the eight, and with time and with the subtle mystery of the human soul.*

—Svetasvatara Upanishad, Part 6, 600–900 B.C.

Wild places are created by the hand of God, but the garden is created through a partnership. God lends us the raw materials, and we combine them in ways that please us, thereby pleasing God. We may group flowers to create a cloud of fragrance rising up to heaven like the prayer of incense smoke. We may plant trees to render a hot, dry place cool and inviting. But none of these things can we do without God's gifts of plants. So let us never forget that God is the architect and we are merely decorators.

Acts and Affirmations

In the tenth century, Spain was occupied by the Moors, Islamic armies from northern Africa. One of their legacies is the great walled gardens, with their traditional re-creations of Paradise, filled with flowers and fruiting trees. Another Islamic-influenced Spanish tradition is sangria, a refreshing wine punch. On a hot afternoon, mix up a punch bowl of sangria by blending red wine and fruit juice. Add slices of fresh citrus and other fruit. Share it cooled with friends and family in the spirit of the Persian moguls, whose gardens of Paradise were a daily reminder of heaven itself.

june 27

> *Therefore, let us build houses that restore to man the life-giving, life-enhancing elements of nature. This means an architecture that begins with the nature of the site. Which means taking the first great step toward assuring a worthy architecture, for in the rightness of a house on the land we sense a fitness we call beauty.*
>
> —Frank Lloyd Wright, *Frank Lloyd Wright: An Autobiography*, 1932

Frank Lloyd Wright was born into a period when the house symbolized dominance of architecture over nature. Wright's genius was in knowing that nature must actually dominate or dictate the architecture. He believed the site comes first, for only with an intuitive, almost spiritual understanding of the land's forms and qualities can a vision of harmonious architectural form be conceived. Similarly, when we as garden makers fail to respond to qualities and conditions of our homesite, the result is inevitably an incongruous failure.

Acts and Affirmations

Frank Lloyd Wright saw in his architecture a sense of spirituality, treating it like the vernacular of his personal religion. Through light and wood, metal and glass, he sought to express the essence of his soul. If you are not familiar with Wright's work, seek out books on the origins and early design of his prairie homes. Then discover the architectural genius of his later works, which became a miraculous melding of site, structure, and landscape.

Shouldst thou attempt to drive out nature by force, yet it will be ever returning, and in silent triumph break through thy affected disdain.
—Horatius Flaccus, first century B.C.

Weeds are incredibly tenacious creations. They send down roots that fight for life even in the most inhospitable places. They cling and claw as we hoe and pull them out, but many are virtually impossible to eradicate once they are established. Though we curse them for this, we may find comfort in them, too. It is wise to remember that these tough fellows will survive virtually any natural or man-made disaster. This is God at work, a living promise that Earth shall forever have plants and that there is always hope, even in the worst situation.

Acts and Affirmations
Who is to say what is a weed and what is an herb or flower? A weed doesn't refer to any particular species; in fact, the word simply means "a plant out of place." Don't turn your nose up at the wayside weeds—consider them flowers of lesser value than those of your garden. As you pick your herbs and flowers to dry for winter, add some of these often maligned species for diversity, and put them to work for holiday decorating.

june 29

He that can discern the loveliness of things, we call him poet, painter, man of genius, gifted, lovable; and whether it be pagan peasant of old, or Christian king of the moyen age, who learned a sacred lesson from flower, or bird, or star, each in his own fashioned, and to the extent of his own inner light of conscience, was poet and priest in one.

—Alfred E. P. Raymund Dowling, *The Flora of the Sacred Nativity*, 1900

Those of us who garden know that the secrets of the universe are all concentrated in the blossom of a single flower. There are many lessons in a flower's beauty: harmony, peace, humility, and above all the finite nature of life. To see these lessons at once is a profound experience, and it is clear that through gardens we become both poet and priest. To find such pure truth in this age of deceit and artifice is to discover the essence of the spirit.

Acts and Affirmations

Even if you are not a priest or poet, you may find the cool dewy morning of a beautiful June day such an inspiration that you are compelled to capture it in some way. Keep a little notebook, and enjoy these peaceful times by painting images and writing poetry without concern for punctuation or structure. Bring out your notebook again in the dead of winter, and your words and pictures will evoke pleasant memories of these contemplative moments of summer.

The man who has planted a garden feels that he has done something for the good of the world. He belongs to the producers. It is a pleasure to eat of the fruit of one's toil, if it be nothing more than a head of lettuce or an ear of corn.
—Charles Dudley Warner, *My Summer in a Garden*, 1870

Generations of children raised in the city have never experienced the miracle of eating something they have grown. They are so separated from things of the earth that the notion of growing something on vacant land is incredibly foreign. Realizing this, many public schools are beginning more aggressive gardening programs. There are community gardens springing up amid the ruins of urban blight. Imagine if all the vacant lots in Detroit were planted and tended by the poor people living there. Can the garden solve our social ills and at the same time heal the heavy heart or the neglected soul? Perhaps.

Acts and Affirmations

Urban gardening projects are a valuable social program for young and old. If you have the time and organizational skills, start a community garden in your area. Or donate your time and knowledge to an existing project. Help the children become more involved because, if you can inspire just one child to become a producer in life through a food-growing project, you can offer him or her a glimpse of a very bright future.

summer

THE TIME OF FRUITING

The seeds sown in spring are now growing vigorously, triggered by the long days and the heat. They have reached their vegetative zenith, and they begin to transfer their energy into the flowering and eventual fruit that follows. The farmer keeps a watchful eye on the crops, protecting them against foraging wildlife and the ever-present threat of drought. Weed and water is the mantra of this season, for the plants are now yielding their greatest benefits of beauty and food. The first pickings—tender young squash, new potatoes, and the leafy greens—occur in this time, when the sun is high. The herbs are rich in oil and at their most powerful around the solstice. Roses are producing faster than we can cut them, and all around us, the vegetable kingdom is in high gear to reproduce and set seed before the end of the growing season.

july

The tribal peoples of old Europe named July "Mead-monath" after the meadows or meades, which were filled with grass and flowers. It was the time when grains ripened in the hot sun and the farmer watched over his crop for the first signs of ill weather. It is the time when the Dog Star rises in the night sky, and the dog days of summer begin on the fourth to extend into August. The water lily blooms in ponds, lakes and swamps, recalling Monet's fascination with a particular pond of them in his garden at Giverny. It is also the month when all New World maize-growing peoples watched carefully over their crop as it produced silk and tassels, the male and female parts for that marvelous process of pollination so unlike any other plant in the world.

MANDAN (MEAD-MONATH): MONTH OF MUCH RIPENING

july 1

We cared for our corn in those days as we would care for a child; for we Indian people loved our gardens, just as a mother loves her children; and we thought that our growing corn liked to hear us sing, just as children like to hear their mother sing to them.

—Buffalo Bird Woman, *Buffalo Bird Woman's Garden,* 1917

Buffalo Bird Woman was a member of the Hidatsa tribe of Minnesota. Their cultivation of corn, sunflowers, and squash had an enormous influence in developing the strains of these plants that we grow a century later. The planting of the corn was done by women, and they indeed sang corn songs to their fields to help the plants grow. In turn, the corn rustled back at them, murmuring softly in the dry winds of later summer. The women carefully maintained the fields while they sang, and it was common for young men to court the girls when weeding or watching. These fields, worked with nothing more than bone and wood tools, became the center of Hidatsa culture, just as our gardens today become the center of outdoor summer living.

Acts and Affirmations

There is little doubt that singing helped the Hidatsa women pass the time as they hoed out the weeds and guarded their fields against marauding wildlife. We too may sing to our gardens to make the plants feel as though they are cared for by a mother or father. When you work in your garden, or while picking from a kitchen plot, try humming or singing out loud. Compose songs about plants as you go, or sing favorite tunes remembered from childhood.

july 2

Keep your eyes clean and your ears quiet and your mind serene.
Breathe God's air. Work, if you can, under His sky.
—THOMAS MERTON, *Seeds of Contemplation*, 1949

To breathe fresh air and work under a bright sky is the perfect antidote to a long week in the office. Contemplative Trappist monk Thomas Merton found it to be the inspiration of his hermitlike existence. The working of the body in a physical sense is crucial to the way our minds think, for when engaged in labor, our brain is free to wander into creative and problem-solving realms. Until we learn to give ourselves over entirely to gardening, we may never truly understand the depths of its therapeutic potential.

ACTS AND AFFIRMATIONS

The best time to work outdoors during this hot season is in those magical hours of dawn and dusk. At that time there is no sun to scorch the skin, but the air is still warm enough to be comfortable outdoors. Venture out at dawn before you leave for work, and feel the cool dew in the gathering light. Or go out at dusk when the air feels like powder on the skin, the crickets sing, and all living things are settling in for the night.

july 3

RISE OF THE DOG STAR
FEAST OF CHERRWIDEN

The sum total of heaven and earth, everything in nature, is thus won to use and purpose. It becomes a temple and altar for the service of God.
—HILDEGARD VON BINGEN, *Meditations,* twelfth century

Cherrwiden, the Celtic goddess of grain, moon, and abundance, like so many other female deities oversaw the growth and ripening of the grain crop. Pagans, and later Christians, said blessings and prayers when planting and harvesting grains, a dietary staple that could easily be damaged by wet weather and summer hail. The original pagan incantations were reworded in medieval times to invoke Mary, the Christian embodiment of all previous female deities. This and so many old agricultural rites illustrate how deeply the feminine was integrated into farming—and how natural it is for this aspect to dwell in our gardens.

ACTS AND AFFIRMATIONS

Honor the goddess of grain by offering the birds a bowl of seed in your garden. Birds will come to feed, and in the process they will snatch up unwanted insects that can become prolific this time of year. The birds are your best friends, and a garden that welcomes them enjoys natural pest control as God created it.

july 4

Independence Day

I have often thought that if heaven had given me choice of my position and calling, it should have been on a rich spot of earth, well watered, and near a good market for the productions of the garden. No occupation is so delightful to me as the culture of the earth, and no culture comparable to that of the garden. Such a variety of subjects, some one always coming to perfection, the failure of one thing repaired by the success of another, and instead of one harvest a continued one through the year. . . . Though an old man, I am but a young gardener.

—Thomas Jefferson, letter, 1811

Thomas Jefferson, one of America's greatest founding fathers, tells us just a few decades after independence how deeply he values his land at Monticello. This former president, politician, and statesman knew how many had died that he might live in liberty on the landscape of America. This makes all of us the benefactors of those bloody battles. The very earth that we cultivate around our homes was purchased for us with great sacrifice over 200 years ago. Let us always honor those who made the ultimate sacrifice on those battlefields of the Northeast by treating hard-earned earth with appropriate sanctity.

Acts and Affirmations

Share the spirit of Jefferson on this sacred birthday of the United States. Send for the Monticello seed and plant catalog, which sells the progeny of plants originating at this historic Virginia garden (see Resources). To celebrate our freedom of choice and the diversity of people that settled America, grow these heirloom varieties from this most historic and patriotic garden.

july 5

Apache Ceremonial of Ghan: Spirit of Fire and Sun

> *When we Apache go on the warpath, hunt, or plant, we always throw a pinch of hoddentin to the sun, saying "with the favor of the sun, or permission of the sun, I am going out to fight, hunt or plant," as the case may be, and I want the sun to help me.*
>
> —Tze-go-juni, Mescalero Apache, *Medicine Men of the Apache*, 1887

We may find the sacred in ordinary things as the Apache did with *hoddentin*, the name given to the fine yellow pollen of the wild cattail of the Southwest. It was carried everywhere in the medicine bag, and the sick were sprinkled and smudged with it in healing ceremonies. No man would consider going to war without a small pouch of hoddentin attached to his belt. And no child was ever without a small medicine bag of it hanging around his or her neck. This is a beautiful example of how the cattail, a species that signified water, became a holy plant in a very dry climate. For when a plant is so closely linked to survival, it is often raised above its humble botany to a sacred status.

Acts and Affirmations

Create a Native American ceremonial meal with fresh cattail and other traditional foods. Simply pull a whole cattail out of the water and peel off the outer layers of its main stalk. At its center is a tender, white fleshy core that is edible as is, tasting like a cross between tender celery and heart of palm. Chop and flavor with seasoned vinegar for a fresh summer salad to complement a Native American meal of corn, beans, and squash.

july 6

Just carry on, don't try to estimate whether things are improving or not. We are the worst possible judges about that ourselves. There is often a temptation to pull up the plant and see how it is getting on. But roots grow in the dark and unseen and unknown and when they are strong the flower blossoms and the fruit comes into being.

—Raymond Raynes, *The Life of Raymond Raynes*, 1963

It evolves gradually but surely, although there may be no outward signs. In the garden we may nurture a young plant or seedling without seeing much change above ground. Yet unseen its root system grows to better support future needs of stem, leaf, and flower. Similarly, the inner spiritual life of every person grows in the dark recesses of the mind, heart, and soul. We are too impatient for obvious miracles of change within ourselves, for this evolution is often so gradual it cannot be perceived. If we abandon the spiritual path for lack of earth-shattering revelations, we risk damaging the roots that are growing slowly. But if we nurture the young plant and have faith in the growth, our roots will be strong and broad, holding us steadfast against ill winds.

Acts and Affirmations

God: When I become discouraged with my spiritual growth, remind me that my internal soul is in a continual state of evolution. Help me to resist the weakness that breeds impatience caused by our culture of instant gratification. Remind me that great trees are not supported by small roots, and my life must grow its roots, too, in their own time.

july 7

The religious and magical writings of the great nations of antiquity, that is to say, the Chinese, the Indians, the Sumerians and Babylonians, the Persians and Assyrians, and the Egyptians and Nubians, contain abundant evidence that these primitive peoples believed that the first beings who possessed a knowledge of plants and their healing properties were the gods themselves.

—E. A. Wallis Budge, *Origin of the Craft of the Herbalist*, 1928

Knowledge of the powers of plants has, since the dawn of humankind, been among the most revered skills. The keepers of knowledge have, until recently, been healers, whether shaman, medicine man, or diviner. In the past there was little division among religion, magic, and the healing arts, so it is natural that the mythology surrounding the origin and activities of many gods was the first record of important plants within each culture. Many of these connections have been lost in the mists of time, but those that remain are a glimpse into the minds of the ancients, who saw each plant as a living spirit of the gods. Science has severed this connection, yet it still touches us through the beauty of plants and their individual myths. These tales connect us to the past and inspire us to ponder the origin of a beautiful flower or a mighty tree.

Acts and Affirmations

Discover the origin of the names of common plants in Greek mythology. Read the tale of how the god Narcissus was changed into this early spring-flowering bulb. Find out why the iris is named after the Greek goddess of the rainbow. Immerse yourself in the sensual love of goddess Aphrodite and her favorite flower, the rose. Not only will you gain a deeper understanding of the link between contemporary gardens and ancient times, you will never forget the names of these plants again.

july 8

Corn-blossom maidens here in the fields. Patches of beans in flower, fields all abloom. Water shining after rain with blue clouds looming above.
—He-Hea Katzina, Hopi song

Native American corn songs are among the most beautiful. Sung by women and children, these musical chants are joyous, often calling for rain. They are also subtly romantic, for as corn maidens sat upon elevated platforms in the fields to guard against foraging wildlife, the corn songs also beckoned young men to approach the girls in relative privacy. We no longer court in the fields as our agrarian ancestors did: lovers' trysts now occur more often in cars than among the tall green corn. Perhaps corn still calls with its promise of courtship and music amid the tasseled green stalks of July's fields.

Acts and Affirmations

Each time you husk sweet corn this summer, take a close look at the cluster of corn silk that's revealed. The silk is actually made up of hundreds of tiny tubes that allow the pollen grain to grow down to the kernels deep within the husks. It was smoked by Native Americans and pioneers alike when tobacco was in short supply. If you find some beautiful corn silk, save it by setting it aside to dry away from direct sunlight. Then add a few strands to cards and letters over the winter, a wonderfully tactile legacy of the golden sun of summer.

july 9

PANATHENA: GREEK FEAST OF GODDESS ATHENA

O blessed queen of heaven . . . thou who illumines all the cities of the earth with your feminine light, thou who nourishes all the seeds of the world with your damp heat, giving your changing light according to the wanderings, near or far, of the sun: by whatever name or form it is right to call upon you . . .

—APULEIUS, second century A.D.

The legacy of the Greek goddess Athena is inextricably tied to the olive tree, from which oil was derived that fueled the rise of the great Mediterranean civilizations. When seeking a name for their new city, the people asked the gods for a patron who would be chosen according to who could give them the greatest gift. Poseidon gave them the horse, and Athena offered the olive. The goddess won the day, for no wealth was greater than a plentiful supply of oil for light and health. Surely Athena's spirit inhabits olive trees to this day, rendering them an eternal symbol of the Greeks' favorite goddess.

ACTS AND AFFIRMATIONS

Honor Athena by splurging on a bottle of extra virgin olive oil, which is made from the first pressing. Create a purely Mediterranean meal by slicing eggplant. Slowly sauté the slices in the oil at medium temperature. Crumble feta, Greek goat cheese, on the hot slices, and flavor with dabs of pesto. Serve with a full-bodied Greek wine, and be sure to toast the goddess with your first cup.

(*Olea europaea*)

The olive tree

The olive tree of today is the descendant of an African species and the shrubby wild olive native to the Mediterranean region. The fruiting olive tree was developed over 6,000 years of selective breeding, dating back to the Copper Age. The olive tree, which is able to grow in very dry conditions, produces a fruit that, if pressed, yields a tasty and highly nutritious oil. It was highly valued since oils and fats were in perennial short supply in ancient times. Cultures rich in this oil became strong and healthy, and their armies were better able to claim new lands from weaker peoples. The oil also provided a reliable fuel for lamps, extending the day until after sunset with illumination for study and social activity. The ancient Greeks were the first to exploit the olive, and, since they controlled the entire industry, their great civilization rose on the back of the olive. Their empire grew through olive oil trade, and without it there would be no classical texts and no great classical architecture. The Roman Empire, modeled on Greek civilization, would never have had such a monumental effect on the Western world.

july 10

Simplicity of life, even the barest, is not a misery, but the very foundation of refinement; a sanded floor and whitewashed walls and the green trees, and flowery meads, and living waters outside.

—WILLIAM MORRIS, *The Decorative Arts,* 1882

As the cramped, overdecorated Victorian home yielded at the turn of the century to the open simplicity of the Craftsman style, architecture tore down its walls to receive the mystical influences of grasslands, mighty trees, and life-giving water. A century later we have a different kind of clutter to contend with: fast-paced technological living. The antidote once again is found in nature—to live more fully and simply through our gardens. For as one wise philosopher believed, the secret to a happy life is a small house and a very large garden.

ACTS AND AFFIRMATIONS

Vow to pay more attention to the simple pleasures in life. When was the last time you ate a watermelon outdoors and spit the seeds onto the lawn? To an adult it will evoke memories of a simple childhood existence. Don't cut up your melon into neurotic little squares; just slice a slab and sit outdoors in the sun and see how far you can spit the seeds.

july 11

The outer world, from which we cower into our houses, seemed after all a gentle habitable place; and night after night a man's bed, it seemed, was laid and waiting for him in the fields, where God keeps an open house.

—Robert Louis Stevenson, *A Night Among the Pines*, 1879

It is all too often that we set ourselves above others who are deemed less fitting for our company. They may be poor, unattractive, uncultured, of the wrong race or class, or a dozen other reasons. The result of this self-segregation is that our lives are less diverse, and we cease to learn the vital lessons that others have to teach us. As gardeners, let us never discount any species as too common for the landscape. Just as we have much to learn from a variety of people, each plant has its own lesson to teach us.

Acts and Affirmations

Discard your preconceived ideas concerning plants. Forget what is a weed and what is an ornamental because every species on earth has its own set of unique qualities. Strive to know more than just what color a flower is or how big the tree grows. Make a point to discover whether a plant is edible, if it provides habitat for wildlife, and what its role in natural and human history has been. These values teach us that, like human beings, each plant is an individual and should never be discounted as unworthy of a garden.

july 12

God is the ground of our being, and we in a sense are like plants in this ground, living as separate entities but as closely connected to Him as a plant is to the earth and not able to exist otherwise.

—MARCIA HOLLIS, *Down to Earth*, 1971

There are profound relationships in the natural world, and few are as inextricable as that of plant to soil. Without soil to anchor itself, a plant cannot stand up straight, nor will it be able to withstand the pressure of wind and the weight of snowfall. While some plants can be grown hydroponically under controlled conditions without soil, they must be supported with special structures to compensate for lack of anchorage. We too must find suitable anchorage against the storms of life, or we will crumble. Spirituality, when deeply rooted in all aspects of life, is our most reliable anchorage. Faith is vital to helping us cope and remain steadfast against the winds of change.

ACTS AND AFFIRMATIONS

God is integrated into our lives like veins that run through the soft green flesh of a leaf. The flesh is our physical being, and the veins are the spirit of God. To symbolize our life and its spiritual connections, create a leaf skeleton using a large, freshly picked tree leaf. Hold the leaf down flat on top of a flat board or cutting board. Use a stiff scrub or natural bristle hairbrush held bristles down toward the leaf. Begin tapping the leaf with the flat tips of the bristles in a straight up-and-down motion. This will pulverize the flesh of the leaf while the skeleton remains intact. When all the pulp is gone, you are left with a perfect skeleton, which represents the physical part of your nature. Let this item be a reminder of how barren life is without the spiritual.

july 13

And even in these days to understand what plant life means to the true countryman is to get into very close touch with him. Not only has suburban life separated the great concentrated masses of our people from their birthright of meadows, fields and woods; of Nature in her untamed splendor and mystery, most of them have never had so much as a momentary glimpse.
—Eleanour Sinclair Rohde, *The Old English Herbals*, 1922

We cannot always get out into the fields and meadows to rekindle our primal connection with wild places. Fortunately, we may find vestiges of it in the plants that inhabit our gardens. In the microcosm of the garden grows representatives of these wild places. Trees that shade us and flowers are a legacy of the great forests. Lawns, no matter how manicured, are little more than a civilized meadow. And a small plot of lettuce or tomatoes is a miniature farmer's field. No matter where we live, we have an opportunity to enjoy these reminders of nature.

Acts and Affirmations

Many suburban gardeners are shocked to find out that disadvantaged inner-city children have never been in a garden or seen the countryside firsthand. These kids see little more of the plant kingdom than an occasional battered street tree or a dandelion springing up through a crack in the sidewalk. To make a real difference in their lives, give your support to programs for summer camp, community programs, and excursions to the country. There is no greater miracle than what happens when a child encounters the magnificence of the natural world for the first time.

july 14

The garden must be prepared in the soul first or else it will not flourish.
—English gardening proverb

The gardeners of England share a passion for plants that is unrivaled anywhere else on earth. It is a practice that has reached near-religious devotion in these people's lives. Their proverbs and superstitions related to gardening are filled with religious meaning, and their gardening and agricultural dates are linked to the feasts of Christian saints, no matter how obscure the saint. St. Patrick's Day governs pea planting, St. Michael marks the bloom season of the aster, and St. Swithin forecasts the weather. Perhaps this is the most natural calendar for Christian gardeners, because, as we mark the passing of seasonal tasks, our souls are naturally inspired by their spiritual connections.

Acts and Affirmations

Strive to become more familiar with the feast days of Christianity because many of them are also auspicious dates of the ancient pagans. Find a Catholic calendar, which is usually available through the nearest parish office. These are the only ones that still include the old feast days of saints and holy days of the year. Over time, you will develop a sense of what saints and rites are connected with each season, and these will become the guideposts of your spiritual planting and harvest.

early calendar of english saints and english flowers

The Snowdrop in purest white array,
First rears her head on Candlemas day;
While the Crocus hastens to the shrine,
Of the Primrose love on St. Valentine,
Then comes the Daffodil beside
Our Lady's Smock on our Lady-tide,
About St. George when blue is worn,
The blue Harebells the fields adorn,
Against the day of Holy Cross,
The Crowfoot gilds the flowery grass.
When St. Barnabie bright smiles night and day,
Poor Ragged Robin blossoms in the hay,
The scarlet Lychnis the Garden's pride
Flames at St. John the Baptist's tide,
From visitation to St. Swithin's showers,
The Lily white reigns Queen of the flowers;
And Poppies, a sanguine mantel spread,
For the blood of the dragon St. Margaret shed.
Then under the wanton Rose again
That blushes for penitent Magdalen,
Till Lammas Day called August's wheel
When the long corn stinks of Camomile
When Mary left us here below
The virgin's bower is full in blow;
And yet anon, the full Sunflower blew,
And became a star for St. Bartholomew.
The Passion Flower long has blowerd
To betoken us signs of Holy Roode.
The Michaelmas daisies, among dead weeds,
Bloom for St. Michael's valorous deeds;
Till the Feast of St. Simon and St. Jude
Save Mushrooms and the fungus race,
That grow till All Hallowtide takes place.
Soon the evergreen Laurel alone is green,
When Catherine crowns all learned men.
The Ivy and the Holly berries are seen,
And Yule Log and Wassaile come round again.

july 15

ST. SWITHIN'S DAY

St. Swithin's Day if thou dost rain . . . for forty days it will remain.
St. Swithin's Day if thou be fair . . . for forty days 'twill rain no mair.
—ENGLISH GARDEN RHYME

In A.D. 971 St. Swithin's remains were dug up in the country and moved to a more suitable resting place in Winchester Cathedral. Legend says that he was so unhappy over this that he began to weep, his tears becoming a heavy rainfall for the next forty days. In rural England, no one ever ate of the fresh apple crop until after this date in deference to Swithin, the patron saint of the apple harvest. But if a light rain should fall, it was deemed the saint himself "christening" the apple crop. That forty days of rain no doubt precipitated a horrible famine as the crops mildewed and rotted in the wet. Therefore the rhyme, like many other legends, grew out of the suffering that followed that fateful year, and the English have sought forgiveness by invoking St. Swithin on this day ever since.

ACTS AND AFFIRMATIONS

Dedicate an evening with old-fashioned English St. Swithin's apple lights. You'll need some good-size firm apples and a package of tea candles in their aluminum cups. First slice the bottom of the apple so it sits upright on the table, then core the apple and cut the opening wider to fit the candle. Sprinkle it with lemon juice to reduce discoloration and insert the candle. Arrange a group of them on your tabletop and all evening enjoy the fresh fruit fragrance as the little flames warm the center of each apple.

july 16

Tao, the Way—the basic Chinese belief in an order and harmony in nature. This grand concept originated in remote times, from observation of the heavens and of nature—the rising and setting of the sun, moon, and stars, the cycle of day and night, and the rotation of the seasons—suggesting the existence of laws of nature, a sort of divine legislation that regulated the pattern in the heavens and on earth.

—Mai-Mai Sze

The peaceful beauty of all Asian gardens is rooted in the idea that they are a microcosm of nature and reflect the rites of passage in both the annual cycle of the seasons and the birth and death of human beings. The seasonal expressions in that garden are reflected by the flowers of spring, the water lilies of summer, the maples in the fall, and the twisted evergreens in winter. These correspond with the cycles of our own life: our birth, which is the spring; our maturation over the long days of summer; our begetting of children, which is the ripe seed of the harvest; and the winter, our own final decline until the circle of life is complete.

Acts and Affirmations

Chinese mark the pilgrimage to a holy place by carving beautiful characters into living green bamboo poles that will heal and retain the message. Create your own spiritual message by painting or carving a green bamboo pole for your garden with meaningful words and names. You need a green pole one to two inches in diameter. (You'll find a bamboo stand in the neighborhood or the woods, or purchase a much harder bamboo pole from the garden center.) When you're through, add Tibetan bells and colorful prayer flags to the pole, then plant it securely in that special place in the garden.

july 17

Feast of the Egyptian Goddess Isis

Indeed all men have Isis and know her and the Gods of her company; . . . they should take very good heed and be apprehensive lest unwittingly they write off the sacred mysteries and dissolve them into winds and streams, and sowing and ploughings, and passions of earth and changes of seasons.
—Robert Graves, *The Greek Myths*, 1955

Isis, the mother goddess of ancient Egypt, was also among the pantheon of Roman gods. She is the true Mother Nature, who created all things. In an ancient manuscript, she is referred to as "Green goddess, whose green color is like unto the greenness of the earth," "She who has given birth to the fruits of the earth," and "Mother of the fruitful furrow's wheat-rich path." Isis is also a goddess of great healing power, and she is evoked by herbal healers as they harvest the plants and prepare their botanical medicines. She represented the rich plains of Egypt, while the god Osiris represented the Nile, which fertilized the land each year as it rose to flood and then recede.

Acts and Affirmations

The ancient Egyptians had a love affair with flowers, which represented the living plants so plentiful along the river that were virtually nonexistent a few miles into the surrounding desert. To honor a guest on the feast of Isis, the Egyptian host always offered a wreath or a large, very fragrant flower to wear behind the ear. Pick a fragrant flower such as a stock, gardenia, perfume rose, or jasmine, and wear it all day. If you go to work, put it inside your shirt or bra so that the fragrance will rise with your body heat to remind you of Isis, Mother Earth herself.

july 18

My garden is surrounded by cornfields and meadows, and beyond are great stretches of sandy heath and pine forests, and where the forests leave off the bare heath begins again; but the forests are beautiful in their lofty, pine-stemmed vastness, far overhead the crowns of softest gray-green, and underfoot a bright green whortleberry carpet, and everywhere the breathless silence; and the bare heaths are beautiful too, for one can see across them into eternity almost, and to go out on to them with one's face toward the setting sun is like going into the very presence of God . . .

—Elizabeth von Arnim, *Elizabeth and Her German Garden*, 1930

Let us never forget that nature provides the models from which we can learn the appropriate plants for a particular environment. On the wind-swept tablelands, low-profile heather hugs the ground where it is more protected from the persistent drying breeze. In the forest under the great old trees grow the ferns, which are compatible with small woodland wildflowers and shade-loving shrubs. When striving to become a better gardener, look to God's natural arrangements of plants that have evolved to grow together in divine perfection.

Acts and Affirmations

Take a drive through the countryside to observe God's clues to great gardens in models of nature. Note how trees are dominant on hillsides where soils are shallow, and the grasses are dominant in areas with deep soil. Should a tree sprout in the grassland, the grasses are far too greedy to allow it to survive. Conversely, should grasses sprout on the hillside, they may not have enough nutrients to become established. This model of how plants are distributed on the land is universal, and when you come to recognize it, the countryside will never look the same to you again.

july 19

You have noticed that everything an Indian does is in a circle, and that is because the Power of the World always works in circles, and everything tries to be round. . . . The Sky is round, and I have heard that the earth is round like a ball, and so are all the stars. The wind, in its greatest power, whirls. Birds make their nest in circles, for theirs is the same religion as ours. . . .

—Crowfoot, Blackfoot warrior and orator

The circle is sacred geometry in nearly every culture. It represents the never-ending cycles of seasons, of the moon, and of natural phenomena. Hopi sand paintings depict crops inside a circle made of a Rainbow Girl figure. At the center of the circle is the sacred pollen, and in the four cardinal directions there grows outward the symbols of the corn plant to the east, squash to the west, beans to the south, and tobacco to the north. Thus the four cardinal directions divide the circle into four quarters, which represent the seasons. This is a beautiful example of sacred geometry manifest in nature, the sun, earth, and ultimately the garden itself.

Acts and Affirmations

If there is a dry spell this summer, use tobacco in your own rainmaking ceremony, which releases the spirit of the plant to coax water from the sky. Place a few pinches of tobacco or crushed cigar into a ceramic bowl and burn it in the garden. As it smolders, turn in a circle, pausing to face east and let the smoke rise. Turn to north, south, and west. This circle of the four directions and the four sacred plants will surely be noticed by the gods as the smoke carries the spirit of the tobacco toward heaven.

(NICOTIANA RUSTICA)

native american tobacco

This very potent, nicotine-rich native tobacco plant of North America has traditionally been cultivated wherever native peoples practiced agriculture. Its relative, *Nicotiana tabacum*, and its far milder progeny gave birth to an enormous worldwide industry, from English pipe tobacco to Cuban cigars and American cigarettes. But grown by the Indians, rustica tobacco served as a medicinal as well as a ritual plant. It was smoked in the peace pipe of the Great Plains, used for healing and divination by Pueblo shamans in the desert Southwest, and grown deep into Mexico. The desert Pima believe that it was a gift of the gods, and when smoked the spirit of the plant was released and could join the other great spirits to influence the future of the people. It was also smoked in rainmaking ceremonies throughout the Southwest. Tobacco is a member of the nightshade family, an annual that is as easy to grow as its relatives, the tomato and chile pepper. Tall plants may exceed four feet when flowering and are night-flowering plants that are more attractive at dusk than any other time.

Each phase of nature, while not invisible, is yet not too distinct and obtrusive. It is there to be found when we look for it, but not demanding our attention. It is like a silent but sympathizing companion in whose company we retain most of the advantages of solitude.
—Henry David Thoreau, *Journal*, 1906

Though you may not realize it, each day in the garden contributes something new to your consciousness and stocks the storehouse of your horticultural wisdom. Gardeners learn from osmosis, which is the scientific word for absorption of a substance through seemingly solid barriers. Each year, subtle lessons of weather, soil, and plant and wildlife behavior are absorbed by us this way, almost unconsciously. Each piece of knowledge adds to our bigger understanding. Such is the discovery of things of the soul as well. We absorb the nuances of spiritual life one experience at a time: through silence, peace, introspection, prayer, and physical expression.

Acts and Affirmations

Use your ever-expanding skills as a gardener by saving seed from your garden. When you grow rare or heirloom varieties of plants and flowers, let one plant of each variety go to seed. Simply leave the spent flowers on the plant so they develop into seed. Treat the other plants normally, harvesting flowers or fruit often to keep them blooming as long as possible. Collect and store the special seeds in a cool, dry, dark place until it is time to grow even more of the rare ones next year.

july 21

MAYAN NEW YEAR

Maize gods native to Central and South America were far more ancient than Christian saints or the crucified God whose image the Spaniards planted in maize fields red with the bloom of conquest. For these Maya descendants, the association of maize with blood is as old as the oldest Maya memory, as old as the first planted seed. As their culture evolved, ancient Maya fertilized seeds of corn with the sacrificed blood of their enemies and the blood of their own kings. For the Maya a single kernel of corn is symbolic of what Christians symbolize by the holy cross—the tragic and monstrous truth that the seed of life is death.
—BETTY FUSSELL, *The Story of Corn*, 1994

Corn is deeply integrated into Mayan mythology, ritual, and religion. Their tree of life, carved into the walls of countless temples of Palenque, is that of a complex branched cornstalk. Each ear is a human head; the ends of the cross piece are tassels and leaves; the roots stretch down into the watery underworld. Today, an ear of Guatemalan corn found with a rare red kernel is dried and stored in the house as a talisman, which, by the blood of the old religion and that of Christ, has the power to miraculously heal and protect.

ACTS AND AFFIRMATIONS

Fertilize your corn or the summer garden with a sacrament of blood, just as the Maya did on this sacred day. Blood is high in nitrogen, the nutrient most needed by lawns and corn, which is nothing more than a giant grass itself. Buy organic powdered blood meal at the garden center and ritually sprinkle it around your corn patch, or around any other plant that could benefit from a little richer diet. Then witness the results as the organic nitrogen, iron, and other nutrients push your vegetable plants, as it did the Mayans', into high gear.

july 22

If the earth is holy, then the things that grow out of the earth are also holy.
—Liberty Hyde Bailey, *The Holy Earth*, 1915

The name of an ancient Greek earth goddess, Gaia, is being used today to describe a philosophy that views the Earth with its many organisms as a single living thing. It supports what Liberty Hyde Bailey, the father of American horticulture, said eighty years ago: that the earth itself and all that grows out of it are sacred. Gaia consciousness helps us understand the interconnectedness of all things. This holistic global view makes us realize that catastrophic soil erosion in Sudan or pollution in Siberia should be as important to us as the health of our own backyard garden.

Acts and Affirmations

If you find the Gaia idea intriguing, begin searching this spiritual path to global ecological consciousness. Learn more through the Internet. Go to any search engine and type in the key words "Gaia Ecology" and browse through the many deeply inspiring websites dedicated to global environmental consciousness.

july 23

There are some days during the summer when the quality of light seems to tend to be an extraordinary beauty of effect. I have never been able to find out how the light on these occasions differs from that of ordinary fine summer days, but, when these days come, I know them and am filled with gladness.

—Gertrude Jekyll, *Color Schemes for the Flower Garden*, 1908

Gertrude Jekyll was a turn-of-the-century artist and garden designer. Her success in transforming the use of color in the English landscape was much needed after the heavily regimented and unnatural Victorian gardening fads. Like the French Impressionists, who lived when she did, Jekyll preferred exuberant color. She also encouraged the use of plants in their natural forms. Psychologists believe color in gardens can actually heal, or at least improve the way we feel. A garden designed to soothe us would include lots of green, the color of growth and peace. It would be heavy in violet, the hue that brings inner calm. And of course, lots of blues—for they are a gift to the spirit and inspire contemplation.

Acts and Affirmations

Capture the magic of your summer garden through photography. What Gertrude Jekyll was trying to identify is that on days when the sunlight is diffused by high fog or thin overcast there are few shadows. Colors captured on such days are richly saturated and free of reflected glare and dark contrast. Learn to see this light as an artist would, and devote these magical days to capturing the color of the garden forever through the lens of your camera.

july 24

It is to this age that the ceremonies in the picking of the herbs transport us, to the mystery of the virtues of herbs, the fertility of earth, the never-ceasing conflict between the beneficent forces of the sun and summer and the evil powers of the long, dark northern winters.

—Eleanour Sinclair Rohde, *The Old English Herbals*, 1922

Each time you pinch a bit of basil, pick a summer tomato, or cut a zinnia for the living room, you are sharing in the very ancient ritual of picking. To participate in the summer harvesting, you must first plant months in advance. Then you must water and weed for weeks or months. By helping our plants thrive, we become an active participant in the miraculous cycle of the seasons where summer and winter battle each other, winning or losing through the transitional seasons of spring and fall.

Acts and Affirmations

Herbs are plentiful this time of year, and the act of running to the garden for a fresh pinch of this or that is taken for granted. Come the winter solstice, you'll regret not having the flavors of summer herbs available in the cold, dark months. Think ahead this year. Each time you go outside to pick some herbs, bring an extra bunch back to the house with you. Tie them with string, and hang them upside down in a dark closet to dry. These herb bundles will accumulate, then come in handy for gift giving, holiday decorating, and for herb-flavored cooking all winter long.

july 25

Hopi Kachina Festival of Niman

He partakes in the springing of the corn, in the rising and budding and earing of the corn. And when he eats his bread, at last, he recovers all he once set forth, and partakes again of the energies he called to the corn, from out of the wide universe.

—D. H. Lawrence, *Mornings in Mexico*, 1927

Every aspect of the Hopi world has a duality that is physical and spiritual. The kachinas are spirits that represent the spiritual aspects of everyday things such as stars, animals, and plants. The Hopi calendar divides the year into two halves, with December to July devoted to the kachinas or spiritual aspects and the rest of the year focusing on the physical aspects. The last kachina festival is Niman, or the Home Dance, the going-away feast for the kachinas before the transition to the physical. Now, the corn matures and people dance in thanksgiving. Kachinas are represented by costumed dancers and or by painted carvings hung from the rafters. Many believe these kachina dolls were the precursors of the carved statues of the Catholic saints, or *santos*.

Acts and Affirmations

Create a kachina to watch over your garden. Use a clean corncob dried in the sun and sanded smooth. Cut the stem flat so the cob can stand up on its own. Round the other end into a smooth dome and use a sharp knife to whittle a neck and waist. Paint the head turquoise, the top half of the body red-orange, and add a white skirt. Legs may be gray with red knee-high moccasins. Paint eyes, a tubelike nose, and a triangle mouth. Decorate the head with bright feathers and tie a piece of felt at the waist. Set it in a wood box nestled in a tree to watch over your crop until the kachinas come again.

(*Populus fremonti*)

desert cottonwood

Cottonwood trees are among the few hardy shade trees capable of surviving the desert climate of the American Southwest. They are usually found in seasonally dry stream canyons, where the roots reach deep into the earth for moisture trapped far below the surface. When the streams do run briefly following the summer thunderstorms, fast-moving waters erode the banks where the cottonwoods grow, exposing these very thick roots. The Hopi believe that a true sacred kachina doll or statue is carved only from the root of a cottonwood tree. The maker must be male, and the work should be done in the kiva, the subterranean, round ceremonial house where the kachina dancers originate. Cottonwood trees and the Hopi will forever be linked through the sacred wood of the kachina, and though it may look the same, a doll carved from any other wood will never be a true kachina.

july 26

Everything has its beauty, but not everyone can see it.
—Confucius

An object that you might consider a piece of junk may to someone else be garden art. Just a few years ago rusted items were banished from gardens, but recently the rusted patina of oxidized metal has become very trendy and expensive. The same is true for so many common plants, because a tree that some may cherish as beautiful, and even spiritual, may to others be little more than a noxious weed. The ability to see art in the rust, or in the beauty in a much-maligned plant, is to be conscious of all things as valuable to a larger scheme. Such a positive outlook guarantees an emotionally fruitful life, whether it is applied to the components of the garden or to relationships with family and friends.

Acts and Affirmations

Visit a local junkyard to explore this idea of finding beauty in unexpected places. Your wanderings amid the debris may turn up a now-stylish piece of rusted cast iron, an old window with flaking paint, or a forgotten gate. Make these architectural salvage pieces the centerpiece of a special garden. Know that, although the object was once discarded as ugly, you've exercised your ability to make it beautiful again through the art of creative perception.

july 27

He who sows the ground with care and diligence acquires a greater stock of religious merit than he could gain by repetition of ten thousand prayers.
—Zoroaster, fifth century B.C.

Zoroaster was a Persian religious poet who lived around 600 B.C. His followers were later assimilated into Islam, and only a small population in the mountains of Asia Minor still belongs to the original Zoroastrian religion today. His beautiful words about the religious merit of sowing and caring for our garden remain valuable spiritual wisdom today. The question remains: On a beautiful spring morning, is it better to celebrate the nearness of God in our gardens or to do so in the unnatural enclosure of a church, synagogue, or mosque?

Acts and Affirmations

The biblical commandment dictated one day in every seven be given over to God and considered a day of rest. Few people rest on Sunday any more, but it can become your holy day in the garden. Make your Sundays in the garden a spiritual time to contemplate the wisdom of a God who demanded that people rest the body and attend to the soul after a hard week in the secular world.

july 28

But the great, gashed, half-naked mountain is another of God's saints. There is no other like it. It is alone in its own character; nothing else in the world ever did or ever will imitate God in quite the same way. And that is sanctity.
—THOMAS MERTON, *Seeds of Contemplation*, 1949

Just because we deem something sacred doesn't mean that it is—there must be a reason, an underlying truth that leads us to this conclusion. As Merton so beautifully explains, the scale and majesty of mountains imitate the infinite nature of God. So too, the most minute creations—a tiny wildflower, or smaller yet, the mysteries of its DNA—are equally sacred, for they are so miraculous in their tiny scale that they are undeniable proof of divine creation.

ACTS AND AFFIRMATIONS

The longest days of summer are the best times to go to the mountains. If you are fortunate enough to live within driving distance of a mountain range, be it the Berkshires or the mighty Sierra Nevada, make an effort to climb a mountain. The mountain wildflowers are in peak bloom in July, and the diversity of dainty alpine flowers found above the timberline is awesome. In the process you will experience the sanctity of mountains and discover why many people, from Tibetan Buddhists to the Sioux of the Black Hills, find them so holy.

White floating clouds. Clouds, like the plains come and water the earth. Sun, embrace the earth that she may be fruitful. Moon, lion of the north, bear of the west, badge of the south, wolf of the east, eagle of the heavens, shrew of the earth, intercede with the Cloud People for us that they may water the earth.
—Pueblo rain song

Thunder and lightning, particularly during summer storms, display an awesome power. In the American Southwest, summer storms are often spectacular shows of black thunderheads, booming thunder, and chain lightning followed by deluges. The chants and corn songs of the Pueblo peoples are beautiful requests for rain or prayers of thanks. Summer rain, particularly to gardeners in dry climates, is like a baptism of renewal, cleansing and revitalizing the landscape. Yet we rarely think to thank the heavens for their blessings.

Acts and Affirmations

Create a lightning stick totem on a rainy summer afternoon. Choose a twisted dried branch from the garden that suggests a bolt of lightning. Peel the bark if it is loose or sand it. Use bright craft paints in shades of turquoise, crimson, golden yellow, olive green, and royal blue. Paint the entire stick with contrasting bands, dots, simple figures, and animals. Lash bunches of dried grass to the top with raffia or calico cloth cut in strips. Stand it in the corner of your garden as a totem of summer rain, or keep it indoors on the porch as a summer remembrance of the great power of lightning.

july 30

In front of the drum was spread a blanket, and on this a great number of cakes were deposited, shaped to represent animals, such as the deer, turkey, rabbit, etc. They are made from a certain seed which is ground and mixed with water. The seed and the plant from which it is obtained are called wa-ve; being yellow, it belongs to the god of fire. The tribe probably made use of this grain before it had corn.

—Carl Sophus, *My Life of Exploration*, 1921

In remote regions of Mexico and Central and Latin America, people still bake small "god cakes." Made out of amaranth flour, not corn, they are consumed in a Eucharist-like ritual at various times throughout the year. The consumption of amaranth grain is very ancient—it has been traced to prehistoric cave dwellers—and even when it was surpassed by maize cultivation, it remained important as a religious food. Though we see amaranth today as a pesky pigweed in our garden, it is really a plant of the gods that may someday again bless the Third World with a reliable and resilient staple food.

Acts and Affirmations

If you use stable or stockyard manure in your garden, chances are you've seen pigweed, or amaranth. If you pick it but leave the root, the single stem branches out on the ground and grows sideways. Once identified, you can allow the heads to mature, and shake out the shiny black seeds. Then create your own little cakes or mix them into polenta and shape into animal forms for your next summer meal under the stars.

july 31

He created all things, the far-off heavens, mankind, the animals, the birds; our eyes are strengthened by his beams, and when he shows himself all flowers grow and live; at his rising the pastures bring forth, they are intoxicated before his face, all the cattle skip on their feet, and the birds in the marshes flutter with joy.

—King Amenhotep IV, king of Egypt, fourteenth century B.C.

The people of Egypt depended on the great Nile River for everything. Its seasonal ebb and flow renewed the floodplain soil so that these desert dwellers could grow enough food to build an empire on two narrow strips of arable farmland. Variations in this seasonal pattern, when the river rose too much or too little, had a serious impact on survival. This dependence imbued the river with a deep spiritual significance. Although today we live separated from rivers by levees, cities, or simply distance, humans first settled on the fertile banks of rivers. The river still runs in our collective unconscious, and the beauty of the fluid landscape is the most nurturing environment for the soul.

Acts and Affirmations

In many cultures, rivers are believed to contain spirits of the water. Sometimes the spirits heal and sometimes they flood and kill. It is an ancient practice to appease the river spirits by leaving gifts along the riverside perched on rocks or other prominent places. Common offerings are tobacco, beer, or incense. Take a day to spend at a river and listen to its incessant murmuring voice. Before you go home, with your primal soul at peace, leave a pile of sesame seeds or ground-up corn chips on a rock—an offering sure to please the river and the local bird life as well.

august

All over northern Europe, the corn harvest begins in August and extends until September. ("Corn" was the name collectively given to all grains.) The harvest marks the end of the farmer's growing season, and the festivities, known as Harvest Home, often revolve around the threshing of wheat, the grinding of grains, and the baking of the first yeasty bread of the season. It is also the Celtic sabbat of Lughnassadh, when sun and plants produce annual fruit. The flower of August is the corn poppy (*Papaver rhoeas*), an annual wildflower of Europe that got its common name because it grows in the grain fields, blooming scarlet among the maturing seed heads of rye and barley.

CELTIC ARN-MONATH (HARVEST MONTH)

HARVEST HOME IN ENGLAND

RISING OF THE DOG STAR

august 1

Lammas (Loaf-Mass; Lughnassadh)

There came three men from out of the west, their fortunes for to try.
As they had sworn a solemn oath, John Barleycorn should die.
—*Ballad of John Barleycorn*, traditional English harvest song

The season of the harvest in old Europe began on August 1, and the ballad of John Barleycorn describes the harvest and the preparation of the grains for the making of whiskey. The death of the Celtic sun god Lugh was celebrated on this date as well, his presence manifest in the wheat fields. Thus the "death" of John Barleycorn referred to the cutting down of the wheat to bundle into sheaves. The Celts followed a different calendar than other ancient people; they celebrated the death of the sun in August rather than at the summer solstice in June. As the grain was cut and bundled in August, Lugh began to wane until his rebirth at the end of winter.

Acts and Affirmations

Lammas (also known as Loaf-mass) was the English harvest festival. On this day it was traditional to winnow and grind the first ripe wheat, rye, or barley to bake it into bread. Until recently, flour was a rare and coveted food, and many believe a shortage of it among the poor ignited the French Revolution. Join in the Lammas tradition by baking some simple biscuits, cut in circles and scored on top like spokes of a wheel, just as the little round Lammas loaves represented this auspicious date in the wheel of the agricultural year.

august 2

DAY OF THE DRYADS

In these days, as we walk in the park or in the woods, we no longer see a god or a dryad in a tree. Indeed, our dependence upon cities, our life in cities—what we have achieved of the Wellsian nightmare—has made us forgetful of trees and other wild things.

—DR. HAROLD WILLIAM RICKETT, foreword to *Make Friends of Trees and Shrubs*, 1962

Nature spirits, or nymphs, were believed by the Greeks to inhabit all natural places. The wood nymphs that lived amid trees and forests were known as dryads. This day in ancient Greece was dedicated to these mythical beings. The notion that things of nature contain their own spirits is not merely a Greek concept, for the Druids and other pagan religions thought so as well. Modern-day pagans call such spirits devas, and communication with them is the technique of dowsing. Many dowsers attribute their success in the garden to their ability to hear and follow the suggestions of the devas, which dictate what the plants need and when. Whether or not devas exist, it is always beneficial to take time to study your plants often, for through their behavior you, too, will discern their wishes.

ACTS AND AFFIRMATIONS

It was customary to avoid cutting or damaging any plants during the day of the dryads. The year's fertility and harvest were tied to these spirits, so these taboos were strictly followed. Offerings were made to the spirits by pouring honey, vanilla, rose water, or essential oils onto the soil at the base of a tree. In the evening, honor the dryads by making a circle of green-glass, seven-day candles underneath a large tree canopy. Inside, set a small offering for the dryads, to grant you prosperity, fertility, and abundance.

august 3

> *The devil's weed has four heads: the root, the stem and leaves, the flowers, and the seeds. Each one of them is different, and whoever becomes her ally must learn about them in that order. The most important head is in the roots. The power of the devil's weed is conquered through the roots. The stem and leaves are the head and cures maladies; properly used, this head is a gift to mankind.*
>
> —CARLOS CASTANEDA, *The Teachings of Don Juan*, 1968

What young Castaneda learned from Yaqui sorcerer Don Juan was to use the great datura plant of the Southwest as a spiritual ally. He consumed the plant and had visions that would reveal to him great wisdom, images of flying, and the ability to divine the future. Datura, found around the world, is the shaman's most powerful plant for healing and divination. As a member of the notorious nightshade family, its duality is prominent: it is both a medicine that can save a life and a dangerous poison that can quickly take it away. Datura teaches us that all living things have a dual nature. We must recognize this duality to live wisely in a world where good and evil, light and dark are always waging war for dominance.

ACTS AND AFFIRMATIONS

God: You have created a duality in all living things. As a human being I too share the duality, for I am composed of both good and evil. Give me the strength to always seek out the good in myself so that the evil will never have a chance to take root and grow. It is my choice, but with your help I will always choose wisely.

(*Brugmansia suavolens* and *Datura inoxia*)

angel's trumpet and devil's weed

The datura—also known as angel's trumpet and devil's weed—is indeed the most notorious wildflower of the Southwest. A beautiful perennial, *Datura meteloides*, bears huge, snow-white, trumpet-shaped flowers up to seven inches long atop mounded bushes. It grows in very dry ground and tends to occur in colonies. This plant can be found elsewhere in the Americas, and no matter where it grows, it is the subject of local myths and legends because of its very toxic nature. Few who encounter the plant realize that it is an important plant in the spiritual and medicinal rites of Native Americans. Native American shamans have long used it to induce a divination trance, but the slightest overdose brings quick death from heart failure. (Datura also contains atropine, which is used in modern medicine.) Datura is a common plant in sacred gardens of the New World, and its larger and showier relatives, the *Brugmansias*, are popular exotics in tropical gardens. Datura, a member of the nightshade family, is most beautiful at dusk, when its trumpets open wide to receive the night-flying moths that are its pollinators.

august 4

The act of putting into your mouth what the earth has grown is perhaps your most direct interaction with the earth.
—Frances Moore Lappé, *Diet for a Small Planet*, 1971

There is a unique dynamic to the growing of fruits and vegetables that is lacking in the cultivation of strictly ornamental plants. When we consume what we grow it is both a creative and nutritive process. The plants become a part of us—a component of our bodies. This communion among the soil, plant, and human body is so primal, it helps us get in touch with our essential role as gatherer and grower. It satiates us in many ways, rekindling the spiritual connection of our species to the kingdom of plants. It is also a deeply natural act that links us to every human being who has ever scratched the soil to yield the miracle of life-sustaining food.

Acts and Affirmations

We tend to think of the needy as just the poor and homeless. You may be surprised to discover how many people have never eaten homegrown vegetables. Imagine never tasting the sweetness of a fresh-picked sun-ripened tomato. What would it be like living without ever eating a lemon cucumber, crisp and right off the vine? Make your friend's or co-workers' day more flavorful by offering them a bag of fresh-picked produce from your garden.

august 5

As long as I retain my feeling and my passion for Nature, I can partly soften or subdue my other passions and resist or endure those of others.
—Lord Byron, letter, June 1822

Lord Byron was an English poet afflicted with manic-depressive mental illness. He struggled, as many creative people do, to reconcile his roller-coaster moods with the world around him. We, too, can seek out a garden or the wilds of nature as a healing therapy for depression, anxiety, or other emotional challenges. Enough time amid the forests, meadows, and flowers can be medicine that makes us stronger and better able to resist the inevitable difficulties of life.

Acts and Affirmations
A passion for nature is not always preexisting—sometimes it must be cultivated. Anyone who learns more about the miracles and mysteries of plants and animals cannot help but develop a passion for acquiring ever more knowledge. Nurture your passion by taking a course in botany, plant identification, or propagation. Not only will you learn more than you ever imagined, you'll become caught up in the collective passion shared by the other students.

august 6

As long as one has a garden one has a future;
And as long as one has a future, one is alive.
—John Richard Moreland, nineteenth century

We have a choice today in the era of lightning-fast news, which brings the ugliness of world events to our doorstep. It is easy to become overwhelmed unless we live as though each day was our last. On that final day, who would be concerned with wars and politics? Suddenly they don't seem so important, but what does grow in value is a beautiful, peaceful existence. This is not to mean that we frenetically pack as much as possible into that short time, but rather it is a state of mind that helps us experience each moment to a greater depth. Of all the activities we may choose for our final day, to spend it living amid the beauty and peace of the garden with those we love seems most appropriate.

Acts and Affirmations

To create and tend a garden is to verify we are alive and that we and the plants will share a future. As your flowers go to seed this year, gather the mature seeds to store over the winter. This act of saving living things for the future is a testament to your belief in tomorrow. And whenever the gloom-and-doom news comes on your TV or radio, change the channel—or better yet, turn it off!

From the dawn of China's primitive folk religion, the relationship between man and nature has been conceived as a deep, reciprocal involvement in which each can affect the other. As the forces of nature can bring prosperity or disaster to man, so can man disrupt the delicate balance of nature by his misdeeds, for Heaven, Earth and man constitute a single, indivisible unity, which is governed by cosmic law . . . the tao.

—"The World's Great Religion," *Life* Magazine Special Edition, 1958

The interconnectedness of all things is expressed in Eastern religions. Indeed, what we do as a people has far-reaching implications on other organisms, both large and microscopic. If we understand this connection, we may gain a greater reverence for nature or for the larger consciousness of living things, that makes us respectful and peaceful in the knowing. And it is in the knowing that we ultimately discover our true spirit and that of the living world around us.

Acts and Affirmations

Traditional Chinese culture saw symbolism in every flower. Flowers meant different things in the home, garden, or in art, and the expression of a sentiment could be compounded by repeating a flower. To paint one or two peony blossoms was to express love, but to paint dozens of them expressed infinite love. Grow in great quantities the flowers that are most meaningful to you to make their symbolic values more profound. Fill bowls or vases all around your house with them to multiply the good feelings they give you.

august 8

Grass feeds the ox: the ox nourishes man: man dies and goes to grass again; and so the tide of life, with everlasting repetition, in continuous circles, moves endlessly on and upward, and in more senses than one, all flesh is grass.

—Kansas senator John James Ingalls, *In Praise of Bluegrass*, 1872

Few have captured the great significance of grass as well as Ingalls. Perhaps it takes someone who has grown up in one of the largest grasslands of America to understand how healing grass can be. As the dietary mainstay of domestic livestock, it is a crucial element in the food chain. Grasses feed the world, cloak the soil, hide the lion, cover the dead, and exist where no other plant can survive. This plant shows us that the meek have truly inherited the earth.

Acts and Affirmations

As the tall, weedy annual grasses turn brown this month, cut some sheaves of them before they scatter their seed. Save these for winter, then bundle them up and tie the bundles to fence posts around your garden. Your offerings stand out beautifully in the snow, and they are welcomed by winter birds and small animals that are still foraging. Although this practice has lost its religious significance and is now done out of a love of winter wildlife, it is a legacy of the old corn spirit traditions of northern Europe.

august 9

No man ever grew so learned as to exhaust the significance of any part of nature. Nature never became a toy to a wise spirit. The flowers, the animals, the mountains reflected all the wisdom of his best hour as much as they had delighted the simplicity of his childhood.

—Ralph Waldo Emerson, journal, 1835

Anyone on earth can accumulate vast amounts of knowledge, but it is wisdom that dictates how well we put it to use. Wisdom is hard-earned, more often discovered through our most grievous errors than magnificent successes. The ability to take renewed interest in the little things of nature, to frolic in a meadow or marvel at a stone made lustrous under water, is one of the greatest secrets of true happiness.

Acts and Affirmations

"Loves me, loves me not" is a very ancient form of divination traditionally practiced by young women throughout Europe. They used a daisy to help divine solutions to other questions as well. Next time you want the wise flower spirits of the garden to answer your dilemma, ask them . . . one petal at a time.

august 10

You herbs, born at the birth of time, more ancient than the gods themselves. O Plants, with this hymn I sing to you our mothers and our gods. The holy fig tree is your home, a thousand are your growths. You, who have a thousand powers, free this my patient from disease.

—Rig Veda, *Hymn in Praise of Herbs*, 2500 B.C.

In India there is a great emphasis on ayurvedic healing with herbs that treat body, mind, and spirit as one. The fig may be considered a common fruit tree elsewhere, but in India it is revered for its power to heal. Our perception of plants is far more limited than it should be, for plants have more value than just food or beauty. They can be far more valuable both physically and spiritually if we leave our Western minds behind to explore common plants and their uses around the world.

Acts and Affirmations

You have probably tasted fig bars, but it's surprising how few people have eaten fresh figs. Figs don't keep well after picking, so you may have to go to a gourmet market or produce stand to find them. Their unique texture and sweet taste make them a very sensual eating experience. Try eating them outdoors on a balmy summer night with a special friend or lover, wearing little clothing and playing Indian sitar music softly in the background.

august 11

We are closer to the Vegetable Kingdom than we know; is it not for man alone that mint, thyme, sage, and rosemary exhale "crush me and eat me!"—for us that opium poppy, coffee-berry, teaplant and vine perfect themselves? Their aim is to be absorbed by us, even if it can only be achieved by attaching themselves to roast mutton.

—Cyril Connolly, *The Unquiet Grave*, 1944

Perhaps it is a miracle that so many plants contain delicious aromatic oils, though these are actually nature's way of protecting plants from insects and herbivores. They are truly a gift to humanity, for the animals don't seem to appreciate their pungent qualities. This points to the fact that herbs are a gift to humanity, a beautiful offering from our Creator. No wonder herbs and their uses have come down to us from ancient cultures, their uses in food and medicine and cosmetics still as valuable as they were millennia ago.

Acts and Affirmations

Enjoy the mint from your garden with fresh mint iced tea. Cut fresh mint leaves, place them in a pitcher or jar, and pour hot (not boiling) water over the top. Allow to steep for ten minutes, pour off the liquid, and refrigerate for a brisk, garden-fresh summer tea.

august 12

Our Father, pure and clean as a mirror, will give us a little to eat. He will aid us. Tilling the fields is our life. We sow corn, chile, tomatoes. If we don't work, how are we to eat? Our Lord will give us enough to sustain our lives. We will toil, we will sow, we will seek out food for our survival. Thus it was ordained by our God.

—TRADITIONAL NAHUATL RAIN CHANT

The "Father" invoked in this chant is Tlaloc, the earth god who controlled rain. His temples were often high in the mountains of Mexico, where the rain clouds formed. Tlaloc had four aspects corresponding to the four cardinal directions. They were different types of rain: a gentle fertilizing rain, harsh storm rain, destructive hail, and the persistent moisture that causes mildew. The Nahuatl identified with water in all its aspects, for this single element is more important to cultures in arid climates than any other substance on earth.

Acts and Affirmations

While reciting the rain chant to Tlaloc, it was customary for women and children to throw handfuls of flower petals into the air off roofs and other high places. The petals were to simulate rainfall and urge the god to be more generous. In contemporary times, the practice evolved so that now people fill swimming pools with fragrant gardenias. To invite rain in this dry month, cast petals about your patio for color, or float flowers on your pool next time someone comes to swim.

The borders of the streams were woven in stripes, and between these borders tiny stones, the size of pearls, gave the impression of water. The stems and branches of the trees and flowers were woven from gold and silver, the leaves from silk like the rest of the plants, and the fruits from brightly colored stones.

—DESCRIPTION OF THE GARDEN OF THE PALACE OF CHOSROES IN PERSIAN CARPET DESIGN, sixth century A.D.

The Islamic peoples of the dry Middle East found it difficult to create refreshing gardens due to a limited water supply. Some were nomadic, living off their flocks, and never settled down long enough to grow plants. The scarcity of true gardens, combined with the gardenesque description of Paradise in the Koran, made gardens a common theme in decorative art, especially beautiful hand-knotted carpets. It was as though the threads woven into patterns were a stylized act of planting the flowers depicted. The earliest designs were the four-quadrant garden of Paradise rich in water and flowers. Later came the Tree of Life pattern. Each Persian carpet is actually someone's garden, planted in symbols and colors that reflect their spiritual love of a verdant landscape they may never see.

ACTS AND AFFIRMATIONS

If you have no place for a garden, create one indoors with a beautiful Persian carpet. Through special programs in Afganistan, weavers have been urged to return to their old vegetable dyes to reduce dependence on imported aniline dyes. Natural dyes are vivid and bright, broad-spectrum colors compared to one-dimensional anilines. Simply inquire at a reputable Persian carpet dealer as to whether they carry natural-dye products. These visions of Paradise, of four-quadrant gardens and trees, make a beautiful symbolic garden in any home.

august 14

Water and protect the root;
Heaven will watch the flower and fruit.
—Chinese proverb

Asian culture is filled with beautiful and wise proverbs that say so much in very few words. This Chinese proverb talks about roots, which, though hidden underground, are the most important part of a plant. We tend to care for the flower and fruit and forget that it is the condition of the roots that support them that matters most. So it is with us: our roots, or our spiritual life, must be healthy and well-tended; otherwise, we can never be truly beautiful nor bear the fruits of happiness.

Acts and Affirmations

As we go about the activities of each day, it is easy to ignore our spiritual roots. Psychologists recommend we create symbolic reminders around our homes and workplaces. Borrow a ritual from China, where they tie little red ribbons to trees to enhance fertility, and tie red strings to a tree limb or a flower stalk. Let the ribbons remind you as you enter your garden that it is the place both to nurture plant roots and cultivate your spiritual roots. If you do that, heaven will take care of the rest.

The greatest delight which the fields and woods minister, is the suggestion of an occult relation between man and the vegetable. I am not alone and unacknowledged. They nod to me, and I to them. The waving of the boughs in the storm, is new to me and old, it takes me by surprise, and yet is not unknown. Its effect is like that of a higher thought or a better emotion coming over me, when I deemed I was thinking justly or doing right.

—Ralph Waldo Emerson, *Nature*, 1836

Who hasn't heard the rustling of dry cornstalks in late summer or twigs tapping against a fence or roof? Yet plants are so quiet that the overactive mind often fails to hear their murmurings. We must cultivate an inner quiet to hear them—that still, silent voice that is new and yet old, in a language that is far more ancient than words. When plants speak, God speaks. When we are quiet and puttering in our gardens, or perhaps wandering amid wild places, our subconscious is open to the messages of plants, and they fill our hearts with peace.

Acts and Affirmations

It's easy to get started meditating in your garden, and there are many variations on this simple process. Choose a comfortable place such as the lawn or a chair, and sit with your spine and head in a straight line. Then close your eyes and pause a moment to become fully aware of your own presence. Repeat a word such as "relax" or a short phrase to yourself over and over very slowly, becoming aware of your breathing. You will begin to grow aware of all sorts of sounds, the temperature of the air on your skin, and many other things you never noticed before. After about ten minutes you should feel far more peaceful, and the more often you practice this the more profound the benefits.

august 16

Salem Heritage Day, Massachusetts

Why not walk in the aura of magic that gives to the small things of life their uniqueness and importance? Why not befriend a toad today?
—Germaine Greer, *The Change: Women, Aging and the Menopause*, 1991

In the days of old Salem, the warty toad was thought to be the witch's familiar—one of the animals she became to travel about unnoticed. It was also a common component in a witch's brew. Both of these bits of folklore do not do justice to this marvelous amphibian, which is actually a beneficial fellow to have around. Perhaps the toad was the colonial woman's best friend, as it kept her dooryard garden pest free and became her prince of beautiful herbs and flowers. At night the toad may truly become the gardener's best friend as it consumes quantities of insect pests and voracious slugs. The toad is a wonderful gift to the world as it sings and croaks out the nighttime hours while it tidies up our pest population. Avoid using chemicals that might reduce their numbers.

Acts and Affirmations

Knowing how vital toads are to pest control in the garden, you can buy cute toad houses from your nursery that offer toads a cool place to wait out the daytime hours. You can easily make your own toad house in a shaded, moist corner of the garden with a large, overturned clay flower pot set over a shallow depression in the soil. Any enclosure that the toad can enter and be protected from the hot sun will eventually become a home, making sure it stays your neighbor and friend.

august 17

FEAST OF THE MOON GODDESS DIANA

There is something haunting in the light of the moon; it has all the dispassionateness of a disembodied soul, and something of its inconceivable mystery.

—JOSEPH CONRAD, *Lord Jim*, 1900

Diana is the Roman goddess of the hunt and the moon, and though decidedly female, she is a powerful, virginal figure. Diana becomes the embodiment of the relationship between the moon's and women's twenty-eight-day cycle. Her temples lacked roofs so that she could look down upon her subjects and their midnight rites from the dark skies. Although today we live under roofs, which separate us from the daily changes in the moon, this relationship is still among the most mystical of all. Perhaps it is time to rekindle this connection by following the moon's quarters as they wax and wane through every month of the year.

ACTS AND AFFIRMATIONS

Silver, with its shining, reflective quality associated with the moon, is a metal sacred to Diana. The ancient way to celebrate the Feast of Diana is to bring something silver out into the garden under moonlight—perhaps an old vase, a candelabra, or nothing more than a silver spoon suspended on a gossamer thread from the eaves or a high tree branch.

august 18

The Giant Sequoia must have afforded pride and pleasure to the Creator for it is the finest tree He ever made. Of a truth, there is not in all the world a tree more wonderful.

—Rodney Sydes Ellsworth, *The Giant Sequoia*, 1924

Few trees have inspired more awe than the mammoth redwoods. They are so revered that many have been individually named and today are avidly protected. Such trees are awe-inspiring because they remind us that creation is a mystery and a miracle, not only in its diversity, but in its extremes. Such experiences are so dramatic they lift us out of our everyday existence into a new realm in which great and mighty acts of God fill our lives with infinite richness.

Acts and Affirmations

Do your part to preserve and protect the redwood trees. Avoid purchasing any lumber or products that are constructed out of redwood because demand and dwindling forests are driving prices so high that these trees are threatened everywhere. If we do our part to reduce this demand, our collective actions will force industry to use a more renewable wood source. As a result, more young trees will survive, and future generations will also be able to marvel at their immense size.

august 19

We see the world piece by piece, as the sun, the moon, the animal, the tree; but the whole, of which these are shining parts, is the soul.
—Ralph Waldo Emerson, *The Over-Soul*, 1841

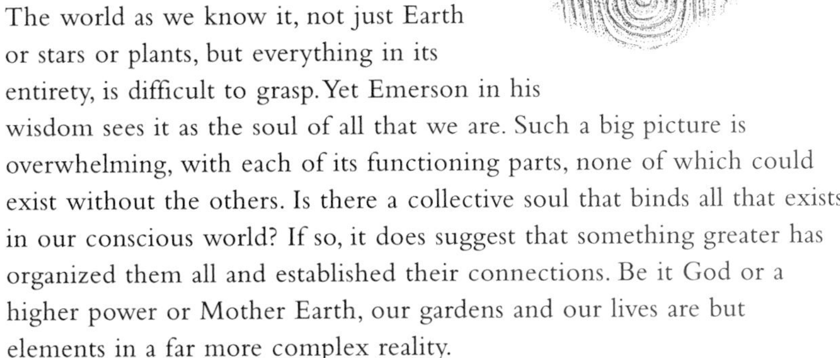

The world as we know it, not just Earth or stars or plants, but everything in its entirety, is difficult to grasp. Yet Emerson in his wisdom sees it as the soul of all that we are. Such a big picture is overwhelming, with each of its functioning parts, none of which could exist without the others. Is there a collective soul that binds all that exists in our conscious world? If so, it does suggest that something greater has organized them all and established their connections. Be it God or a higher power or Mother Earth, our gardens and our lives are but elements in a far more complex reality.

Acts and Affirmations

Ancient passage graves made of enormous stones arranged into a tunnel-like enclosure have been found in Great Britain and northern France. Inside them, the most common decorative motif is the spiral, which is the most ancient symbol of life and fertility. The spiral also makes a beautiful temporary tattoo when applied either with a henna kit or fresh blackberry juice. Use a paintbrush or the crushed tip of a wooden toothpick to express the soul of all things by staining spirals on your skin.

august 20

FEAST OF ST. BERNARD OF CLAIRVAUX

What I know of the divine science and Holy Scripture I learnt in the woods and fields.

—ST. BERNARD, *Epistle 103*, twelfth century

At the tender age of twenty-two, St. Bernard was given twelve monks and ordered to found a new monastery in the valley of Wormwood in medieval France. Wormwood is a shrubby plant of the sagebrush clan that grows on the poorest of soils. Bernard and his brothers lived poorly in the woods for a long time, proving their devotion as they cleared enough land to support themselves with a garden. Despite such meager ascetic lives, their numbers grew as word of their holiness spread. Those years in the woods clearly taught the young abbot truths that provided valuable insights into both holy scripture and the divine presence.

ACTS AND AFFIRMATIONS

The powerful bitter scent of wormwood, *Artemisia absinthium*, made it a common plant of mourning in cultures around the world. It was made into a "mourning necklace" worn as a sign of grief. A mourning necklace is composed of little cloth bundles of fresh-cut wormwood tied onto a cord worn around the neck. It is a most suitable gift for someone grieving or worn as a personal decoration to remember a departed loved one.

august 21

Nature uses human imagination to lift her work of creation to even higher levels.

—Luigi Pirandello, *Six Characters in Search of an Author*, 1921

Gardens are the result of a collaborative effort between nature and human creativity. God supplies the materials, such as plants and trees, stones and earth. We take the materials and arrange them in a way that is beautiful, be they a model of the natural environment or a more abstract composition. When we arrange natural things to make them more beautiful than they were originally, we honor creation as a whole.

Acts and Affirmations

Use your imagination to expand your garden from one that is merely ornamental to a landscape filled with aromatic, culinary herbs. The stately haze of feathery purple fennel can reach five feet tall and is a favorite perennial border accent. Chamomile is both a cheerful edging plant and ground cover. Creeping thyme was a popular plant for scented medieval lawns and is a great filler between flagstones. Creeping rosemary can be clipped into tiny formal hedges or allowed to spill over the edges of walls. Let your imagination run wild to explore a more useful mix-and-match landscape to lift your work to higher levels.

august 22

A river seems a magic thing. A magic, moving, living part of the very earth itself—for it is from the soil, both from its depth and from its surface, that a river has its beginning.

—Laura Gilpin, *The Rio Grande*, 1949

Unlike static bodies of water, rivers are more like living, moving organisms. Day and night the fluid landscape passes down the channel, lapping at the shores. People have always built settlements on riverbanks, for the fresh water cleanses the refuse of daily life and offers a convenient means of travel. A river is never the same two days in a row as water levels rise and fall with the seasons. Where the riverbed is irregular there are rapids and waterfalls, which are the dramatic voice of the water as it speeds down the stream. Large or small, deep or shallow, cold or warm, rivers have captured our primal selves and our contemporary hearts with their animated character. The next time you have a chance to visit a river or stream, sit down and listen to its song, and you will hear the voice of nature whispering to your heart.

Acts and Affirmations

Moving water is mesmerizing, and its sight and sound work magically to refresh the wearied mind. To experience the same sensations primitive peoples did as they slept in their riverside shelters, purchase a small tabletop fountain. Choose carefully because each fountain is slightly different. Find one that has a variable speed so you can adjust it to fit your mood. After a hectic day at the office, sit back in a comfortable chair, start the fountain, and imagine life by the riverside.

august 23

A tree that can fill the span of a man's arms grows from a downy tip; a terrace nine stories high rises from hodfuls of earth; a journey of a thousand miles starts from beneath one's feet.
—Lao-tzu, *Tao-te-ching*, sixth century B.C.

When you look at a backyard or a piece of land that is neglected, weed-infested, and dismal, it's hard to find the courage to begin creating a garden. The task may seem overwhelming, but it is like other things in this world that as a whole seem insurmountable. But when the whole is broken up into tiny pieces, each little one seems far easier to accomplish. With the garden, the first step is to pull or hoe off the weeds one by one. Suddenly you'll look up to find that neglected ground has become fertile land ready to cultivate and plant.

Acts and Affirmations

What the quince lacks in taste it makes up for in beauty and fragrance. The trees bloom in the spring, but they become nondescript during the summer months. If you can find a quince tree nearby, pick the fruit and place them in a wide bowl to scent your rooms. Enjoy this traditional Asian summer aroma, knowing that the wise Lao-tzu probably enjoyed it in exactly the same way.

august 24

If God created the earth, so is the earth hallowed; and if it is hallowed, so must we deal with it devotedly and with care that we do not despoil it, and mindful of our relations to all beings that live on it. We are to consider it religiously: Put off thy shoes from thy feet, for the place whereon thou standest is holy ground.

—Liberty Hyde Bailey, *The Holy Earth*, 1915

In contrast to popular scientific theories about creation, American botanist Liberty Hyde Bailey believed that all things, both living and nonliving, are created by God. This belief is the basis for Bailey's deeply rooted conviction that farmers and gardeners who work the soil are high priests who serve at the altar of God.

Acts and Affirmations

As children, we often shuffled barefoot through the powdery dust of late summer. Indigenous peoples still wander the deserts and bushlands of the world with calloused bare feet. Chances are it's been a long time since your bare toes have left their imprint on the earth. Next time you're in the garden or wandering in the country, take off your shoes and walk on the sacred earth. Feel the dust and cracked soil, the scratchy chaff of dead spring grass, and know that this primal act will reconnect you with the sacred ground.

august 25

> *To have been placed on this earth "to dress and keep it" was the divine intention; to make it a garden of delights for ourselves and our children, where the healthy prodding and stirring of the soil should produce, not only nourishing fruit for the body, but also most nourishable food for the mind.*
>
> —St. Augustine, *City of God*, sixth century

One of the first commands God gave Adam and Eve in Genesis was to tend the Garden of Eden. This places the act of gardening as the primary devotion for the Judeo-Christian world. The garden is the one place where both the body and mind may be nourished at the same time. We grow God's creations, which give us food that energizes the body and fills it with vitamins and minerals. The time we spend nurturing the plants in the garden allows us hours of quiet for the mind amid a very simple place composed of earth and plant and sun. Preparing the plants for meals by harvest or cooking becomes almost a ritual act that binds our spirit with those we serve at the table. Is there any more suitable place for human beings to nurture mind, body, and spirit?

Acts and Affirmations

Choose a tree in your landscape to become a tree of life. Find one that feels familiar and that offers a generous crotch or knothole. Let this become a place where you privately express the feelings surrounding events, changes, and memories of your life by leaving mementos in the crotch or hole. Each visit to the tree will become an emotional journey back to the feelings or memories sparked by the offerings you have left there.

august 26

REBIRTH OF VISHNU AS CHILD KRISHNA

As the sheath and branching leaves of the plantain are seen in its stem,
so You are the stem of the universe and all is visible in You.
—HINDU PRAYER TO VISHNU

The banana, or plantain, grows in a stalk shrouded in layers of leaves. The leaves are tightly packed, but they open one at a time as the stalk elongates. A similar structure occurs inside an onion bulb and in the rosette of a lettuce plant before it "bolts" prior to flowering. Vishnu is likened to the banana tree because within him all the universe resides. This omnipotent, all-seeing deity exists in all of the plants that hide so many layers inside in preparation for future growth. In India, Hindus celebrate Vishnu's reincarnation in his most beloved form, Krishna, in a feast that honors rebirth and resurrection.

ACTS AND AFFIRMATIONS

Yellow is the traditional color of Vishnu and of his tree, the banana. Honor the child Krishna today with a feast of fried bananas sprinkled with petals of yellow nasturtiums, squash blossoms, and rose petals. Burn incense as you dine on this traditional tropical meal of India.

august 27

CHOOSUK: CHINESE HARVEST FESTIVAL

When the tea is well-brewed and the incense has pure fragrance, it's a delight if friends drop in; when birds twitter and flowers drop their petals, even solitude is contentment for the soul.

—CONFUCIAN PROVERB

Writers and artists must find an environment of quiet peace to create beautiful work. Such an atmosphere is difficult to find these days, as the pace and complexity of everyday life seem to push the peaceful hours into a small corner of our day. Yet peace is crucial to more than just artists, because every living thing strives to think creatively in one way or another. Peace and happiness free the soul to soar, and sunny hours spent in the garden can be the perfect setting to set your creative process in motion.

ACTS AND AFFIRMATIONS

Chinese scholars often receive gifts of decorative pots planted with *Liriope muscari*. In older times when handmade rice paper was far more costly, it was wasteful to use it for bookmarks. Instead these plants grown on the desk or nearby windowsill provided the user with long, thin leaves for bookmarks. Give your favorite book fan one of these plants in a Chinese ceramic pot. Print a short poem on a piece of rice paper, fold it up, and nestle it inside the leaves for an evocative inspirational greeting.

august 28

The earth is not selfish. It is open and free to all. It invites everywhere. The naturist is not selfish; he shares all his joys and discoveries, even to the extent of publishing them.
—Liberty Hyde Bailey, *The Holy Earth*, 1915

One of the most beautiful truths about the garden is that it is open and free to all who wish to cultivate the earth. But there is a charge, that we learn from each garden we plant. A person does not need to go to school to obtain this learning, although it is very helpful to become friends with others who till the soil to glean some of their accumulated wisdom. Knowledge must most of all be learned from personal trial, followed by error and some success. No amount of money will bring back a dead plant. Wealthy or poor, everyone will make mistakes and be forced to start over. If you persist you will profit from your mistakes in the long run, not in a heavier crop this year, but laying up treasures of knowledge that will lead to a bumper crop in years to come.

Acts and Affirmations

Staffs, particularly those made of elderberry wood or ash, were prized for the protective powers they granted to the user. If there is elder near you, choose a good, straight branch to make a five-foot-long staff, or choose one from any hardwood tree. Allow it to season many months if not already seasoned, then sand the surface smooth. Use a simple electric wood-burning tool to make the staff meaningful by burning words and names, symbols and decorations into the shaft. Take the elder staff whenever you walk, and it will protect and guide you.

august 29

What is man without the beasts? If all the beasts were gone, man would die from a great loneliness of spirit. For whatever happens to the beasts, soon happens to man. All things are connected.

—Chief Seattle, letter to President Franklin Pierce

Gardens are not just composed of plants. They suppport and are supported by many species of birds and insects, each with its own place in the natural ecosystem. The birds keep the insects at bay, and the insects devour weak plants to ensure only the strong live to reproduce. Even the worms and pill bugs fill an important role, aerating the soil with their tunnels and helping organic matter decompose. Native Americans endowed nature with a deep spirituality, realizing that there are many strands in the larger web of life and that they are all interconnected.

Acts and Affirmations

The praying mantis is perhaps the most valuable of all predators, and even if you find these largish insects revolting, you should treat them like VIPs. They are God's gift for pest control and thus are sacred in all gardens. Avoid pesticides in your garden if you want to keep the praying mantis alive. Know how to identify this good insect and its egg cases, which are often laid on twigs and wire fences. Salvage the eggs for next year's garden by leaving them in a sheltered place outdoors as you clean the garden in autumn and prune throughout the winter.

august 30

There seem to be but three ways for a nation to acquire wealth. The first is by war, as the Romans did, in plundering their conquered neighbors. This is robbery. The second by commerce, which is generally cheating. The third by agriculture, the only honest way, wherein man receives a real increase of the seed thrown into the ground, in a kind of continual miracle, wrought by the hand of God in his favor, as a reward for his innocent life and his virtuous industry.

—Benjamin Franklin, *Positions to Be Examined Concerning National Wealth*, 1769

Gardens are a continual miracle, and the hand of God is in every flower and tree and leaf. Gardening is an endeavor that grants us the quiet hours of industry that set our minds to thinking about the good things, of sun and earth, of dawn and dusk, and the thousands of little miracles that are witnessed only when we spend a lot of time outdoors. Without gardening we would lose our memory of such nuances, for there would be nothing to rekindle us, to renew our inspired wonder at the continual miracle.

Acts and Affirmations

At this time of year, there are abundant increases from the seeds thrown to the ground. All plants recognize that the solstice is passed and the days are noticeably shorter. It is time to begin gathering the seeds of all the plants you wish to cultivate next year. This is the divine payoff for the honest labor of gardening: a free garden come spring. Seeds also make great last-minute holiday gifts. Put them in pretty little decorated envelopes bearing your personal message!

august 31

Climb the mountains and get their good tidings. Nature's peace will flow into you as sunshine flows into trees. The winds will blow their own freshness into you, and the storms their energy, while cares will drop away from you like the leaves of Autumn.

—John Muir, *My First Summer in the Sierra*, 1911

In the forests of the West, August is dry, and the great pondersoa pines emit a unique fragrance that is as soft as a grandmother and as sweet as honey. Muir wrote of the wind blowing its freshness, no doubt while he was perched on a great cliff looking east across Yosemite Valley into the rising sun. There the raging, late-summer storms energize your whole consciousness, their power both a threat and therapy. It is rare to feel a landscape so deeply as Muir did, but all who visit the wilderness in these last days of summer before the leaves of autumn blow have these gifts to gain.

Acts and Affirmations

High places have long been favored as a contemplative environment for many religions, such as the Buddhist monasteries in the Himalayas or Incan shrines of the Andes. There is something unique about high places, for they make us feel more a part of the sky than the landscape below. It is an uplifting experience to go to a high place to spend some contemplative time in the sky surveying the view. You can find it easily even if you live far from the mountains, because you will feel much the same at the top of the Statue of Liberty or on the roof of a skyscraper. If you cannot climb a natural mountain then at least climb a man-made one.

september

The harvest continues into September, with the late-maturing grains the last to be cut from the fields. It is the time when the farmer takes stock of the size of the stored harvest.

The autumnal equinox falls this month, providing an auspicious date to mark thanksgiving rites to God or the spirits of nature and vegetation. The aster is associated with the month of September because it is among the latest-blooming flowers and is inextricably linked to the September Feast of St. Michael. It is also the pagan sabbat of Mabon, which was the original pagan thanksgiving celebration before it was made Christian by pilgrims in the seventeenth century and later became an American holiday in the nineteenth century.

ARAPAHO MOON OF DRYING GRASS

CELTIC GERST-MONATH, OR BARLEY MONTH

september 1

Feast of St. Fiacre, Patron of Gardeners

The evil peasant woman Becnaude, lurking in the forest, saw Fiacre raise his staff and walk forward, his lips moving in prayer. To her surprise and horror, a great furrow appeared in the rich earth, stones were turned aside, bushes were uprooted as the miraculous plough continued—until a tract of land great enough for a garden and a church was surrounded and properly marked.

—Adelma Grenier Simmons, *Saints in My Garden*, 1932

The sixth-century saint Fiacre was born to wealth, but he literally gave up the world to spend the rest of his life in a garden. According to legend, his land was miraculously cleared and plowed by the angels of God soon after he began his hermitlike existence in the French countryside. The garden produced healing herbs, flowers for church, and food for the poor. Over his eighty years, the monk used his garden to generously care for others. As late as the seventeenth century, Fiacre's shrine still drew a vast number of pilgrims seeking healing.

Acts and Affirmations

Everyone who grows a garden may learn from the example of St. Fiacre, who used plants to treat the sick, feed the poor, and beautify the altar. We, too, grow God's gifts of useful plants to enrich our own households or to share with friends and neighbors. With each new plant added to the garden, we naturally expand our knowledge of its uses and increase our ability to make our familiar world a better place. We continue the tradition of utilizing the gift of plants as a form of devotion, reaping the many benefits they bring to us and the world around us.

(*Hyssopus officinalis*)

hyssop

In the Bible, sprigs of a plant called "hyssop" were used as a prop to anoint or sprinkle people and holy places with water. The plant was probably marjoram, which grew in the Holy Land. Another plant, *Hyssopus officinalis* (the one known today as hyssop), is actually native to Europe. It was named after the plant of the Bible because it was used in medieval times for sprinkling holy water. The plant was grown by virtually every medieval monastery and grew wild in the region of France where St. Fiacre lived. The powerful aroma of its leaves led to its use as an herb that was strewn about the house to cover unpleasant smells. Women pressed leaves in their psalm books or missals to sniff when drowsy during long sermons. Hyssop was also an age-old remedy for coughs and asthma, and was surely used by Fiacre in his renowned healing practices. It remains a beautiful plant for home herb gardens where it serves as a medicinal, a culinary seasoning, an attractive blue-flowered ornamental, a habitat plant for bees, and a beautiful symbol of Judeo-Christian tradition.

september 2

Grape Vine Festival

Drink no longer water, but use a little wine for thy stomach's sake and thine often infirmities.
—1 Timothy 5:23

Wine is integral to the cultures of the Mediterranean, but it can be found in virtually every culture in which grapes or other fruits are cultivated. Wine raises the spirits and courts the muse. Greeks celebrated both the vine and wine on this day, the beginning of the harvest with all its communal celebrations. The coming together to bring in the crop is one of humanity's oldest cooperative ventures. And thus it becomes something more than labor—it is an integral rite in the cycle of the agricultural seasons.

Acts and Affirmations

Wine has long been used to "toast" someone or seal a bargain. On this day, share a good bottle of red or white wine with close friends, family, or fellow gardeners to celebrate the harvest.

Ancient poetry and mythology suggest, at least, that husbandry was once a sacred art; but it is pursued with irreverent haste and heedlessness by us, our object being to have large farms and large crops merely. We have no festival, nor procession, nor ceremony, not excepting our Cattle-shows and so called Thanksgivings, by which the farmer expresses a sense of sacredness of his calling, or is reminded of its sacred origin.
—Henry David Thoreau, *Walden*, 1854

The season of the harvest was the most joyful part of the year in earlier times. It was a continual celebration of abundance as the crops were harvested and stored for the long winter to come. All agrarian peoples have these autumn rites integrated into their spirituality, for at no other time was God closer than when the fields bore their fruit. Let us rekindle the sacredness of the farmer or gardener's calling by returning to the forgotten festivals that make the age-old acts of planting and harvest an integral part of our daily lives.

Acts and Affirmations

Reintroduce the ancient sacrificial fruits of the harvest into your summer's-end experience. Choose flowering heads of grasses, dried flowers, fruit, and colorful vegetables as tangible representations of your garden's diverse harvest. Then arrange them creatively to take advantage of their forms, colors, and textures. Place them in a shrine in your garden or home, or in a basket to remind you to celebrate the end of the season and the beginning of autumn.

september 4

Great is a ripe sunflower, and great was the sun above my corn-fields. His fingers lifted up the corn-ears, his hands fashioned my melons, and set my beans full in the pods. Therefore my heart is happy, and I will lay many blue prayer sticks at the shrine of Ta-wa.

—Traditional Pueblo women's harvest song

Until you have tried to garden in a desert, you can't come close to understanding the great sense of accomplishment people must have felt when they had a good crop ready to harvest there. The Pueblo songs are among the most beautiful of all Native American prayers, and this one dedicates the successful harvest to Ta-wa, the Creator who makes things grow. There is also an example of how the gods are honored at harvest time with a thousand different ceremonies around the world. The blue prayer sticks represent through color the spiritual qualities of sky, water, and plants.

Acts and Affirmations

Create your own blue prayer sticks to thank the Creator for your harvest. Choose some stout, dry sticks from garden refuse. Clean them up and paint them bright turquoise blue. Either add them to a garden shrine, or stick them deeply into the soil so they stand upright in the garden. Use them to remind you to offer thanks, because every flower, fruit, and herb is a gift.

september 5

FESTIVAL OF MAMA QUILLA, INCA MOON GODDESS

The moon is a white strange world, great, white, soft-seeming globe in the night sky, and what she actually communicates to me across space I shall never fully know. But the moon that pulls the tides, and the moon that controls the menstrual periods of women, and the moon that touches the lunatics, she is not the mere dead lump of the astronomer.

—D. H. LAWRENCE, introduction to *The Dragon of the Apocalypse* in *London Mercury*, 1930

This same moon that makes seeds sprout has governed the monthly cycle of tasks that every farmer and gardener have followed since time immemorial. Almanacs, with their strange signs and forecasts, were the official guides to the phases of growth and destruction. Farmers waited for the dark of the moon to pull a weed, cut wood, or plow their fields. The waxing moon was a time of fertility, and the full moon was the night light of magic abundance. Though few people garden by the moon phases any more, those who do swear it is the key to a successful garden.

ACTS AND AFFIRMATIONS

To truly become a soulful gardener is to be ever alerted to the status of the moon. You should know when it is waxing and waning, and notice the full moon, while conscious that this is the halfway point of the month. The moon is always represented by a goddess in virtually every culture and is decidedly female.

september 6

Miracles are not in contradiction to nature. They are only in contradiction with what we know of nature.

—St. Augustine, sixth century

What was yesterday thought to be miraculous is today explained by science. Yet each scientific explanation opens the door to a thousand new miracles. We still do not fully grasp that ephemeral thing called life sequestered in a small, hard seed. Though we understand DNA, we do not know the depths of a plant species' ability to evolve, nor the nature of those changes. Thus a phenomenon once miraculous is merely transformed by science into a well-designed blessing from God.

Acts and Affirmations

There is no more profound example of miracles than the dawn redwood tree, a plant known only through fossils as the ancestor of the California redwoods. In the 1940s a living grove of this primitive deciduous conifer was discovered in a remote part of inland China, which is a miracle for paleobotanists. As a gardener I will strive to be a free thinker and believe that miracles occur every day in the most ordinary ways. I will always look for them, knowing that surprises like the dawn redwood are waiting to be discovered by the believing soul and adventurous mind.

Grass is the forgiveness of nature—her constant benediction. Fields trampled with battle, saturated with blood, torn with the ruts of cannon, grow green again with grass, and carnage is forgotten. Streets abandoned by traffic become grass-grown like rural lanes, and are obliterated. Forests decay, harvests perish, flowers vanish, but grass is immortal.

—Kansas senator John James Ingalls, *In Praise of Bluegrass*, 1872

The grasses are everywhere, springing up with the warmth of spring, growing quickly to flower, and sending their seed off into the autumn breeze. They cloak the prairie earth to hold it against the perpetual wind and occasional drought. Grass is the hardest-working plant in the world; it feeds us, covers our houses, is weaved into clothes and beds, feeds animals and provides them bedding—the list is endless. To know grasses is to bathe in the constant benediction of nature and to obtain a rare glimpse at the seeming immortality of these remarkably tenacious plants.

Acts and Affirmations

Strive to adopt a new attitude toward grasses and see them as nature's problem solvers rather than merely weeds or lawns. Grasses are beautiful in all their diversity and deserve a new appreciation of their many talents. They are the perfect symbol of the triumph of the spirit over the challenges of adversity.

september 8

The tradesman, the attorney comes out of the din and craft of the street, and sees the sky and the woods, and is a man again. In their eternal calm, he finds himself.

—Ralph Waldo Emerson, *Nature*, 1836

Every time we trudge to the office, we lose a bit of ourselves somewhere in the chaos of commuting and the workplace. Schedules, traffic, and daily conflict and stress combine to separate us from the things of the spirit. We need not venture far to reclaim some of this lost calm, for if we cultivate a garden of our own, we may rest there awhile and rediscover the self. Emerson knew a hundred years ago that, while commerce threatens the soul, nature offers a simple remedy.

Acts and Affirmations

God—May I exchange neon for sunshine, foliage for walls, and under my feet give me soft green grass to cushion my weary body at the end of a long day.

september 9

Chrysanthemum Day, Japan and China

To go to see the prune flowers after snow, pay a visit to the chrysanthemums during frost, tend the orchid during rain, or listen to the swaying bamboos before the breeze—such are the joys of leisure of a rustic fellow, but they are also moments of the greatest meaning to the scholar.

—Confucian proverb

Chrysanthemums are China's most beloved herbaceous plants. They are celebrated on this, the ninth day of the ninth month, with festivals and drinking chrysanthemum-flavored rice wine. This consummate flower of autumn marks the season when the yang of summer yields to the yin of winter, and though it is a celebration, there is a hint of melancholy as people look toward the hard winter months ahead. Because these flowers blossom so late in the season, they are also a symbol of old age and wisdom.

Acts and Affirmations

Express your respect for wisdom and old age by giving a bouquet of chrysanthemums to a special friend who is in the later years of his or her life. Seniors are rarely shown respect in Western culture. Before you give them away though, choose a few stems of this easy-to-root perennial for a chrysanthemum garden of your own next fall.

But I do know that there are people who are like flowers, just as simply in touch with God and as incarnate with His spirit as the flowers; and I do know that there is no greater thrill that one can get than reaching out and touching these great souls.

—George Washington Carver, *The Man Who Talked with Flowers*, 1939

It is unlikely that the people Carver longed to touch were the movers and shakers of society. Those he recognized were typically humble and quiet like this former slave. They go about their daily life living spirituality with each step and act, but few words. If Carver were a flower, there is little doubt he would be a dandelion, golden yellow in spring, its leaves and root food for all mankind. Mother Teresa would be a small field aster that stands brilliant and pure amid the tangled wayside weeds. Often it is the small common flowers that lodge in our hearts, loved for their pure souls and their deep humility in the shadow of gaudy hybrids.

Acts and Affirmations

Strive to see the little flowers, the tiny ones that live and die without much attention. Yet they are tenacious and come back season after season. Next time you're out walking, stop and pick them for a tiny bouquet of miniature perfection—a reminder that the greatest gems in life are often found in the shadow of much more demanding plants.

september 11

I often think, when working over my plants, that Linnaeus once said of the unfolding blossom: "I saw God in His glory passing near me, and bowed my head to worship." No deeper thought was ever uttered by a poet. For in this world of plants, which with its magician chlorophyll, conjuring with sunbeams, is ceaselessly at work bringing life out of death.

—John Fiske, *A Century of Science and Other Essays*, 1899

Sixteenth-century botanist Carolus Linnaeus devised the binomial system of Latin genus and species that not just names plants but indicates their relationship to one another. Fiske quotes Linnaeus to show that the man was more than a scientist: he was deeply moved by the miracles of plants around him. Like George Washington Carver and Gregor Mendel, he made discoveries that transformed our view of the plant kingdom. Most important, all three came away awed by the perfection of creation. And they all came to the same conclusion: that a higher power is indeed behind it all.

Acts and Affirmations

As gardeners, we may expand our sense of the plant kingdom by integrating Latin names into our learning. Unlike common names, Linnaeus's Latin names reveal the nuances of relationships that are highly valuable in understanding the genetic origins of plants. Like Linnaeus, let us see God in each flower, knowing that it is just one individual in an enormous divine order.

september 12

. . . and have sent down out of the rain-clouds water cascading that We may bring forth thereby grain and plants, and gardens luxuriant.
—Qur'an, *The Tiding*, 78:15–16

The Koran is filled with images of gardens and paradise, because the regions where Islam was born are arid and barren. No one treasures the verdant beauty of the garden more than someone who lives in a parched land. The garden is truly a metaphor for spirituality, with the dry land representing humanity without God and lacking things of the spirit. Yet anywhere in that dry land an oasis may spring up, watered by the spirit, which will flower under the nourishing rain of God's love.

Acts and Affirmations

God—Help me to remember that my spiritual life is as important as a water-filled oasis in the desert. When I am overwhelmed by the desert, let me envision your love as an oasis in my mind that will refresh my soul on those very long and difficult days.

september 13

There is not a flower that opens, not a seed that falls into the ground, and not an ear of wheat that nods on the end of its stalk in the wind that does not preach and proclaim the greatness and mercy of God to the whole world.

—THOMAS MERTON, *The Seven Story Mountain*, 1948

We are entering an age of global consciousness that knows no distance or boundary. Today any organism from virus to elephant is just a twenty-four-hour airplane flight away, and the Internet makes communication around the world as simple as the click of a computer mouse. The geographic separations that previously prevented both travel and communication with remote parts of the world are vanishing, and we are now learning to consider issues that exist well beyond our nation's boundaries. Perhaps the advent of technology has caused Merton's vision of a single divine Earth to grow clearer by the day, prompting us to contemplate the meaning of our own presence within it.

ACTS AND AFFIRMATIONS

One by-product of a global community is the invasion of native ecosystems by more aggressive exotic plants. In North America, invasive species include Japanese honeysuckle in the Midwest or the yellow star thistle in the grasslands of the West. Become aware of problem plants in your region and help stem the tide by participating in eradication efforts or funding such efforts through native plant societies.

september 14

What the mystery of plant life which has so deeply affected the minds of men in all ages and of all civilizations meant to our ancestors, we can but dimly apprehend as we study these ceremonies. They carry us back to that worship of earth and the forces of Nature which prevailed when Woden was yet unborn.

—Eleanour Sinclair Rohde, *The Old English Herbals*, 1922

It is natural to view the earth and its processes as God-like, for they govern all aspects of life. This veneration of the earth is the foundation on which the contemporary religions are based. Islam had a concept of paradise, the Judeo-Christian Bible Eden; to Buddhists, nature is the consummate reality. To ignore these botanical roots is to lose the most colorful aspect of religion.

Acts and Affirmations

No matter what spiritual path or religion you follow, there is bound to be a tree somewhere in its origins and literature. Make a point to find out what it is, and make that species your own sacred tree. Develop the attitude that wherever you go, whenever you see that tree, you will let it bring your mind to its spiritual aspect.

creation trees

The creation myths of many world religions are tied in some way to a tree. In Eden, there was the Tree of Knowledge of Good and Evil. Nigerian spirituality recognizes the big tree of the village, into which the souls of the dead enter when they die. The northern European tree of life is an ash called Yaggsdril, the only deciduous tree to survive in the coldest climates. The Druids believed the oldest oaks were oracles containing the spirits of nature. Why does the tree appear more than any other single image? Because they are the largest living things, and perhaps more important, because they are crucial to survival. People relied on them for protection from the elements, for building materials for shelter, for fuel for warmth and cooking, and for food in the form of fruit and nuts. Today they continue enhancing the human environment by filtering pollution and adding oxygen to the atmosphere.

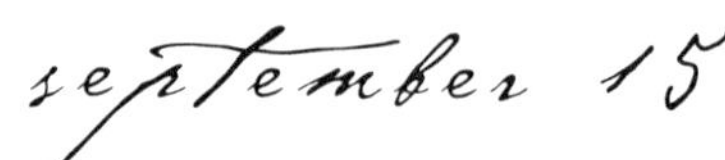

There is something most appealing about a private shrine or chapel, particularly when it is placed in the woods or fields, with the green world surrounding it, the wings of the birds caressing it and the sweet odor of the earth rising as incense to further add to the sense of enchantment. A kind of holiness is achieved there.

—Adelma Grenier Simmons, *Saints in My Garden*, 1932

The shrine is a very ancient idea reshaped in our modern world to enclose gods and other holy images of Catholics, Hindus, or Buddhists. But shrines need not be exclusive to one faith, for they are a vital form of personal expression that gives sanctity to anything vital to the spiritual path. To create a garden shrine and to tend it regularly provides the place for ritual recognition of the sacred seasons, holy days, celestially auspicious occasions, and personal remembrances. Most of all, we may discover a very special kind of holiness while creating it and later spending time there.

Acts and Affirmations

If you don't already have a garden shrine, use the coming winter to plan one. Choose a secluded place in the garden, one that you can see from indoors. Decide if it will have a theme and whether a special piece of art, such as a standing stone or perhaps a statue of St. Francis, will become the central element. Then provide it with a beautiful enclosure and a flat stone or table on which to place offerings and flowers. Remember that shrines are ever-changing and over time yours will evolve as you do.

september 16

It seems as if a child had not had his rightful share in this world when he has been limited to some pent up court or narrow street. Every child is born with a love for flowers. Yet many a little one must be satisfied with the dandelion that comes up in the backyard, which the eager fingers reach for as a miser would for gold.

—Amanda B. Harris, *Wild Flower Papers*, 1882

There is nothing more beautiful than a limp, crushed, and wilted bouquet of wildflowers grasped in a grimy little hand offered up to a mother or father. Children see flowers and run to pick them, only to discover that part of what makes flowers so precious is their short life. Children remind us that all flowers—whether bright or dull, large or small—are beautiful. Their young minds still retain that innocent eye for beauty that is uninfluenced by their culture's sense of style or monetary value. If we are to learn from them, the lesson would be to see all things just as they are, and thereby discover that all that is made by God is equally and uniquely beautiful.

Acts and Affirmations

God—Help me to pay more attention to the little things in life. Keep me from becoming blinded by big glorious flowers so that I will not overlook the tiny jewels scattered among them. Keep my heart as open as my eyes for other small things that make life spiritually rich and deeply fruitful.

september 17

FEAST OF ST. HILDEGARD VON BINGEN

Holy Spirit, Through you clouds billow, breezes blow, stones drip with trickling streams, streams that are the source of earth's lush greening. Likewise, you are the source of human understanding. You bless with the breath of wisdom. Thus all of our praise is yours, you who are the melody itself of praise, the joy of life, the mighty honor, the hope of those to whom you give the gifts of light. Amen

—*THE OXFORD BOOK OF PRAYER*, 1985

The Holy Spirit is the invisible aspect of God, and to many it is the manifestation of God's energy that enters human beings to aid and animate their spiritual lives. This energy is also called the Paraclete, a Greek word meaning "to invoke." Thus to pray to the Holy Spirit is to invoke the powers of God. Hildegard's prayer indeed invokes the Holy Spirit, honored as the power of nature, invited to enter the soul with all its gifts. Among these gifts are wisdom, knowledge, faith, healing, and miracles. This prayer uses nature as the environment in which the Holy Spirit is most powerful and asks that its powers increase our understanding and wisdom and enlighten us. The energy of the Holy Spirit as it breathes life into the natural world is universal, although expressed in as many different ways as there are faiths.

ACTS AND AFFIRMATIONS

Pray Hildegard's prayer of enlightenment every day. Remember that the Holy Spirit is the Paraclete, the comforter, the consoler. As the source of all understanding, the Holy Spirit is vital to all who seek spiritual enlightenment.

september 18

CHINESE HARVEST MOON FESTIVAL

The nature of water is to soak and descend; of fire, to blaze and ascend; of wood, to be crooked and to be straight; of metal, to obey and to change; while the virtue of earth is seen in seed-sowing and in gathering.
—LAO-TZU, Chinese philosopher, sixth century B.C.

The concept of yin and yang in Chinese philosophy describes the universal opposites, the two aspects of one nature. They can be manifest in light and dark, sweet and salt, or male and female. Yin is female—a cool, quiet, and moist aspect represented by the moon. Yang is male—hot and active and represented by the sun. Feng shui, the Chinese art of placement, seeks to balance these two influences to create harmony in the home. And part of this practice is to use "moon doorways" or arched gateways as protection against harmful energies that might enter the home and disturb the harmony.

ACTS AND AFFIRMATIONS

Strive to keep positive energy in your home and garden by avoiding designs that place gateways and doors to the house in a straight line. The key is to offset them, forcing the energy, or "chi," to work harder to get out. This underscores the natural order emphasized by feng shui principles—that nature rarely positions anything in a straight line. Design of home landscape should avoid this unnatural linear layout to retain harmony, both in the place and in the people who dwell there.

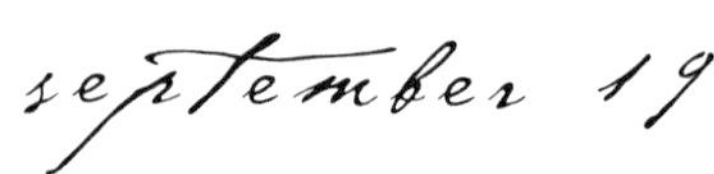

As you drop the seed, as you plant the sapling, your left hand hardly knows what your right hand is doing. But Nature knows, and in due time the Power that sees and works in secret will reward you openly.
—Oliver Wendell Holmes, *When We Plant a Tree*, 1886

So many people over the millennia have referred to the "Power"—the great force of Earth and universe that creates life. We use religions to capture the idea and define it in human terms, but it is such an awesome presence that amid the beauty and mystery of nature more concrete definitions seem inadequate. Twelve-step programs stress the recognition of a higher power in life, and the members are free to manifest it any way they wish. The important thing is simply to recognize that the power exists and that we can give ourselves over to it for the infinite rewards of an ever-deepening sense of peace.

Acts and Affirmations

Autumn planting is a discipline that many gardeners never get used to. But if you don't add to your tired flower beds now, you'll regret it come early spring, when the first hardy bulbs appear. This year make a point to plant the most outrageously colored tulips you can find—try striped and ruffled ones, too. Plant them in pots or beds, even around garden shrines and art pieces in your garden.

september 20

ROSH HASHANAH (VARIES)

God also said: "See, I give you every seed-bearing plant all over the earth and every tree that has seed-bearing fruit on it to be your food; and to all the animals of the land, all the birds of the air, and all the living creatures that crawl on the ground, I give all the green plants for food." And so it happened. God looked at everything he had made, and he found it very good.

—GENESIS 1:29–31

This very holy holiday is near the end of the annual cycle of Jewish agricultural festivals. New year's celebrations of every faith and culture are bittersweet, like youth and old age, for we must bid good-bye to what was, while looking forward to the birth of what will be. Introspection is a big part of Rosh Hashanah, when we explore our failings and strive to work harder to overcome them. These periods are vital to the spiritual life of all people because they demand we pause and take stock of our behavior. For Jews, this is a beautiful occasion when they celebrate the passing of the final season of the spiritual year.

ACTS AND AFFIRMATIONS

Create an arrangement of branches from a willow tree to evoke the Holy Land. To grow your own willow tree, take a cutting in late winter and put it into moist sand or right into the soil. Then take a bundle of dormant willow cuttings many feet long and put them in a faux-antique, narrow-mouth ceramic water jar to create a beautiful arrangement.

september 21

Autumnal Equinox
(varies)

The sun was like a great visiting presence that stimulated and took its due from all animal energy. When it flung wide its cloak and stepped down over the edge of the fields at evening, it left behind it a spent and exhausted world.

—Willa Cather, *One of Ours*, 1922

The autumnal equinox, midway point between the peak of summer brightness and the darkest day of winter is a subtle celestial event marking the close of the agricultural year. The sun's position in the southern sky orders the agricultural year, telling the primitive farmer by its shadow length when the corn is ripe and when the crops must be brought in before the weather sours. It also influences our own gardens, for the equinox marks the end of growth and the dying back of life to lie dormant in the earth for winter. The spent, exhausted world lies down to sleep as ordered by God, while the gardener rests and renews over the long, dark months to come.

Acts and Affirmations

If you already have a pole, a tall stone, or a column large enough to cast a shadow on the garden, mark the center of its position today. This marking indicates one of the four primary positions of the sun and will help you appreciate the solar journey. It also teaches you to better understand what influences plant exposures from season to season. Over time you will awaken to the nuances of the sun's position and begin subconsciously recognizing each season of the solar cycle.

september 22

FEAST OF ST. PHOCAS, THE GARDENER

Thorns and thistles shall it bring forth to you, as you eat of the plants of the field. By the sweat of your face shall you get bread to eat until you return to the ground from which you were taken; for you are dirt, and to dirt you shall return.

—GENESIS 3:18–19

The Cathedral of St. Mark in Venice bears a mosaic and statue of an old man with a long beard, clutching a spade. They depict Phocas of Sinope, who cultivated his garden outside the gate of the city on the Black Sea, sharing its abundance with travelers and the poor. An early Christian, he lived in fear of Roman persecution. One day, two soldiers came to his door to execute him. Before revealing his name, the old man fed them a meal of wine and vegetables. When they were through, he went outside and dug a grave for himself in the garden. After announcing his identity, he submitted to execution, knowing his soul would enter heaven and his body would remain earth-bound to fertilize the rich soil he so loved to tend.

ACTS AND AFFIRMATIONS

Let St. Phocas inspire us to be buried close to the earth. There are alternatives to unnatural separation from the soil in a heavy casket inside a concrete vault under the turf of a neatly manicured city cemetery. Choose instead a simple pine box in a country cemetery, where a tree may be planted upon the grave. Or perhaps we prefer to have our ashes strewn over a forest or meadow to fertilize it with all that remains of us on earth.

september 23

I have . . . a terrible need . . . shall I say the word? . . . of religion. Then I go out at night and paint the stars.
—Vincent van Gogh

What Impressionist painter Vincent van Gogh sought was his own sense of spirituality, which he celebrated through his art. We, too, may express our spirituality in our gardens and the plants that dwell within them. For no one who knows the deep truths of horticulture can help but feel a divine presence, a force that orders the never-ending cycle of the seasons, the microscopic soil flora, and the monumental trees. Whether our religious rites are best expressed by turning the earth, arranging beautiful flowers, or composing the essential palette of a living botanical painting, our creative endeavors touch the very soul of our being.

Acts and Affirmations

The Impressionists painted what they felt rather than striving for a photographlike depiction of their subjects. To van Gogh, painting was a truly emotional experience that he felt to the tips of his toes. Open yourself up to the same level of expression by painting a picture to capture a spiritual love of your garden. Use large sheets of heavy paper, watercolors, and a big fat brush. Free yourself of constraints and preconceived ideas by using great swaths of color that capture the essence of the colors in your garden. Let the paintings become your lasting connection to seasonal flowers, which are with us only a few glorious weeks of the year.

september 24

Nature always wears the colors of the spirit.
—Ralph Waldo Emerson, *Nature*, 1836

As the nights cool, trees stop producing chlorophyll and the leaves gradually die out in a blaze of autumn glory. They are nature in her garments of change, ranging through every color of the sunset. Each color speaks to us in a spiritual language. The golden leaves are the spirit of divine energy and light. Red is the spiritual color of passion, blood, and fire. Brown is spirit of earth, home, and humility. Orange is strength, healing, and adaptability. What message does your spirit hear when nature parades through this glorious season?

Acts and Affirmations
Preserve autumn leaves in the pages of last year's telephone book. Choose small leaves that will fit easily into cards and letters. They hold up far better than pressed flowers over time, and their colors will suggest energy, passion, earth, and healing in your correspondence.

september 25

I like to think of God in the music of the winds among the trees, in the delicate blossoms of the sweet wild rose, and in all other creations of His hands; this is the only explanation I can give as to how I became a lover of nature.

—NINETEENTH-CENTURY ENGLISH LABORER

Nature touches us in a most intangible way. We love to dwell among its flowers or wander in the woods as it quiets the continual voice of the mind and brings us nearer to God. Often these places are far more holy than churches, their quiet filled with rustling leaves, the hum of the bees, and the twittering of birds overhead. These are the sounds and feelings we experience when we work in our gardens. God is manifest in the music of the wind and the purity of a petal and in every other created thing on earth.

ACTS AND AFFIRMATIONS

God—Let me find you in the sunshine, in the cool summer breeze, in the petals of every flower. I will never forget that they are all living reminders of your infinite creative powers.

september 26

Native American Festival of Green Corn

She also strewed sacred corn meal all around her until the front-door steps and the sidewalk are much daubed with dough. This is not the corn meal in common use in the United States, but is sacred meal ground in Zuni with sacred stones.

—John Simpson, *Expedition to Navajo Country*, 1849

Ceremonial corn is treated very differently by the Zuni than staple corn. It must bear the colors of the cardinal points: yellow for north, blue for west, red for south, and white for east. Only perfect ears can be chosen, and often the costumed traditional dancers hide one of them in their waistband. These are the essence of the ceremonial corn, ground not by women for food but by men in sacred places such as the kiva, where the cornmeal is imbued with all of its mystical powers. The Zuni used this holy cornmeal to anoint themselves and their homes and to offer healing powers to the sick.

Acts and Affirmations

In Zuni tradition, it is the custom to offer a packet of ceremonial cornmeal when visiting a distant friend or the home of someone who is ill. To create your own packet, choose kernels of Indian corn in the four colors described above. Grind them with a clean electric coffee bean grinder, or grind them the old-fashioned way with stones. Take the colorful meal and fold it up into a neat little two-inch packet wrapped in a fresh or dry corn husk. Tie it with brightly colored yarn or raffia in red or turquoise, and offer it as a beautiful gift.

september 27

In the woods we return to reason and faith. There I feel that nothing can befall me in life,—no disgrace, no calamity which nature cannot repair.

—Ralph Waldo Emerson, *Nature*, 1836

Ralph Waldo Emerson suffered from fear of unknown calamities or social disgrace, but he found that these feelings waned in the woods. Compulsive fear is an irrational emotion that can destroy our faith, shatter our self-confidence, and turn everyday events into emotional nightmares. But, like Emerson, many people find that their fears can be brought into realistic perspective amid nature and the garden. The more time we spend among plants, the greater our faith, and what fears and difficulties once existed in our minds, nature repairs far better than countless visits to the psychologist.

Acts and Affirmations

The next time I begin to feel fear or anxiety building, I will remember to go walk in a large park or take a ride in the countryside to walk in wild places. Nothing in this world is more important than my spiritual well-being, and I will cancel all my obligations and take a break from home and work until I find inner peace again. I will let go of all worries, so that faith may rush in and renew my body and soul.

september 28

If you would be happy for a week take a wife; if you would be happy for a month kill a pig; but if you would be happy all your life, plant a garden.
—Chinese proverb

For many people, an interest in gardening gears up in midlife. Around the age of forty, many people slow down to enjoy the subtle rewards of this age-old pastime. Planting a garden is the start of a very long, gradual process that requires patience and perseverance. It is a lifelong learning experience. We enjoy the subtle changes of each new year, which is so unlike other creations—architecture, art, or crafts, for instance—that once made never change. But the garden is forever evolving, and over time it becomes more intensely rewarding. It is this reward that brings us a deep sense of happiness so crucial to the balance of influences from mind, body, and spirit.

Acts and Affirmations

In China, the combination of bamboo and flowering plum trees in the garden signifies the harmony between partners. If you are married or in a committed relationship, devote a tiny place in your garden for plum and bamboo to grow side by side. Put petrified wood in the composition to symbolize the everlasting nature of this relationship.

september 29

Michaelmas: Feast of St. Michael the Archangel

The Michaelmas Daisies, among dead weeds, blooms for St. Michael's valorous deeds
And seems the last of flowers that stood, till the feast of St. Simon and St. Jude.

—old English garden rhyme

This beautiful little rhyme refers to the ritual mass dedicated to St. Michael the Archangel on this, his feast day. The aster is blooming now when all else in the garden is fading, and it has been dedicated to the angel as the Michaelmas daisy. St. Michael is deeply integrated into British culture because it is believed he appeared on a mountain, now called St. Michael's Mount in Cornwall. Such a place of apparition connects him with the earth, particularly high places. He is famous for battling the devil and remains a central figure in the rite of exorcism. We love angels because they are beautiful and because these transcendent heavenly beings are well integrated into our culture. And when the angel is powerful, like Michael, there is an additional benefit—protection from evil.

Acts and Affirmations

If there is no angel to guard your garden, shop for a beautiful winged cherub that you find personally appealing. Place it carefully amid the plants and flowers, where it will remind you that these heavenly spirits do exist as our invisible guardians.

september 30

The green book of Nature is one of God's witnesses to Himself no less than the book of the Scriptures,—in both, deep calls to deep; the strange and inscrutable pleasure that those gifted with the power of keen perception feel in the presence of natural beauty.

—Alfred E. P. Dowling, *The Flora of the Sacred Nativity*, 1900

The Bible speaks of God in a written language, but the green book of Nature speaks of God perhaps even more clearly. For there among the plants is order and beauty, life and death, and a thousand occurrences that teach us the very same lessons of scripture. The ability to perceive these lessons can be cultivated by anyone with the time and desire to discern the signs of God in nature. And this is learned through weeks and years in the garden, studying many things—the earth, plants, sun, weather, and water—and thereby ultimately gaining greater wisdom with the passing of each growing season.

Acts and Affirmations

Next time you encounter a garden that touches you deeply, spend a few moments contemplating whether it is the color, the arrangement of space, the prevalence of green, or some other quality that makes it compelling. Such analysis reveals not just our taste and preferences but perceptional biases we never realized we had before.

autumn

THE TIME TO HARVEST

The shadows grow long again, and light in the garden is mellow. As a result of the cooler nights and shorter days, plants slow their growth and leaves change from green to the fiery hues of fall. The garden becomes a skeleton of summer, and in this season all signs point to the coming of the eventual death of winter. As the plants fade, so does the spirit of the vegetation, to make this also a time of remembrance of the dead and ancestors. It is the time of firing the fields to burn off the lingering stubble and to drive out overwintering pests. Such fires surround the postharvest period, when people give thanks to the gods who divide years of plenty from those of famine.

october

The Germanic nations called the full moon of the tenth month *Winter-fyllith.* It meant "the full moon that begins the winter season." It is the time of decay, when all that remains of the summer growing season is cut back by the cold and smothered by snow. The month concludes with the great sabbat of Samhain, when the spirit of the vegetation dies for winter. Many believe that during this sabbat, the veil separating the world from the afterlife is temporarily drawn back and the spirits of the dead walk the earth.

This recognition of death has become a universal day when many cultures remember departed loved ones. The Christian feast of All Saints' Day (the old name was All Hallows') falls on November 1, and the mass celebrated the night before is All Hallows' Eve, or Halloween. The flower of this month is the European pot marigold, *Calendula*, which means "little first day of the month." It was so named because it blooms nearly the whole year through.

ALGONQUIN MOON OF WHITE FROST ON GRASS

october 1

FEAST OF ST. TERESA, THE LITTLE FLOWER

To strew flowers is the only means of proving my love, and these flowers will be each word and look, each daily sacrifice.
—ST. TERESA OF LISIEUX

St. Teresa was born in 1873 in a small French town. At fifteen she entered the Carmelite convent, where conditions were simple, austere, and devoutly pious. There she deemed her life was the "little way," the sanctifying of every act by committing it with spiritual devotion. Before she died at twenty-four, she promised that "After my death, I will let fall a shower of roses. I will spend my heaven doing good on earth." After her death the rain of roses began, not as flowers, but as a series of miracles that led to her canonization in 1925. St. Teresa became the patron saint of florists and roses.

ACTS AND AFFIRMATIONS

Be inspired by the little way of St. Teresa and make small sacrifices of time, money, and skills to help those in need. Give something you cherish to someone who has admired it. Offer a few hours of precious time to someone lonely. Plant a few flowers in the garden of someone who has none. Spread the little way and it will multiply, just as the young nun's followers have now reached around the world.

october 2

O Circle of Stars, whereof our Father is the youngest brother, marvel beyond imagination, soul of infinite space, before whom Time is ashamed, the mind bewildered, and the understanding dark, not unto Thee may we attain, unless Thine image be Love. Therefore by seed and root and stem and bud and leaf and flower and fruit do we invoke thee.

—Aleister Crowley, *Magick in Theory and Practice*, 1960

This old incantation illustrates just how sacred herbs were to the practice of healing, which was intertwined with other forms of magic. It was believed that a plant should be picked at the correct phase of the moon and handled in a specific way that ensured its potency. We have lost our magical connection to healing, but we do know that the mind and soul play an important part in whether a person survives serious illness. Perhaps the medicinal use of herbs, together with modern medicine, will increasingly help fight disease on a plane that transcends the mere physical and incorporates the mind and spirit.

Acts and Affirmations

The Earth contributes its all to sustaining our species, but did you ever think of returning the favor? Consciously perform gifts to the environment. Each time you add compost to the soil it receives a boost of microorganism activity. Every new seed you plant increases the mass of vegetation that protects the Earth's surface. Cutting down on invasive exotic weeds, such as kudzu, allows more beneficial plants to grow and relieves the earth of its burden. The key to making these actions meaningful is to be conscious of them as gifts of thanks to Mother Earth.

october 3

Close your eyes. You might try saying . . . something like this: "The sun is shining overhead. The sky is blue and sparkling. Nature is calm and in control of the world—and I, as nature's child, am in tune with the Universe." Or—better still—pray!

—DALE CARNEGIE, *How to Stop Worrying and Start Living,* 1944

When Dale Carnegie wrote this book in 1944, World War II was ending. A traumatic period in history, many of people's relatives had died, and they understood deeply what it was like to live each day with uncertainty. In comparison, some of today's worries seem far less threatening, but we worry nevertheless about what the future brings. If we visualize ourselves as children who belong in nature, we find that quiet peace in the garden and prayer is as applicable today as it was fifty years ago, and probably five hundred years ago as well. The beauty and calm of the plant-filled landscape is our God-given remedy for uncertainty and fear. Although it will not solve all of our problems, it is a place where we may at least find the comfort needed to better cope with them.

ACTS AND AFFIRMATIONS

God: I am a child of your universe, a part of the divine plan. Let me greet each day like a peaceful celestial journey toward self-discovery through my garden. Make every morning a promise so that I might look forward to each new day and a fresh secret revealed.

october 4

Feast of St. Francis of Assisi

Sister lark has a hood like a religious and is a humble bird who gladly goes in search of any little grain, and even if she finds something in the garbage, she picks it out and eats it. In flight she sweetly praises God like good religious who, detached from worldly things, turn ever toward heaven and who long only to praise God. The lark's garb, her plumage, is the color of the earth. Thus she offers religious an example of how not to wear elegant, flashy clothes, but moderately priced things, of the color of earth, the humblest of elements.

—St. Francis, *Mirror of Perfection*, 1317 A.D.

St. Francis believed that because God made all living things, they are reflections of their divine creator. Francis was the first to bring live animals indoors to re-create the nativity, and he was said to step around earthworms lying in his path rather than destroy one of God's creatures. Francis shows us that material things mean little, and that the way to spiritual fruitfulness is through humility integrated into every aspect of life. There is no better place to imitate his spirituality than in the garden, digging in the earth.

Acts and Affirmations

St. Francis has become an icon in gardens all over the world, whether or not their owners are Christian. Such is the pervasive influence of this humble man on our collective spirituality. If you don't already have a small statue of this saint in your garden, choose a humble earthy clay sculpture that is more in keeping with the character of gardens than stark white concrete. Better yet, place it in the center of the birdbath, where little brown birds will appear to remind you of this little brown-robed patron saint of ecology.

october 5

NUBAIGAI: LITHUANIAN FESTIVAL OF THE CORN GODDESS

The early Teutonic peoples had so profound a sense of the sacredness of the very soil that we get our word earth *from their goddess Hertha, whom they identified with it.*

—LIBERTY HYDE BAILEY, *The Holy Earth,* 1915

In Europe grains were vital to survival and vulnerable to the fickle whims of autumn weather. It was thought essential that the fields be protected by a higher power—a belief that gave birth to cultural celebrations integrated with the seasons and cycles of the agricultural year. The grain from seed to harvest was likened to women in three forms: maiden, mother, and crone. The corn goddess feast is that of the old woman, or crone. The last sheaf of grain was dedicated to her and was carefully protected over the winter. It would provide the first seed to be sown in spring, when it was reborn again as the maiden.

ACTS AND AFFIRMATIONS

The last sheaf of grain was woven into a female doll and hung in the rafters to protect the stored harvest. This ritual gave rise to the art of making corn-husk dolls or weaving long-stemmed dry wheat into beautiful artistic creations. Corn husks can be found in the Mexican foods section of your supermarket. The key is to presoak the husks to make them pliable, then fashion them into the desired shape and tie them securely and dry stiff. Celebrate the Lithuanian way by creating your own doll to add a hint of the corn goddess to holiday decorations.

The Lord hath created medicines out of the earth: and he that is wise will not abhor them. Was not the water made sweet with wood, that the virtue thereof might be known?
—Ecclesiastes 38:4–5

This passage is the source of the Doctrine of Signatures, which herbalists took literally to mean that each plant bears a visible clue to its ability to cure disease. This theory has long been disproved, but the passage illustrates how God has filled the earth with many powerful healing plants—from the poppy's white sap, which dulls pain, to the chinchona tree bark, for malarial fevers; and the miraculous fungus plant penicillin, so vital to curing infection. He who is wise will always respect our healing herbs as gifts from the Lord.

Acts and Affirmations

Make an infusion of your favorite healing herb. Harvest fresh leaves and mince them into tiny pieces. Place them in a glass container of distilled spring water, shake well, and allow to steep for two days. The plant material will settle out and the remaining liquid will be infused with the essence of the plant.

october 7

Our Lady of the Rosary

Poor men and women who are sinners, I a greater sinner than you, wish to give you this rose—a crimson one, because the Precious Blood of Our Lord has fallen upon it. Please God that it will bring true fragrance into your lives.

—St. Louis de Montfort, *The Secret of the Rosary*, 1954

In 1206 St. Dominic Guzman decided it was better to teach illiterate peasants just one or two prayers to repeat over and over rather than the litanies of many prayers used at the time. Prayers were originally counted by passing small stones from one hand to the other. Then the first rosaries were used, providing a more convenient way to count prayers. Rosary meant "crown of roses," and to say the rosary daily was to tend one's spiritual rose garden and keep it beautiful. The rosary today remains the most beautiful of all Catholic devotions and forever connects the Virgin Mary, Queen of Heaven, to the rose, the queen of flowers.

Acts and Affirmations

The oldest style of rosary still available today is that with beads made of compressed rose petals. They release their fragrance when warmed by human hands. Created by Carmelite nuns in cloistered convents of Spain, they are sold today in Catholic stores. Rose-petal rosaries are both holy relics for prayer and highly fragrant jewelry, which celebrates the natural beauty of this tradition and the Virgin's sacred flowers.

october 8

Make body the field, the mind the ploughman, honest labor the irrigating water. Sow the seed of the Lord's Name, let contentment be the leveler, and humility the fence. With deeds of love the seed will fertilize.
—Guru Nanak, *The Adi Granth*, fifteenth century

Our spiritual life is like a garden, with branches, roots, and vines that penetrate every aspect of our existence. Though there may be much vegetative growth, we are content only when it flowers and bears fruit. We cannot see the blossoms until we become mindful of others. So many messages today urge us to focus exclusively on self, which destroys community and strangles love. To ensure that our garden flowers and bears fruit, we must strive for the humility to serve others and God, and remember that love is the greatest force behind an abundant harvest in both the garden and life.

Acts and Affirmations

I vow to never again be satisfied with vegetative aspects of my life. I will use love to fertilize my life to make it flower and bear fruit. Love for family, neighbors, co-workers, and everyone I meet will soon cause me to flourish in every way, and the harvest of contentment is soon to follow.

In the knowledge of simples, wherein the manifold wisdom of God is wonderfully to be seen, one thing would carefully be observed; which is to know what herbs may be used instead of drugs of the same nature and to make the garden the shop.

—George Herbert, *Country Parson*, seventeenth century

A simple is a plant supposed to have one single or simple virtue that is peculiar to it alone. But simples were much earlier connected to a single god or goddess with powers, not just of healing, but of protection against elves, dragons, and a variety of other mythical demons. The "lucky" four-leaf clover inserted inside the shoe is a vestige of these ancient beliefs. Plants were often used as amulets, such as a clover wrapped in red cloth and worn next to the body, where the power of the Saxon god Thor protected against creatures of darkness. Such practices of old Europe are remarkably similar to the phylacteries of Judaism, relic medals of early Christianity, and the medicine bag of Native Americans.

Acts and Affirmations

Red clover tea heals a sore throat, but its lesser-known and more powerful ability is to heal poor soils. It is an important cover crop, sown into fallow ground in fall, where it helps to add nitrogen through its roots. When tilled in by late spring, or if left a year and tilled the following season, the soil gains twice the benefit. Clover plants contain an extra dose of residual nitrogen plus organic matter, which can naturally heal soils that are poor from the start or simply exhausted.

A child said, What is the grass? Fetching it to me with full hands;
How could I answer the child? I do not know what it is any more than he.
I guess it must be the flag of my disposition, out of hopeful green stuff woven. Or I guess it is the handkerchief of the Lord.

—Walt Whitman, *Leaves of Grass*, 1882

That simple question, What is grass? may haunt us eternally, for it is impossible to define this most ubiquitous plant. It is a family that illustrates the great range of God's adaptive power through a diversity of annual and perennial species, from tree-size timber bamboo to brilliant blood grass and dense prairie sod.

Acts and Affirmations

During the golden month of October, collect bundles of dry wild grasses. Create your own ritual to end the harvest by binding them up with string and tying them into little human shapes. It was once traditional to throw such dolls into the hearth fire in the spirit of the autumnal bonfires. This ancient rite has been rekindled by modern-day pagans with the enormous Burning Man celebration in the Nevada desert, which draws people from throughout the American West.

october 11

Algonquin Cranberry Festival

The Great Spirit is in all things, he is in the air we breathe. The Great Spirit is our Father but the Earth is our Mother. She nourishes us, that which we put into the ground she returns to us.
—Big Thunder (Bedagi), Wabanaki Algonquin

Native American tribes that were hunter-gatherers viewed their wild food plants as a gift and conscientiously protected them for assurance of future harvest. Tribes that practiced agriculture viewed their manipulation of plants as an interactive sacrament overseen by a Great Spirit. They saw the spiritual in every aspect of the planting, tending, and harvest. Their efforts were viewed as an investment, and its return would be not just the product of labor but a fulfilled promise from Mother Earth.

Acts and Affirmations

Make your holiday traditions this season one of Native American plant foods, which celebrate the role of both aboriginal agriculture and the hunter-gatherer tradition. Combine fresh cranberries with raw sunflower seeds and stone-ground cornmeal to produce breads and muffins that contain the flavor and texture of the traditional foods of the land. These are the true American cuisine, uninfluenced by Europeans and sanctified by both the Great Spirit and Mother Earth.

october 12

COLUMBUS DAY

To the entire world I give my light and my radiance, I give men warmth when they are cold; I cause their fields to fructify and their cattle to multiply; each day that passes I go around the world to secure a better knowledge of men's needs and to satisfy those needs.

—INCA MYTH, *Royal Commentaries*, sixteenth century

The people of Latin America were the first in the New World to see the Europeans who were to change the face of their culture forever. Under the European influence, the great religions of the Incans, Mayans, and Aztecs faded into obscurity but lived on in the countryside under the cloak of Catholicism. Their spirituality was integrated into seasons of growing corn and potatoes, two plants that substantially improved the diet of Europeans. The tragedy is that the peoples of the New World did not gain much from their relationship with the Old, but the agriculture of the Old World was wholly transformed by crops of the Americas.

ACTS AND AFFIRMATIONS

Celebrate this holiday with a meal of purple potatoes, now available in the produce departments of gourmet markets. Bake them, then cut them and sauté in olive oil with parsley and garlic. This colorful dish provides a taste of pre-Columbian Peru in the heyday of Incan civilization.

october 13

Physicians might, I believe, make greater use of scents than they do, for I have often noticed that they cause changes in me, and act on my spirits according to their qualities; which make me agree with the theory that the introduction of incense and perfume into churches so ancient and widespread a practice among all nations and religions, was for the purpose of raising our spirits, and of exciting and purifying our senses, the better to fit us for contemplation.

—Michel de Montaigne, *Essays*, sixteenth century

We are touched by fragrances, which are like messengers to our souls. Each fragrance acts on our emotions in a different way. This idea has been part of Indian Vedic healing, which uses essential oils of plants to balance the chakras, or nerve centers that send messages to the brain. There are twelve sacred plant fragrances in essential oil form considered the most useful in chakral therapy: basil, eucalyptus, geranium, lavender, lemongrass, Mexican marigold, pennyroyal, peppermint, rose, rosemary, sage, and thyme.

Acts and Affirmations

If you suffer from winter depression, essential oil of geranium is one of the best aromatherapies for depression and anxiety. Add two drops of oil to one-quarter cup of water and mix well. Pour into a small, clean spray bottle and use to spritz the face (eyes closed) or apply to neck and temples like perfume. Use daily until depression has lifted.

Why should there be so many different faiths? The Soul is one, but the bodies which she animates are many. We cannot reduce the number of bodies, yet we recognize the unity of the Soul. Even as a tree has a single trunk, but many branches and leaves, so is there one true and perfect Religion, but it becomes many as it passes through the human medium.

—Mohandas K. Gandhi, *Yervada Mandir: Ashram Observances*, 1933

Perhaps the reason that trees are such a universal element in creation myths is that their architecture represents the unity of the human race and how it splits into races, cultures, tribes, nations, and religions. It is very much like a great family tree branching out from a single common ancestor. The tree shows us that it is not the branches that represent the whole of humanity; it is the trunk from which they all spring that is the collective spiritual consciousness.

Acts and Affirmations

Let me always remember that all spiritual paths originate with the knowledge that there is a single divine source of all things. Just as there are many kinds of people in the world, there must be as many kinds of faith. Rather than faith dividing humankind, let us focus not on the branches but on that single trunk, and know that we are part of the spreading, leafy canopy that shelters the whole world.

october 15

Roman Harvest
Festival of Mars

To me nothing else about a tree is so remarkable as the extreme delicacy of the mechanism by which it grows and lives, the fine hairlike rootlets at the bottom and the microscopical cells of the leaves at the top. The rootlets absorb the water charged with mineral salts from the soil and the leaves absorb the sunbeams from the air. So it looks as if the tree were almost made of matter and spirit, like man; the ether with its vibrations, on the one hand, and the earth with its inorganic compounds, on the other—earth salts and sunlight.
—John Burroughs, *The Falling Leaves*, 1921

It is amazing that the largest living thing in the ocean, the whale, is dependent on the smallest living things for its survival. Whales use special structures called baleen to sift microscopic plankton from the water. Trees share this quality because their smallest parts are the most vital to their survival. Root hairs, hardly visible to the naked eye, interact with soil to take up moisture, not the thick main roots, which are merely conduits. The paper-thin cambium just under the bark transports all its vital nutrients. With tiny cells of the leaf it manufactures food from sunlight. These examples illustrate that things are not always as they seem and, if we make an effort to look more closely, there are often wonderful secrets to be discovered.

Acts and Affirmations

Ash tree wood is said to drive away snakes. It was believed among ancient Germanic tribes that if a snake had a choice of slithering through fire or ash branches, it would choose the fire. This makes ash the perfect tree for a walking staff. Cut a straight limb and allow it to dry for several months in a flat, dry place free of moisture. It will become hard as a spear shaft, and whenever you hike with it, the snakes will flee as you and your ash approach.

october 16

> *The* Yeyecameh *[winds] are like little dolls, dressed in gaudy colors. They frolic and play at the edge of streams and in deep rocky gorges. When a person goes to their favorite places it is thought wise to offer them a little food, a few drops of liquor or leave a cigarette lying on a stone or on the ground.*
>
> —Fernando Horcasitas, *The Azetcs Then and Now*, 1979

The Aztecs believed there were many gods representing various aspects of the natural world. The gods required sacrifices from people in exchange for their benevolence. This generated a broad range of rituals from human sacrifice to decorating temples and homes with flowers. We often sacrifice plants for the benefit of the garden. When we encounter volunteers, such as chamomile or tomatoes, we must pluck them out so that our desired plants will not have to compete with them for water and nutrients. This is a gardener's reluctant sacrifice, for it is not easy to do away with such willing plants that in another place and time would be the seedlings of choice.

Acts and Affirmations

As winds of autumn begin to blow through the gaudy leaves, notice that the leaves turn their most brilliant hue just before they fall to the ground. This last flash of beauty is a lesson in the wisdom of advanced age. Though old, we may burn brightly at the end to shed the last of our accumulated spiritual wisdom on those around us. Each soul exists for a purpose, and until that final day we have something to offer—be it comfort, or a listening ear, or to share with children the final shining moments in the short life of the leaf.

october 17

Frost performs its secret ministry, unhelped by any wind.
—Samuel Taylor Coleridge, *Lyrical Ballads*, 1789

As nights grow cool, frost is busy at work transforming the garden. Its "secret ministry" is to touch plants with icy fingers, then shrivel tender flowers and foliage. It causes the sap to fall into the roots from branch down through trunk. There the life of the tree waits, protected deep below the frozen ground. The white hoarfrost takes the lives of the hardiest insects and sends the field mice deep into burrow nests. Frost tells all living things that winter has come and to prepare for the frozen dark months when life rests to renew itself for the work of spring.

Acts and Affirmations

Frost is like a fingerprint of God. The thin, white sheets of frost tell you where the coldest places in your garden are. This visual language must be interpreted by gardeners because it indicates where spring seedlings are likely to be struck if planted too early. Use these frosty mornings to study the patterns of frost, and they will guide you in many ways to create a successful garden in years to come.

october 18

St. Luke's Little Summer

The leafless trees become spires of flame in the sunset, with the blue east for their background, and the stars of the dead calices of flowers, and every withered stem and stubble rimmed with frost, contribute something to the mute music.

—Ralph Waldo Emerson, *Nature*, 1836

The four days around the time of the feast of St. Luke were known in Britain as a brief spell of clear, warm weather before the storm winds of autumn began to rage. It was the date to plant the winter crops, such as cabbage greens and wheat. During this little summer, we encounter many spiritual messages. For while we stare into the face of a ruthless winter, our planting becomes a small act of faith in the promise of spring.

Acts and Affirmations

Celebrate St. Luke's little summer this weekend by planting edible winter greens like leafy kale. The ornamental varieties of winter greens are also edible but not as tasty. Plant them in a terra-cotta French herb trough left on the porch or patio. When the vegetables flesh out, cut an entire head to use as a holiday centerpiece surrounded by fresh vegetables and dip.

october 19

> *You ask me to plow the ground. Shall I take a knife and tear my mother's bosom? Then when I die she will not take me to her bosom to rest. You ask me to dig for stones! Shall I dig under her skin for bones? Then when I die I cannot enter her body to be born again.*
>
> —WOVOKA, Paiute tribe

Not all Native Americans practiced agriculture. Many tribal peoples of California and the Paiute of Nevada were hunter-gatherer cultures. Their nomadic way of life allowed them to travel to places when the plants there were ripe and ready to harvest. These people understood native plants like no others, watching changes in leaf color or the length of days for indications that it was time to harvest seeds, berries, and roots. They shared the holiest of connections to nature and found it difficult, if not sacrilegious, to be forced into an agricultural way of life.

ACTS AND AFFIRMATIONS

As Native American people modernize, they lose the old ways. This vital storehouse of knowledge is dwindling. Some of the people who are rescuing it are those of other races and cultures who realize its infinite value. Become a preserver of Indian medicine and food plants by attending lectures and demonstrations that teach identification, gathering, and preparation. Someday these skills will be passed down to your children and grandchildren, so they, too, may become inheritors of these vanishing life ways.

october 20

God writes the Gospel not in the Bible alone, but on trees, and flowers, and clouds, and stars.

—Martin Luther, sixteenth century

Perhaps the most limiting approach to Christianity is to become myopic in terms of scripture. As Martin Luther, the leader of the Reformation, points out, there is so much around us that expresses the same ideas found in scripture in intricate and beautiful ways. The words of salvation are seen in the aspects of nature. We need not be told that God is all-powerful when we explore the genius of his natural creations. We need not read that God loves us when he surrounds us with a natural kingdom as vast and inspiring as that of the plants. We need not study printed words when the glory of heaven is miraculously evidenced in the unique and beautiful signs of every season.

Acts and Affirmations

God: Help me to look beyond passage and verse to find the spiritual lessons that surround me in nature. You gave me a brain to find the logic in your world and a heart to understand it on an emotional level. Allow my brain and heart to work together to find the ideal combination that inevitably results in spiritual wisdom.

october 21

A woodland walk, a quest for river-grapes, a mocking thrush, a wild rose or rock-living columbine, salve my worst wounds.

—Ralph Waldo Emerson, *Nature*, 1836

To live is to feel pain. Everyone, no matter how confident or powerful, has experienced pain and suffering. It is part of the human condition. Emerson salved his wounds with walks among wild rose and columbine. We, too, have salves at our fingertips. They await planting in the fertile soil of the backyard or are displayed on nursery shelves waiting for us to adopt them. There is no better, more private, or more nurturing place than the home garden, filled with trees and flowers, to soothe our every ache.

Acts and Affirmations

If it's inconvenient to take a walk in the countryside next time you feel the sharp barbs of life, try working in the garden instead. Nothing is more healing than working away the tears. It is as if you drain your sorrows into the newly turned earth. There you have time to pause and regain your composure, then find the courage to continue.

october 22

No effort to create an impossible or purely ideal landscape is made in the Japanese garden. Its artistic purpose is to copy faithfully the attractions of a veritable landscape, and to convey the real impression that a real landscape communicates. It is therefore at once a picture and a poem; perhaps even more a poem than a picture. For as nature's scenery, in its varying aspects, affects us with sensations of joy or of solemnity, of grimness or of sweetness, of force or of peace, so must the true reflection of it in the labor of the landscape gardener create not merely an impression of beauty, but a mood in the soul.

—Lafcadio Hearn, *Glimpses of Unfamiliar Japan*, 1894

The landscape, both natural and man-made, speaks to us in a language of form, color, and light. We find this beautifully expressed in Japan, where the language of the garden is very different from that of the West. Few Japanese gardens contain flowers except for those borne on shrubs and water plants. The garden's silent messages are wrought in sculptural forms of carefully trained trees and shrubs, many of them needled evergreens in the bonsai style. The landscape also whispers through the movement of water over stone and images reflected in its glassy surface. This is a carefully composed garden of stone, water, and plants that speaks to the discerning eye in a visual poem. Through our subconscious we absorb the intangible feeling that is fed though the mind into the soul.

Acts and Affirmations

Small Japanese stone lanterns light the pathways of Japanese gardens for those coming to share in the tea ceremony. To create a Japanese meditation corner in the garden, choose a special stone, concrete, or cast-iron lantern to illuminate a focal point nestled amid the plants. Provide a place for a thick carpet or comfortable meditation chair. Go there often, at all hours of the day and night.

october 23

Each work of art excludes the world, concentrates attention on itself. For the time it is the only thing worth doing—to do just that; be it a sonnet, a statue, a landscape, an outline head of Caesar, or an oration. Presently we return to the sight of another that globes itself into a whole as did the first, for example, a beautiful garden; and nothing seems worth doing in life but laying out a garden.
—Ralph Waldo Emerson, journal, 1839

We tend to constrain our idea of beautiful gardens by classifying them in a style that already exists. English flower, French formal, and Southwestern Santa Fe are all garden styles we aspire to re-create. To live the artistic gardener's way is to surrender to your emotional reaction to plants so that you are not constrained by preconceived ideas of what is right and wrong. If you are daring and willing to take risks, explore offbeat ideas that will make your garden really speak to you. Instead of sowing your vegetable plants in a straight row, make them undulate in fluid parallel lines that turn your veggie garden into a work of modern art. Choose multicolored scraps of granite countertops rather than stodgy red bricks to create a postmodern pathway. Consider strangely colored plants like purple smoke tree and black bearded iris as futuristic sculpture. Take risks and you may discover you've transcended the mundane and created something truly monumental in the garden.

Acts and Affirmations

Tribal people around the world mark their territorial limits with totems or other objects. To take full possession of your land or rented yard, establish its limits or corners with brightly painted stones or stakes. As you place them, consider it an age-old act that claims, in the sight of God and man, that this tiny patch of earth is for now all yours.

october 24

Sunlight made visible the whole length of a sky, movement of wind, leaf, flower, all six colours on tree, bush and creeper: all this is the day's worship.

—MAHADEVI, *Speaking of Siva*, twelfth century

Have you noticed there are days when colors in your garden are richer and seem to leap out at you? This is rarely a moment when the sun beats down boldly from above. It is usually one that is overcast or is just before a fog burns off when there is strong light but not enough to cast shadows. This is the nature of diffused light that allows the color of each leaf and flower to saturate your vision with an incredibly intense hue. A photograph will capture this scene with perfect exposure. In contrast, direct sun on leaves, particularly glossy ones, causes light to reflect off the surface and blind you or your camera to the color. Each plant and leaf casts a bold shadow that will appear in high contrast to the reflections on leaves. To distinguish the difference between the appearance of the garden under diffused light versus bold direct sun will open your mind to the awareness of light and shadow as seen by nature photographers.

ACTS AND AFFIRMATIONS

Become more conscious of light in your garden through experiments in photography. Keep an eye out for that golden moment when the sun is perfectly diffused and your garden glows. Shoot a roll of film under these conditions, and then shoot a comparative one on a bright, sunny day and compare the two. It will be clear how different they are, and you will never photograph outdoors again without considering the nature of the sunlight.

october 25

Chinese Festival of the Harvest Goddess Han Lu

The best quality tea must have creases like the leathern boot of Tartar horsemen, curl like the dewlap of a mighty bullock, unfold like a mist rising out of a ravine, gleam like a lake touched by a zephyr, and be wet and soft like a fine earth newly swept by rain.
—Lu Yu, *Cha Ching*, ninth century

Ceremonial drinks, often containing alcohol or other potent drugs made from plants, are part of religious rites all over the world. Though we consider alcoholic beverages common today, in the past they were limited and enjoyed only on special occasions. Ceremonial drinks may be consumed, used for anointment, and even offered to the earth in exchange for plant crops. They are also part of the shamanistic tradition in divination rites. In Mexico *pulque*, a drink made of fermented juice of the mescal agave, was drunk only by Aztec priests but is now widely used. In the South Pacific the juice of kava provided an intoxicating beverage. In California some Native Americans used drinks spiked with datura in their coming-of-age ceremonies. Whether alcoholic or narcotic, plants have long provided humanity with stimulating drinks, which continues today among wine aficionados who take enjoyment from imbibing a good vintage.

Acts and Affirmations

Celebrate the feast of the harvest goddess by drinking green tea, which has both ceremonial and medicinal uses. Anoint your garden with it by pouring a small cup on your shrine, pagoda light, water basin, or kneeling stone as a gesture of thanks for a long and productive growing season. Then share the rest of the pot with friends.

october 26

Feast of Hathor on the Full Moon

Holy Goddess tell us. Mother of Living Nature, the food of life. Thou meter out in eternal loyalty, and, when life has left us, we take our refuge in Thee.

—SECOND CENTURY B.C. EULOGY

Hathor was the ancient Egyptian goddess of the moon and patron of fertility and harvest. Her flowers, the white night-blooming lily of the Nile, were featured decorations in the Feast of Hathor celebration. Egyptians built altars to her in the threshing barns so that she might continue her patronage as the men separated the grain from the chaff. Her hieroglyphic cartouche and image are the most common decorations in the modest tombs of farmers and landowners. Hathor shows us the vitality of the link between moon and harvest, an awareness that dates back to earlier times. Perhaps there is more benefit than we realize from planting and harvesting by the phases of the moon.

Acts and Affirmations

"Drawing down the moon" is an ancient ritual to imbue water with sacred powers of the moon. To try it, fill a beautiful bowl with water or white wine under the light of the full moon. Use a mirror to reflect the direct moonlight onto the water or wine, and call upon the moon goddess of your choice to make it sacred. Once empowered, use this water or wine to create flower essences, love potions, and many other divination practices.

october 27

A man is ethical only when life, as such, is sacred to him, that of plants and animals as that of his fellow man, and when he devotes himself helpfully to all life that is in need of help.

—Albert Schweitzer, *Out of My Life and Thoughts*, 1937

Environmental ethics have entered the world of the garden in a way that recalls Schweitzer's philosophy. We no longer view all waste as disposable and realize that garden chemicals can too easily find their way into the food chain. Respect for life helps us to garden ethically by using organic methods that utilize the natural processes to support and protect plants in our landscapes.

Acts and Affirmations

Change your attitude toward the garden. Be aware of everything you use from fertilizers to pest killers. Always choose the least toxic alternative to use on your garden to show your respect for life. Choose insecticidal soap over pesticides. Pull weeds or prevent them rather than using herbicides, and choose manure instead of chemical plant food.

october 28

Does a man bare his head in some old church? So did I, standing in the shadow of this regal tree, and looking up into that completed glory, at which three hundred years have been at work with noiseless fingers! What was I in its presence but a grasshopper? My heart said: "I may not call thee property, and that property mine! Thou art the child of summer. Thou art the mighty temple where birds praise God. Thou belongest to no man's hand, but to all men's eyes that do love beauty, and that have learned through beauty to behold God!

—Henry Ward Beecher, *A Discourse on Trees*, 1893

Great old trees inspire us like no other living thing. Our own short life compared to their accumulated age is but a blink of an eye. Do we ever own the tree that grows on our land? At this dawn of the third millennium, we are rediscovering what Druids of old knew since time immemorial—that the spirit of God dwells inside the massive trunk to whisper its truths in the rustling of branches.

Acts and Affirmations

If you live within the range of the bristlecone pine tree, plan a summer pilgrimage to the high country to see firsthand the greatness of this, the oldest of trees. Feel each groove in the twisted bole, and note the economy of its short, stiff needles. While there, know that you are close to God, for the divine no doubt dwells deep within the heartwood of every bristlecone.

october 29

IROQUOIS FEAST OF THE DEAD

The American Indian is of the soil, whether it be the region of the forests, plains, pueblos or mesas. He fits into the landscape, for the hand that fashioned the continent also fashioned the man for his surroundings. Once he grew as natural as the wild sunflowers, he belonged just as the buffalo belonged.

—LUTHER STANDING BEAR, Oglala Sioux

The lives of Native American people were defined in some ways by the native plants of the local landscape. Oak trees defined the lives of California tribes, piñon pine defined the Pueblo people, and prairie grass fed the buffalo that the great Plains tribes depended on. Our own regions are similarly defined by the local native plants. When we use natives in our landscape, it is not only ecologically beneficial to local wildlife and conserves resources but we make a deeper connection to the land and its peoples. This link transcends mere gardening and integrates us into the giant web of plants and animals that is an almost spiritual part of our unique geographic heritage.

ACTS AND AFFIRMATIONS

Pursue a deeper relationship with the native plants in your region by growing them. Look for specialty nurseries that grow local species and integrate these plants into your landscape. With each native tree, shrub, vine, wildflower, or grass you manage to grow, you will come closer to that intrinsic connection to the land so prevalent in Native American consciousness.

october 30

Orare est laborare, laborare est orare.
To pray is to work, to work is to pray.
—MOTTO OF THE BENEDICTINE ORDER

As a society we are consumed with the art of leisure, and television is a big contribution to this problem. But it can be immensely rewarding in both a physical and spiritual sense to spend leisure time working on one's own terms. The gardener knows that his or her labor is both pleasant and therapeutic, particularly after a workweek indoors in offices. To gauge the quality of one's free time simply by hours of pure leisure eliminates the deep satisfaction that is derived after a good day of digging, raking, pruning, watering, or weeding in the autumn sunshine.

ACTS AND AFFIRMATIONS
The quiet hours in the autumn garden are spent cleaning up remnants of the summer and preparing plants for their long winter rest. It is the best time to talk with God during these golden afternoons as we rake leaves, transforming work into a very physical form of prayer.

october 31

SAMHAIN
ALL HALLOWS' EVE

Night is a dead monotonous period under a roof; but in the open world it passes lightly, with its stars and dews and perfumes, and the hours are marked by changes in the face of Nature. What seems a kind of temporal death to people choked between walls and curtains, is only a light and living slumber to the man who sleeps afield.

—ROBERT LOUIS STEVENSON, *A Night Among the Pines*, 1879

On the night of Samhain, an ancient Celtic festival, it is said that time ceases to exist and the doorway opens briefly to the otherworld. Samhain is also the official end of summer and the twilight of the year before the long nights of winter set in. Great bonfires were the traditional celebration in Old Europe. During this short window, the spirits were thought to walk among us, and traditional costumed trick-or-treaters go out to meet them, traveling from house to house seeking sustenance. Though many condemn Halloween (Eve of All Saints' Day; formerly All Hallows' Eve) as ungodly, it is a beautiful expression of our belief that human souls do continue to exist after death.

ACTS AND AFFIRMATIONS

To celebrate Samhain in its pagan tradition, choose the largest turnip you can find in the market. Slice off the stem to create a flat bottom, then turn it upside down to hollow out a place for a votive candle. Place this beside your jack-o'-lantern to bring the Old and New World traditions together on this night.

all hallows' pumpkin

The Halloween pumpkin is rooted in the Celtic rites of Samhain. During Samhain, all lights in the village were extinguished, and a ritual bonfire was kindled in a sacred shrine, fed with wood of the Druid oak and ash. Each family lit their own small candle from the bonfire to bring home, using it to light a fire in their hearth with the new flame of the year. The candles were carried inside giant turnips or a thick-stemmed cabbage to avoid burns. A form of this tradition continued in America, with the easy-to-grow and abundant native New World pumpkin substituting for turnips or cabbage. The faces carved on pumpkins were thought to scare away any "haunts" that might be wandering around on this special night.

november

The early winds of the coming winter blow through in November.

It has long been considered a dark and dreary

time of the year, "when little witches down themselves, and great

ones sell themselves to the Devil" (Reginald Scot,

The Discovery of Witchcraft, 1584).

It has also been called the month of blue devils and suicides.

These superstitions are no doubt a legacy of Samhain and

Halloween, which fall on the last day of October,

and November's All Saints' Day and All Souls' Day,

when the dearly departed are remembered by the church.

The slowing of this season is the time to prepare

for a more housebound life in

winter. The flower of this month is the

chrysanthemum, a perennial featured largely in

Asian festivals as a symbol of wisdom.

CREE WHEN RIVERS BEGIN TO FREEZE MOON

november 1

FEAST OF ALL SAINTS
EL DÍA DE LOS MUERTOS

The flowers form brilliant mounds of colour. Predominant is the vivid orange and yellow of the cempasuchil, *the "Flower of the Dead," which has been associated with festivals for the dead since pre-Hispanic times. Both its colour and aromatic scent are important for they are thought to attract the souls towards the offering. Paths of marigold petals are strewn from the* ofrenda *to the door of the house out into the roadway in the direction of the cemetery.*

—ELIZABETH CARMICHAEL, *The Skeleton at the Feast*, 1991

All Saints' Day, or *Todos Santos*, is among the most beautiful of all Latin American traditions. This blend of Catholic and pre-Columbian ritual brings people to their graveyards to decorate the family tombs with flowers. They offer their dead relatives special foods as nourishment for the spirits' venture out of the grave on these special nights. It is a festive time that helps the families cope with recent losses through remembrance in a healthy, healing way. We find great inspiration by sharing in this festival, which is growing in popularity in the American Southwest and in Latino communities across the country.

ACTS AND AFFIRMATIONS

Create your own Día de los Muertos shrine indoors or in the garden. The central elements are pictures of deceased loved ones. You may want to include a cross, statues of saints, and lots of brightly colored seven-day glass candles and little votives. Decorate with fresh and dried flowers so that the place is beautiful and gay, and sprinkle the petals of African marigolds among the pictures to guide the beloved wandering souls.

(*Tagetes erecta*)

flowers of los muertos

The robust, pompon-flowered annual African marigold is, despite the name, entirely a New World plant. Aromatic and heat-loving, the flowers were a part of pre-Columbian rituals that focused on cut blossoms to symbolize the transience of life and the inevitability of death. The Spanish sent marigold seeds back to the Old World, and this species became prominent in northern Africa (hence the name). Since then, it has become integrated into Hindu rituals and is worn by gurus and used to decorate funeral pyres all along the Ganges. Today this flower, known in Mexico as *cempasuchil*, is the flower of the dead because it is believed the wandering dead can smell its scent and will be pleased wherever it is abundant. The African marigold is ubiquitous during the three-day Day of the Dead festival. They are strung into garlands, arranged in patterns on boards, and heaped into fragrant mounds. Petals are plucked and strewn onto the ground in a path from graveyard to family home in the village, so that the wandering dead may follow it back to the grave as the festival closes. (If not led back to its place of repose, a lost soul may linger to haunt the family all year long.) This marigold should be in everyone's summer garden if for no other reason than for its natural ability to deter certain insects and nematodes from praying on vegetable plants.

november 2

Feast of All Souls

Behold the honor bestowed in your memory, with this humble little offering from our harvest, as a sign of gratitude for your benevolence and your visit to this transient place. You, Lords, Creators and Progenitors, the givers of all vital knowledge, of memory, we offer you the perfume of flowers and the music of our songs.

—Totonac invocation to the dead and to the lords

The altars of Día de los Muertos are the setting upon which mortals offer the dead a special meal (*ofrenda*) to sustain them during this busy time. It is usually composed of special bread made of amaranth grain and traditional *pulque*, the fermented juice of the agave plant. There are also a variety of colorful fruits and skulls made of hardened sugar. This tradition is a living legacy of the Aztec and Nahuatl religion, with sugar skeletons replacing the ancient ritual sacrifice of human beings. Like the Egyptians, the Nahuatl believed the dead passed through many underworlds, and foods are offered to sustain them during the journey.

Acts and Affirmations

Prepare an *ofrenda* for your home shrine with Mexican sweet breads, marzipan, and other traditional Latin American foods. Fill two small glasses with tequila, leave one in the *ofrenda*, and toast the dead with the other. If you don't drink liquor, mango or papaya nectar is a suitable alternative.

november 3

All that thy seasons bring, oh nature, is fruit for me.
All things come from thee, subsist in thee, go back to thee.
—Marcus Aurelius, *Meditations*, 180 A.D.

Days grow short, nights grow increasingly cold, and the garden withers for lack of sun. It is an introspective time when we recall the past summer's garden. Though we are reluctant to see the growing season end, it is a natural occurrence. Perhaps the greatest beauty of fall and winter is that they make us more deeply appreciate the summer. This is true of so much in life, for without sickness we would not value health, and without old age we would take youth for granted. It is the reason there is darkness, pain, and loss, for without them we would never know the precious good things in life.

Acts and Affirmations

I will not pine away for the summer but learn to love every season in its time. I will be more aware of the newly exposed tree trunks, the pattern of fallen leaves on the ground, sparkling ice crystals on a very cold morning, and the fog of my breath as I take it all in.

november 4

The pine is the tree of silence. Who was the Goddess of Silence? Look for her altars amid the pines—silence above, silence below.
—JOHN BURROUGHS, *A Spray of Pine*, 1908

In the silence of the woods in late autumn, the first dusting of snow gathers up sound in its ivory cloak. The only sound is the whispering of the winds in the tall treetops, which in another season would be drowned out by the rustling of a thousand leaves. Pines, our most universal evergreen, are some of the few trees that stay green through the winter, and amid the dense forests we know why Burroughs was so inspired to write of a goddess who dwells there. And should we stand in our winter coats and hats in a dense stand, we would know the altars are there, invisible but calling us to silently contemplate the peace.

ACTS AND AFFIRMATIONS

Gather pinecones this time of the year from wild and domesticated pines that shed their beautiful ornaments where no one except gardeners notice them. Each kind of pine produces a unique cone that is the best way to identify the trees. Cones are nature's free decorating items, and they give us a wonderful excuse to take long walks in the country searching for just the right cone, all the while listening intently to the silence.

november 5

Take God from nature, nothing is left.
—Robert Browning, letters

The more deeply a person becomes steeped in botany and horticulture, the more true Browning's statement becomes. God is manifest in the majestic puzzle of the plant, with its miracle of photosynthesis, its probing roots capable of splitting solid rock, and the mystery of a tiny flower with its intricate parts. This is the difference between mere science, with its table of elements, and the spiritual truth realized by the enormous network of living, breathing creations.

Acts and Affirmations
God: Help me to find my soul in the branches of the trees, in the fluttering wild grasses, and in the tiny center of the smallest flower. Without you they would be but factories that utilize light and water to survive, but with you they are miracles that fill each day with wonder.

november 6

While these clouds and this somber drizzling weather shut all in, we two draw nearer and know one another. The gathering in of the clouds with the last rush and dying breath of the wind, and then the regular dripping of twigs and leaves the country o'er, the impression of inward comfort and sociableness, the drenched stubble and trees that drop beads on you as you pass, their dim outline seen through the rain on all sides drooping in sympathy with yourself. These are my undisputed territory. This is Nature's English comfort.

—Henry David Thoreau, *Journal*, 1906

The barren trees turn dark as the rains come, water streaming down their trunks to be soaked up by thirsty earth. The branches drip with moisture—rain, dew, or fog growing heavy as the dampness sets in. It is the time to abandon the garden and take up residence before the hearth. There the wood warms us and licking tongues of fire are a reminder in a distant way of the heat and light of the far-off summer solstice. We listen to the wind outside clattering the windowpanes, knowing that it is part of the eternal cycle and that we are but small beings in a much larger plan.

Acts and Affirmations

Dark rainy nights prove to be extraordinarily productive for some writers and artists. The sound of the rain dripping sets a mood, and under the small light shed down upon a desk, the world is shut away and the words flow. Use these times for journal writing, to set down thoughts and expressions on paper to send to others, or to simply recall the nuances of the garden and reminders for next year's improvements.

november 7

12 Things for Gardeners to Remember

The value of time. *Seasons are rarely long enough.*
The success of perseverance. *Neither Rome nor gardens are built in a day.*
The pleasure of working. *It is the garden path to daily peace.*
The dignity of simplicity. *Modest garden plans are rarely abandoned.*
The worth of character. *Nature is the ultimate truth.*
The power of kindness. *Grow for others besides yourself.*
The influence of example. *Garden with children.*
The obligation of duty. *Plants require our constant attention.*
The wisdom of economy. *Plant a seed, don't buy a seedling.*
The virtue of patience. *You cannot hurry the plant.*
The improvement of talent. *Each season increases ability.*
The joy of originating. *Your own garden is always the best garden.*

—Marshall Field and Maureen Gilmer

We discover these truths in the garden, from creation to tending to harvest. Gardens cultivate patience, for plants grow at their own pace, and it takes a lifetime for a tree to mature. Virtuous gardening requires our complete participation and teaches us subliminal lessons. In a society that values instant gratification, these virtues are the hidden keys to a happy life.

Acts and Affirmations

Plant propagation—creating new plants from cuttings, layering, or seeds—is an exercise in patience and economy. Learn more about propagation: plants' marvelous regenerative abilities are among the most inspiring aspects of gardening, and propagating plants is one of the most affordable ways to grow a garden—and to grow as a person.

november 8

JAPANESE FESTIVAL OF THE KITCHEN GODDESS

I put upon the field of tranquil mind the water and manure of constant faith, then sow it with unblemished seed of a heart immaculate. Over it, like pealing thunder, reverberates sincere prayer. Grace falls upon it like a shower of rain.

—LIFE AND HYMNS OF MILAREPA, from *A Buddhist Bible*, 1970

The Japanese kitchen goddess, Daidokoro, is honored this day. She oversees the work of both food growers and those who prepare food in the kitchen. In Japan, the art of presentation is as important as the gift or offering itself, and the foods for this little festival are always among the most carefully decorated. The way we present others with the bounty of our gardens should be equally well prepared. When we take care with the presentation of a winter squash or an ear of Indian corn, it adds the new dimension of a human touch that says so much about the value of our interpersonal relationships.

ACTS AND AFFIRMATIONS

When offering friends, family, and neighbors fruits and vegetables from your garden harvest, remember that presentation adds so much more of yourself to the gift. Whenever you attend garage or rummage sales, buy attractive baskets, which sell for pennies apiece. Keep different sizes on hand, so that rather than giving away your precious homegrown produce in brown paper bags, you can offer it in artistically arranged baskets.

november 9

Haitian Yam Feast

I love to think of nature as an unlimited broadcasting station, through which God speaks to us every hour, if we will only tune in.
—George Washington Carver, *George W. Carver*, 1943

The yam was first domesticated in Africa thousands of years ago and was vital to the Yoruba people of the west coast. It is a plant that thrives in hot, humid climates, which are hostile to so many other species. The African cultures that adopted yam farming proved successful in part because of the ready supply of vitamins the plant provided. Healthier people meant a more complex and successful culture. The yam then migrated to the Caribbean and found a new home on the island of Haiti, where the climate was much like equatorial Africa. After Haiti's independence, the Africans and their descendants who had settled there became self-governing and again grew dependent on yams for their staple food. It is no wonder that they celebrate the yam with a feast, for it and the traditions of voodoo are legacies of their West African heritage that survived the slave trade.

Acts and Affirmations

Yams aren't just for Thanksgiving dinner.
They are a beautiful African—and African American—dietary staple that scientist George Washington Carver developed into dozens of new foods and products. This season, use freshly prepared yams for your pies instead of pumpkin, to discover a new-yet-old flavor of the American South in this season of plenty.

november 10

But besides this general grace diffused over nature, almost all the individual forms are agreeable to the eye, as is proved by our endless imitations of some of them, as the acorn, the grape, the pine-cone, the wheat-ear, the egg, the wings and forms of most birds, the lion's claw, the serpent, the butterfly, sea-shells, flames, clouds, buds, leaves, and the forms of many trees, as the palm.
—Ralph Waldo Emerson, *Nature*, 1836

The garden has inspired art and architectural decoration since ancient times. The columns of Egyptian temples were inspired by the lotus, and Greek capitals depict the acanthus plant. The turn-of-the-century Art Noveau style of Arts and Crafts featured plants, flowers, and materials inspired by nature. These universal gardening motifs suggest that the garden is the primary source of all art. To see individual elements of the garden as artists do, we must take them out of context and view them in a more abstract way. Only then will the spiritual beauty of leaf veins, petal arrangement, and the texture of tree bark become fully revealed to us.

Acts and Affirmations

This season, when most trees are bare, is a good time to become acquainted with the nature of tree bark. Though all bark may look the same to you at first, each species has its own unique characteristics. Study the furrowed texture of sugar maple, the scaly surface of spruce, and exfoliation of shagbark hickory. Don't just look at bark—experience it in a tactile way. Smell it to find the trees' essential perfume, such as the vanilla scent of pine bark.

november 11

It is God's love that speaks to me in the birds and streams but also behind the clamor of the city God speaks to me in His judgements, and all these things are seeds sent to me from His will.
—THOMAS MERTON, *Seeds of Contemplation*, 1949

It is so easy to find God in the natural things of the garden and countryside, but it is more difficult in the city. For the gardener that lives in the city, the seeds of peace amid chaos may be found in a collection of houseplants or a container garden on the roof or fire escape. It is not the size of the garden that matters to the soul but whether we experience God's love issuing from the smallest leaves and flowers.

ACTS AND AFFIRMATIONS

If you live in a city, particularly in an apartment without a balcony or yard, it is spiritually therapeutic to surround yourself with living plants. Improve the conditions indoors by installing full-spectrum lightbulbs or fluorescent tubes to allow you to cultivate green growing things far from your windows. Start with easy-to-grow mother-in-law's-tongue (*Sansevieria*), then move on to exotic succulents and orchids. Why live in a lifeless, sterile box when you can turn your apartment into a rain forest jungle on the fifteenth floor?

Unto the plough and oxen of undistracted thought I add the ploughshare of right method and of reason. The oxen is guided by the undeluded person, with a firm grasp of undivided purpose, and goaded on by the whip of zeal and perseverance. They break up the hardened soil of ignorance, clear away the stones of the hardened, sin-filled nature, and weed out all hypocrisies.

—Life and Hymns of Milarepa, from *A Buddhist Bible*, 1970

Past hurts and wrongs can take root in our spiritual life and build up over years. Resentments cause us to build a hard shell around our hearts to protect against painful experiences. The problem is that our spirits become imprisoned as well, for we cannot reach out through such a dense layer any more than others can reach in. It is like the crust that builds up on soil to prevent water from reaching plant roots, which also prevents the roots from spreading out. To break open the soil we must vigorously cultivate it, then feed and water it well. To free ourselves spiritually we must be aggressive in purging all of our resentments so we can grow again from the ground up with a positive, open attitude toward the world.

Acts and Affirmations

Alfalfa can gently heal abused soil, just as explorations of the spirit can heal early physical or emotional abuse. Get to know the effects of alfalfa in your garden this winter. Buy bales of alfalfa from a local livestock feed store tear them apart. Spread the alfalfa evenly over the surface of your kitchen garden to a depth of six inches or more. Then walk all over it to press the dried plant material into the mud. Over the winter months, it will work its magic to transform worn-out soil into a rich living garden of microorganisms.

november 13

With ten characteristics was the earth created: wisdom and understanding; knowledge and strength; rebuke and might; righteousness and justice; mercy and compassion.
—The Talmud

These virtues or characteristics are reflected not only in human behavior but in the ecological processes of the earth. Through knowing the vital interconnections of all species, we earn wisdom and understanding. By being self-reliant through our gardens, we gain knowledge and strength. By taking responsibility for the environment, we express righteousness and justice. And by sharing our labor and crops, we understand mercy and compassion. Thus we can say that all great truths can be learned from the garden as we cultivate, plant, and tend it from childhood to old age.

Acts and Affirmations
God: As I go about my work in the garden each year, help me to intuitively glean the messages of life from every little task. Teach me patience as I wait for the seed to sprout. Teach me devotion as I nurture the little seedling. Teach me faith as I witness its flowering. Teach me hope as the fruit matures. And teach me charity as it delivers a mature crop into my waiting hands.

november 14

In the early days we were close to nature. We judged time, weather conditions and many things by the elements—the good earth, the blue sky, the flying of geese and the changing winds. We looked to these for guidance and answers. Our prayers and thanksgiving were said to the four winds—to the West, which ended the day and brought rest, and to the North, the Mother of the winter, whose sharp air awakened a time of preparation for the long days ahead.

—UNKNOWN SPEAKER, National Congress of American Indians, 1965

Native Americans lived by the signs of nature, which were the first calendars and clocks in a world governed not by minutes and seconds but by sunrise and sunset, solstice and equinox. The migrations of birds and other animals are among the most beautiful signs of seasonal change. As gardeners we may share in these changes in a far deeper way than everyone else, for to look up as you cut your brown cornstalks and see the Canada geese flying in a V-shape overhead is to witness one of the most beautiful sights in the world.

ACTS AND AFFIRMATIONS

The warm breezes of summer are gone, and the icy fingers of the north come down to find openings in our clothes and gaps in our windows. In these last days of autumn make a mental note of directions: that of the wind, that of the migrating birds, and that of the shadows, which are now growing long. For these signs become our natural clock and calendar, notifying our subconscious minds that change is at hand.

november 15

Feronia: Feast of the Roman Goddess of Fire

The world, an entity out of everything, was created by neither gods nor men, but was, is and will be eternally living fire, regularly becoming ignited and regularly becoming extinguished.

—Heraclitus, *The Cosmic Fragments*, 480 B.C.

As the bonfires of autumn render the skies smoky, we are reminded of the ancient firing of the fields to burn off the stubble at season's end. Fire was then and remains today one of the most magnificent natural elements on earth. It is a cataclysmic destroyer, but the resulting ash is a component in regeneration. Fire heats us at our hearth through the winter; it cooks our food and provides light. No wonder it was dedicated to so many gods and goddesses, for who could explain where a fuel went once burned?

Acts and Affirmations

It is our primeval fascination with fire that makes candlelight such a mood maker. The lively, moving character of flame is absent in electric lights. Living flames can turn a dark November night into an enchanting experience. Create a contemplative environment by surrounding yourself with candles: in bed, in the bath, or in that sacred space created in the home. Then contemplate that fire has not changed a bit since the first upright human being traveled the planet so very long ago.

november 16

It is He who sendeth the winds like heralds of glad tidings going before His Mercy. When they have carried the heavy-laden clouds, He drives them to a land that is dead, makes rain to descend thereon, and produces every kind of harvest therewith . . .
—The Koran: Sura 7

The Islamic faith was born in deserts and continues to flourish in the dry, barren climate of the Middle East. The coming of rains to any arid land is like a miracle from heaven, which brings life in so many forms. This is much like our spiritual life. For when the soul is dry and empty, it yearns to be filled with grace, energy, or inspiration. And when God sends the winds, we must open up to the clouds and stand ready for the rain to descend and fill us with spiritual life.

Acts and Affirmations
I will keep my heart and soul open for signs of God in the heavens. I will look up often to watch clouds float by. I will stand to witness each thunderstorm with its lightning flashing in a spectacular expression of power. I will listen to the rain at night drumming on my roof and know that all these things are sent to fill me up with reminders that higher forces are at work.

november 17

Feast of St. Elizabeth of Hungary

Each bud flowers but once and each flower has but its minute of perfect beauty; so, in the garden of the soul each feeling has, as it were, its flowering instant, its one and only moment of expansive grace and radiant kingship.

—Henri Frederic Amiel, *Journal Intimate*, nineteenth century

Elizabeth and her wealthy husband, Louis, were great benefactors of the poor peasants, despite their family's objections. During a great famine, Louis was away at war when Elizabeth secretly began feeding the poor outside the castle gate. One day she sneaked out with an apron filled with bread, only to meet up with greedy family members who accused her of wasting their fortune. When asked what was in her apron, Elizabeth replied, "I am carrying roses," and when an angry man loosed the apron, she was startled to find the bread had been transformed into roses. This is just one of the miracles attributed to this medieval saint, who became patron of bakers and beggars and is always depicted with roses.

Acts and Affirmations

The act of charity is exemplified by this legendary miracle of bread turned to roses in the apron of St. Elizabeth. Such compassion for the poor is repeated today in soup kitchens across America. Charity not only helps the poor but it reminds the givers of their blessings. Volunteer to help feed the poor. Afterward, your garden's abundance will seem like a true miracle in comparison.

november 18

Whatever a man sows, that shall he reap. The law of Karma is inexorable and impossible of evasion. There is hardly any need for God to interfere. He laid down the rules, and as it were, retired.
—Mohandas K. Gandhi, *Hindu Dharma*

The universe is governed by laws of all kinds, from physics to biology. The Hindu and Buddhist law of karma states that what we do comes back to us in the end. This idea is well evidenced in the garden: if we neglect our plants, they will not bloom for us. If we fail to care for the soil, it becomes very hard and difficult to work with. All of these laws are based in practical cause and effect and are integrated into the culture of gardening, of religion, and of nature. Every act has its consequences, and in the garden we may reap only what we have sown.

Acts and Affirmations

Strive to cultivate good karma in your life—and in your garden. When we nurture plants, the positive karma is returned to us with abundant harvest. When we nurture other people in times of need, that nurturing is returned to us when we are needy. And when we are cruel or unkind, we in turn will suffer this brutal treatment at the hands of another. What you sow, you shall reap is more than spiritual—it is simple cause and effect.

november 19

The book of nature lies open to every eye. It is from this sublime and wonderful volume that I learn to serve and adore its Divine Author. No person is excusable for neglecting to read this book, as it is written in an universal language, intelligible to all mankind.

—JEAN-JACQUES ROUSSEAU, *Emile*, eighteenth century

This is the season of quiet rest in the garden, but one of active study indoors. Much of what we learn as gardeners is gleaned from books, magazines, and catalogs saved over more active seasons to digest in the winter. This illustrates why gardening appeals to us on so many levels, for it requires not only physical effort but our intellectual growth. If we add the spiritual and mental health benefits, it becomes more than a hobby but a way of life that makes us happier, more fulfilled people.

ACTS AND AFFIRMATIONS

Spend dreary winter days reading about the relationships of human beings to plants. Read about the legends and myths of great civilizations, which explain the origin of the names of many historic species. Learn about ecology and the roles of native plants in their communities. The better we understand these connections, the deeper our spiritual connection with the earth and its cloak of plants becomes.

november 20

And when we turn to the inner circle of the spiritual masters—the men and women, not necessarily gifted or distinguished, to whom God was "a living, bright reality" which supernaturalized their everyday life and transmuted their homeliest actions into sublime worship—we find that their roots stuck deep into the soil of spiritual silence.

—E. Herman, *Creative Prayer*, 1955

We aspire to become better people and look to those who have a greater spiritual development as teachers and guides. We emulate them on our path to self-discovery. The world of horticulture is also filled with masters who provide us with inspiration to grow. The European monk Gregor Mendel broke open the secrets of genetics through his small garden and the lowly pea. The famous California plant wizard Luther Burbank was driven by a desire to free the world of famine by breeding improved plants. George Washington Carver created whole markets for poor farmers to better their chances of self-sufficiency. The author Vita Sackville-West shared her passion for the English landscape through countless poems and articles that taught readers far more than just horticulture. To turn to this inner circle, to read of these great lives, will indeed help us transform our actions into inspired activities.

Acts and Affirmations

Plant a dwarf juniper in the garden as a symbol of humility and endurance. Let it be the Gandhi or Mother Teresa plant of your landscape, quietly asserting its presence through diligent growth and resistance to adversity. It is better to yearn for spiritual riches and eternal humility than the hollow shroud of fame and material wealth, which vanishes upon death.

november 21

i thank you God for this most amazing day: for the leaping greenly spirits of trees and a blue true dream of sky; and for everything which is natural which is infinite which is yes.

—E. E. CUMMINGS, *Xaipe*, 1950

The ancient trees of Europe inspired the Celtic Druids to believe the spirits dwelled inside them. Some groves were so sacred to them that any unauthorized person found among them would be summarily sacrificed to heal the sacrilege. Druids were expressly forbidden to worship under roofs, so old groves were the first churches. The soaring arches of medieval cathedrals are believed to have been inspired by the branching canopies of trees.

ACTS AND AFFIRMATIONS

Each time you enter a church or cathedral, look up to the soaring heights of its arched ceilings and visualize yourself inside a sacred grove. Consider the church architecture a legacy of pagan Druids, whose tradition has subtly left its mark on Christianity.

november 22

A lake is the landscape's most beautiful and expressive feature. It is earth's eye; looking into which the beholder measures the depth of his own nature.
—HENRY DAVID THOREAU, *Journal*, 1906

Few scenes are as beautiful as a lake in the winter when the trees once crowding its shores are bare and colorless. The reflective surface of the water is among the greatest inspirations of nature and water gardens, for the surface is not so much itself but a mirror of sky and surrounding trees. How many hours or days did Thoreau sit gazing at the surface of Walden Pond? We may never know for sure, but his observations showed us that Walden was never exactly the same two days in a row. All still water is that way, and we may study its changing nature while pondering our own.

ACTS AND AFFIRMATIONS

From today forward, notice the way you look at lakes, pools, and water gardens. Rather than focusing on the surrounding landscape, pay attention to the reflective surface. Note what is pictured there: the landscape, the clouds passing overhead, and perhaps most beautiful of all, a full moon shining upon the waters.

november 23

On the wreck of the year they flourished, sucked strange life from rotten stick and hollow tree, opened gills on lofty branch and bough, shone in the green grass rings of the meadows, thrust cap and cowl from the concourse of the dead leaves in ditches, clustered like the uprising rooftrees of a fairy village in dingle and in dene.
—EDEN PHILLPOTTS, *Children of the Mist*, 1896

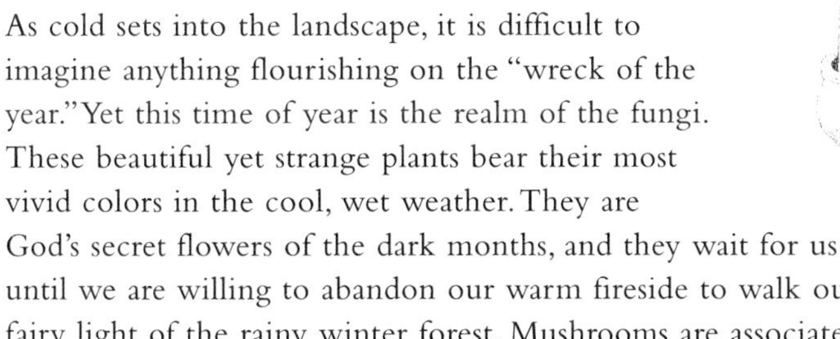

As cold sets into the landscape, it is difficult to imagine anything flourishing on the "wreck of the year." Yet this time of year is the realm of the fungi. These beautiful yet strange plants bear their most vivid colors in the cool, wet weather. They are God's secret flowers of the dark months, and they wait for us silently until we are willing to abandon our warm fireside to walk out into the fairy light of the rainy winter forest. Mushrooms are associated with fairies and witches, mystics and trolls in folklore from the earliest times.

ACTS AND AFFIRMATIONS

This year take walks in the woods during the rainy season, when there is no snow, to look for the many forms of fungi that grow on dead wood. Bring your magnifying glass to reveal this bright and beautiful wonderland that only appears in wet weather. Although often overlooked or destroyed, fungi can be beautiful, with incredibly bright colors and exotic spore-containing structures. These lesser-known gifts of the plant kingdom are among the greatest treasures of the rainy season.

november 24

Nature loves such woods, and places her own seal upon them. Here she shows what can be done with ferns and mosses and lichens. The soil is marrowy and full of innumerable forests. Standing in these fragrant aisles, I feel the strength of the vegetable kingdom, and am awed by the deep and inscrutable processes of life going on so silently around me.

—John Burrows, *In the Hemlocks*, 1871

The beautiful evergreen forests of North America, with their towering trees and ferny foliage, are truly inspiring. Beneath them it is an eerie place filled with fragrant oils exuding from leaf and bark and cone. The wind whistles through the treetops, while underneath all is quiet and still. Each step is quieted by the spongy litter of countless seasons building up like a featherbed. It is truly a separate reality that is more dramatic in winter when the sounds of life have gone to sleep or fled south. Winter is the season of the hemlock and our season to wander these fragrant aisles in quiet contemplation.

Acts and Affirmations

If you long for the inspiration of the forest but live far from it, consider planting a mini-forest ecosystem in your landscape. Nestle it in a far corner and plant with the species of conifer best adapted to your climate, such as redwoods in California and cypress in the southern states. Wait for them to grow large enough to cast their shade, and under the spreading canopies place a comfortable garden seat and surround it with locally native ferns and shade-loving perennials. There in winter or summer, you will enjoy the fragrance and relax in the cool green luxury that is the natural medicine of the soul.

november 25

Each blade of grass has its spot on earth whence it draws its life, its strength; and so is man rooted to the land from which he draws his faith together with his life.

—Joseph Conrad, *Lord Jim*, 1900

Until the end of the nineteenth century, it was common for generations of a family to live on a single homestead. That deep attachment to a piece of land defined the individuals and instilled a true sense of belonging. Today sense of permanence is long gone. We have become transient, and there is but emptiness where the sense of belonging once existed. But creating a garden, which can be a lifelong task, is the act of reclaiming our connection to a spot on earth. Over time, it becomes the well from which we draw our spiritual strength and inner peace.

Acts and Affirmations

Earth becomes sacred when it originates in a place that is meaningful, whether it is a family farm, an abandoned homestead, a religious space, or a place where an important event occurred. We may use such earth to consecrate our own gardens, by mixing a small amount of it into our freshly cultivated soil. As the two soils become one, the garden becomes more than a backyard, more than a place for plants. It becomes a natural reflection of faith.

november 26

The flowers of the earth do not grudge at one another, though one be more beautiful and fuller of virtue than another; but they stand kindly one by another, and enjoy one another's virtue.
—Jakob Boheme, sixteenth century

The lesson of the flowers is one of tolerance, and in a time when competition and physical beauty have become overwhelmingly important, the lesson is even more vital. Television creates a perception that only attractive, thin people are valuable. The garden has a place for every plant and every flower, no matter how squat or lanky, whether its color is pale or vivid. One needs the other, for without quiet color the riotous ones have no contrast or relief. Only when all kinds of flowers are planted and nurtured together do they combine to create a beautiful garden.

Acts and Affirmations
Knowing that it takes all kinds of flowers to make a beautiful garden, and all kinds of people to make the world, I will strive to never compare myself to people on TV, in magazines, or other idealized images. I am as unique as the wood tulip, and my sturdy reliability and natural beauty will make every gathering a garden.

november 27

THANKSGIVING (VARIES)

O gracious Father, who openest thine hand and fillest all things living with plenteousness: Bless the lands and waters, and multiply the harvests of the world; let Thy spirit go forth, that it may renew the face of the earth; show thy loving-kindness, that our land may give her increase; and save us from selfish use of what thou givest, that men and women everywhere may give thee thanks; through Christ our Lord. Amen.
—FOR THE HARVEST OF LANDS AND WATERS, *Book of Common Prayer*

At the first Thanksgiving, it is likely the Puritans prayed something very similar to this traditional Episcopal prayer of the harvest. This holiday celebrates the true wealth of the New World—not gold nor timber but food. The plants developed by indigenous peoples—and shared with the Pilgrims at the first Thanksgiving—so changed the Old World that it is hard to imagine cuisine before introduction of these foods. Squash and corn, cranberry and pumpkin, wild rice, a host of legumes, and sunflowers are all the legacy of that first meal. They represent the real treasure that we honor each time we plant these truly American crops and pray over them before dining.

ACTS AND AFFIRMATIONS

Let us all strive to avoid the selfish use of resources. Let each daily act be the manifestation of this philosophy by living economically, with a deep awareness of how we use water, energy, foods, and other gifts of the earth. For only when we are conscious of our consumption can we show our appreciation of God's greatest gifts to humankind.

november 28

From Wakan Tanka, the Great Spirit, there came a great unifying life force that flowed in and through all things—the flowers of the plains, blowing winds, rocks, trees, birds, animals—and was the same force that had been breathed into the first man. Thus all things were kindred, and were brought together by the same Great Mystery.

—Luther Standing Bear, Oglala Sioux

It is called by many names, but Great Mystery is among the most beautiful expressions to define life and the interconnectedness of all things. Native American spirituality is filled with this recognition of the sanctity of the Earth and its vast populations of living things. They believed that man is an intrinsic part of this mystery rather than separate, dominant beings. This is a very old idea but it is newly appreciated as we explore aboriginal peoples who do not live separate from natural processes but are actually part of them.

Acts and Affirmations

I am as important as the soil beneath my feet, the stars above at night, the animals and the plants that clothe the earth. Through gardening I act out my part in the Great Mystery with the changing tasks of each season. If I can become intimate with the earth in my tiny plot of soil, I will have begun the journey to discovering that the mystery is everywhere.

november 29

God is day and night, winter and summer, war and peace, surfeit and hunger.
—Heraclitus, *The Cosmic Fragments*, 480 B.C.

Harmony is the balance of opposites, and these opposing forces are manifest everywhere in the realm of nature. This idea points out to us that to live happily—or garden well—we must seek the center. Garden soils show this clearly, for the neutral center between acid and alkaline pH is appealing to most plants. Roots prefer soil that is neither saturated with water nor dry and dusty but in between. There, in the place of consummate fertility, our plants will flourish.

Acts and Affirmations
God: Help me to see and understand the full range of your creative powers in every aspect of my garden. Let me know it in sunshine and in the dark. May I love it in the abundance of summer and the barren simplicity of winter. And guide me to seek a harmonious balance in all things so that my life becomes equatorial rather than continuously lurching from pole to pole.

november 30

When lightening flashes like an arrow; when the wind rends the mountains, as though they were earthen pitchers; when at the sound of the abundance of rain, all ears grow deaf; then the beasts of the forests all together take refuge, and all the young doves flee into the clefts in the rocks. But in a moment, with the radiance of its light, the sun shines forth, and breaks through, and dispels all clouds and darkness. Thus likewise, God, who rules the world with might, causes relief from trouble to spring forth within a moment into the contrite.

—MOSES LUZZATTO, *The Way of the Upright*, eighteenth century

Despair is to believe that the lightning and the wind and the rain and the darkness are all that exist at the moment. It is difficult for us to realize that, like storm clouds parting, God can come into our lives to bring the sunshine back. The garden sliding into winter is rarely inspiring and seems to be the epitome of dreariness. But under that wet sod and hidden inside every twig are the flowers and green shoots of spring lying dormant. In the same way, when our lives seem overwhelmed with sadness, when the future appears unpromising, let us imagine the dark winter garden and the life that is sleeping inside it. And may this promise fill us with faith that God will dispel the clouds and fill coming days with light.

ACTS AND AFFIRMATIONS

If the winter storms to come fill you with dark thoughts, use creative visualization to help you through the difficult times. Find a comfortable place to sit or lie down and create mental images of the sun shining through the clouds that now block its rays. Or imagine wisteria running across the eaves of your house bursting into long sprays of flowers and glittering under the last raindrops as the bright morning sun rises.

december

Many people and cultures relate this month to smoky skies because

each home or hut or lodge burned fires to keep warm.

It was the month of the god Thor,

whose celebrations are the origins of the Yule, for he

dwelled in the yule logs burned at Christmas.

Celtic Christians called December Heilgh-monath, or holy month,

as it was the birth of Christ. But earlier in history

December was significant for the birth of the sun at the

winter solstice, falling just days before Christmas.

In agricultural cultures, this month was spent celebrating

at the hearth. Narcissus became the flower of the

month even though holly and mistletoe

are the true plants of the season, since they

were rare broadleaf evergreens of the northern climates.

The Christmas color scheme was borrowed from the holly,

with its red berries and green prickly leaves.

SIOUX MOON OF THE POPPING TREES

December 1

O ancestors, powerful spirits, who live amongst us: your tombs are the mountains, your waterfalls are the clouds, the plants are your jewels.
—Sumatran incantation

The idea that ancestral spirits live in nature is not so foreign when you imagine the soul as eternal. Peoples all over the world worship their ancestors. One reason is that it provides a means of gauging the passage of time; another is that it soothes the pangs of grief. It is comforting to imagine our departed loved ones dwelling in the most beautiful aspects of nature, inhabiting the plants and the mountains or floating through the skies. For who is to say what happens to the eternal soul after it is freed of the body?

Acts and Affirmations

Gardens are important places of ancestral remembrance. The burial grounds of the South Pacific, for example, are filled with trees and shrubs planted by the families of the dead, and the planting memorial was a popular Victorian practice. The plants that derive their sustenance from the decomposing body become a form of reincarnation. To give each new tree or shrub in your garden meaning, dedicate it to a loved one who has passed on.

December 2

BEGINNING OF ADVENT
(VARIES)

I asked the earth and it answered me: 'I am not it,' and all things whatsoever made the same confession. I asked the sea and the deeps and the creeping things and they answered me: 'We are not thy God; seek beyond us.'
—ST. AUGUSTINE, *Confessions*, sixth century

Advent is the season of expectation of two great events. It is a preparation season over four weeks leading up to the birth of Christ. It also coincides with the ancient pagan rite of the birth of the sun on the winter solstice, around December 21. Both are parallel events in the natural and spiritual worlds. We tend to ignore Advent in the hustle and bustle of holiday shopping, but it is good to keep our eyes turned toward these great holy days rather than on cash-register totals. For we feel the spirit of both the pagan and Christian holidays not according to how much we spend but by how much time we spend sharing love.

ACTS AND AFFIRMATIONS
The Advent wreath is a flat circle of evergreens with brackets for four candles: one purple and three pink. Each night the candles are lit as a rite of anticipation—the first week just one candle, second week two, and so on. Create your own Advent wreath and share in this candlelight tradition, or just light four candles in the evenings as you await the coming of Christmas or the winter solstice.

December 3

How earthy old people become—mouldy as the grave! Their wisdom smacks of the earth.

—Henry David Thoreau, *Journal*, 1906

Each season presents its own glory, just as each phase of a person's life yields its own treasures. The desire always to be surrounded by perfect weather and young, beautiful people is to reject the universe and to dwell only in a small corner of it. This cuts us off from the full experience of life, where we witness both the storms that rage and the most brilliant sunshine, birth and death, pain and love. This is the art of living well and experiencing each year with its changes rather than fighting tooth and nail to cling to youth. Because only when we embrace our true age, will we understand every dimension that makes up the range of life of the human spirit.

Acts and Affirmations

The people most often overlooked this time of year are those suffering alone from old age or long-term illness. Their needs are more than physical, for their universe has shrunk to one lonely soul and four confining walls. It is very easy to give money and things, but it is far more beautiful to provide something of yourself—your time and attention. Mother Teresa explains: "The biggest disease today is not leprosy or tuberculosis, but rather the feeling of being unwanted." Use the time you would otherwise spend shopping to brighten someone else's very limited universe.

December 4

Blessed are they who never read a newspaper, for they shall see Nature, and through her, God.

—Henry David Thoreau, *Journal*, 1906

Television, radio, print, and the Internet are filled with stories of crisis and chaos. The most horrendous acts of the day crash into our world, filling us with suffering, sadness, and negativity. We need not listen to the stories or become enslaved to the perpetual crisis mentality. Why wallow in it? Even in Thoreau's day, he knew it was better to leave the world behind and return ourselves to nature, and through her ultimately find our way to God.

Acts and Affirmations

We are far less dependent on the daily news than you think. As a spiritual exercise, shut off all news programs on radio or TV, and do not pick up a newspaper for a few weeks. You will find that you are happier and more upbeat. Continue to the new year, and then reassess if you want to go back to following the news or if you would find the coming year's promise brighter without it.

December 5

It has been said that the very fact of winter and summer, of cold death and warm life springing up again, should speak to us of resurrection and a life after death.

—Marcia Hollis, *Down to Earth*, 1971

Nature is the model of a circular process, that of birth, maturation, bearing fruit, and death. It is the story of life, the cycle of the seasons. This natural model of the return of life each spring suggests that all living things may be resurrected, or reborn, at some time. Physics tells us that matter does not go away, it simply changes form. By combining the concept of ever-present matter with the cycle of regeneration, we see a subtle promise that even when we die we do not go away—we simply change form.

Acts and Affirmations

Enjoy the resurrection of bulbs months before their time by forcing them in special Tye vases. Use these decorative transparent glass containers on a sunny windowsill, and watch bulbs put down their roots and then flower. Now is the time to hunt down Tye-style colored glass vases and the bulbs you want to force. The fragrant hyacinth is the most popular species of bulb for this.

December 6

There are times when God may suggest very quietly some duty, or action, that he desires us to do; but we are not on the alert, and the thought scarcely stirs a ripple on the surface of our mind. Only later do we find that we have let someone down, or forgotten some urgent duty. To live in this careless way causes prayer to droop and wilt, like houseplants in a stuffy room.

—Olive Wyon, *Prayer*, 1961

Living carelessly is to fly through life without pausing for reflection, mechanically reacting to things that come our way rather than living consciously. Careless living can be illustrated by how we shop for plants. Do you race through the garden center, compulsively choosing plants by their immediate impact, size, or color? An alternative approach would be to shop deliberately, deciding beforehand what plants you need to perfect your scheme. If you try to live with similar deliberateness, you will be rewarded with a well-ordered life.

Acts and Affirmations

God: Help me slow down my pace, to live less by reaction than through deliberate intent. Let the order make me more receptive to small suggestions that creep into my consciousness so that I always rise to my ultimate destiny. I must be forever mindful that personal growth happens in tiny ways, and if I neglect them, I will never become a more spiritual person.

December 7

Haloia of Demeter

Here the earth will celebrate this grave; the earth will bring its wild thin grass, its nodding blooms of simple buttercups and daisies and poppies, colors of blue and yellow and pink, the mellow shades of the rampant untended and eternal garden.

—Anne Rice, *Violin*, 1997

The ancient Greek Haloia of Demeter was a celebration of the beginning of winter. Demeter was the Greek goddess of tillage and plant fertility. According to myth, her daughter Persephone was gathering wildflowers when she was captured by Hades, god of the underworld, and made his queen. In sorrow Demeter stopped all plants from growing until Zeus intervened with the compromise that Persephone would live half the year with her mother and half with Hades. Thus Demeter ceases growth while her daughter is in the netherworld, initiating winter until it is time for Persephone to return. The homecoming celebration is spring.

Acts and Affirmations

Demeter was honored by placing carved pig figurines, branches of pine, and small cakes on her shrines. Honor the goddess of the grain by placing on the garden shrine a small, weatherproof pig figure made of ceramic, stone, or wood.

December 8

The outdoors was glorious. Conscious of the tingling cold, I felt a kinship with everything—with the crusted snow, the sparkling ledges on Bear Mountain, the restless, hidden lake, the muffled brook flowing under huge covers of glittering ice. Every bird sounded the universal theme.

—Brooks Atkinson, *Smoke from a Valley Cabin*, 1972

Hiking in winter is very different from summer hiking. It is more of a contemplative experience, cold and blustery. Why did many hermit monks choose this setting, whether it be a barren and cold North Africa or the Himalayas? Perhaps because there are fewer distractions. The wind is a reminder to retain focus, its fingers of ice digging into exposed skin reminding us not to let our consciousness stray. To find this state of peace, let us go out and return to the simplicity of winter.

Acts and Affirmations

During these cold winter days, take walks into the most remote and rugged places you can find. Bundle up and go alone so you can spend time in meditation. In that quiet place, you may discover what the Buddhists have known for centuries: that when we are surrounded by the drama of nature in all her power, the self falls away.

December 9

Jesus said: "I am the light that is over all things. I am all: From me all has come forth, and to me all has reached. Split a piece of wood; I am there. Lift up the stone, and you will find me there."
—Gospel of St. Thomas

This unauthorized gospel found near the Dead Sea Scrolls has stirred much controversy over the sayings of Jesus. This saying emphasizes the fact that God is everywhere, not just in churches or sacred places. Split the wood and he is there. Lift the stone and underneath with the sow bugs and the worms—he is there. This suggests that our gardens are filled with God and that divinity is everywhere. And only when we finally grasp the nature of the Creator will we truly understand that God is, was, and always will be.

Acts and Affirmations

The Gospel of St. Thomas reminds us that our bodies as well as our gardens are temples of the spirit. This suggests that abuse of self or of the landscape is an abuse of the divine. Treasure life and all of nature, for the supreme being is in the lowliest of places.

December 10

When we behold the fragrant rose and lily, we see His love and purity. So the green trees and fields and singing of birds are the emanation of His infinite joy and benignity.
—Jonathan Edwards, *Sermons*, eighteenth century

In these cold days, the birds and small animals that remain around home and garden struggle to find food. In this dormant season, the birds are all that remain of the animated summer landscape. In return for our enjoyment of their beautiful colors and cheerful presence during these dark months, leave seed to help them through the winter.

Acts and Affirmations

Provide your local wild birds with most welcome, high-quality food supplements. Use large pinecones to create beautiful feeders for the winter garden. Tie a hanging string to the top of the cone, then tightly pack its nooks and crannies with fresh peanut butter. Roll the cone in birdseed and hang it from eaves or tree limbs. Then watch the birds feast.

December 11

The various energies that make up, for example, the carrot. The Carrot Deva "pulls together" the various energies that determine the size, color, texture, growing season, nutritional needs, shape, flower and seed process of the carrot. In essence, the Carrot Deva is responsible for the carrot's entire physical package.

—Machaelle Small Wright, *Behaving as if the God in All Life Mattered*, 1983

The art of dowsing is more than merely finding water with a forked stick. As practiced today, it is the art of communicating with the devas, or spirits of light, that inhabit all things. This practice by sensitive individuals has produced the great garden of Findhorn, Scotland, where the founders turned a cold, wet wasteland into the most productive landscape in Britain. They contend that the ability to communicate with the devas of that landscape so pleases these spiritual beings that they respond with preturnaturally proportioned flowers and vegetables.

Acts and Affirmations

If you are sensitive to psychic energies, follow Machaelle Wright's example and contact the devas yourself. Before going into the garden, take a moment for centering meditation and wait quietly for the small voices. Machaelle asks them to tell her what they need for growth and what her tasks in the garden should be that day. Whether or not the devas speak to you, a moment for thinking about the day's tasks before digging in is always fruitful.

December 12

Feast of Our Lady of Guadalupe

I was born again in the polychromatic junction of all sorts of flowers, skin-colored, rose-colored which burst out miraculously spreading their rainbow in thy presence, Mother of Us, Most Blessed Mary. I am the bush with the loveliest buds, the creation of the One God, the God of Perfection, I am the most perfect of all His creatures. Thy Soul is alive there in the Painting.

—Nahuatl proclamation, 1531

Our Lady of Guadalupe is the patron of all Latin America, at once an incarnation of the Christian Mary and the Aztec goddess Tonantzin. The "shining woman" appeared to a poor Indian, Juan Diego, on Tepeyac Hill above Montezuma's capitol. She instructed him to gather roses, which could never have bloomed in such a place in the middle of winter. With his cloak filled, he brought her message to the bishop, and when he let the flowers fall, her image was left on the cloth. The agave fiber cloak remains over the altar of her basilica in Mexico City, where she is today recognized as the Holy Mother of all Latin American people.

Acts and Affirmations

Our Lady of Guadalupe is a Christian saint cloaked in Nahuatl imagery. See if you can find these buried Nahuatl Indian symbols in Our Lady of Guadalupe's image: She is looking down—symbol of humility. Hands are together—symbol of offering. Maternal tassel (*cinta*)—symbol of pregnancy. Small flower called *nagvioli*—Nahuatl symbol of their sun god. Stars on her cloak—luminous skirt of goddess Ometeotl. Rays around image—presence of sun god, Quetzalcoatl. Standing on a moon—Nahuatl god of night. Turquoise mantle—color of the great god Omechihuatl. Rose red gown—color of the war god and blood sacrifice.

December 13

ROMAN FESTIVAL OF SATURNALIA (CONTINUES UNTIL THE SOLSTICE)

Before meals the blessing of the gods was asked, and after the meal, but before the dessert, there was a short silence, and a portion of food was placed on the hearth and burned. If the hearth and the images were not in the eating-room, either the images were brought and put on the table, or before the shrine was placed on a table, on which were set a salt-cellar, food, and a burning lamp. On these and other joyous days the images were crowned, and there were presented offerings of cakes, honey, wine, incense, and sometimes a pig.

—J. N. FRADENBURGH, *Departed Gods*, 1891

Such a daily rite would have occurred in every Roman household during Saturnalia, the holiday of Saturn, god of agriculture. His hollow statue in the center of Rome was filled with olive oil as a symbol of fertility and abundance. The feasting of Saturnalia is the reason why our Christmas rites are so festive, for Romans saw this as the season when all things were turned around—slave became master, master served slave. Gifts, small statues, and sweet treats were exchanged generously in the spirit of Saturn's abundance. This season is a beautiful example of how the often brutal Roman Empire became peaceful and happy in the name of this of their oldest god.

ACTS AND AFFIRMATIONS

Celebrate Saturnalia the Roman way by giving friends and co-workers little sprigs of ivy to wear in honor of Bacchus and the Golden Age of Saturn. Pin artificial silk ivy sprigs to friends if no fresh ones are handy. Better yet, throw a Saturnalia party and provide every guest with a wreath of artificial silk ivy and dine on classical Italian cuisine.

December 14

He showed me a little thing, the quantity of a hazel-hut, in the palm of my hand; and it was round as a ball. I looked thereupon with eye of my understanding, and thought: What may this be? *And it was answered generally thus:* It is all that is made.
—Julian of Norwich, *Revelations of Divine Love, 1393*

Often the smallest things have the greatest impact on humanity. A virus is invisible to the eye yet is more powerful than our greatest armies. A seed barely larger than a pinhead may someday produce a towering tree. A beetle slightly bigger than the seed can bring down the towering tree. Diamonds, embryos, bacteria, and the single cell with its strands of DNA hold great mysteries for us and serve as sources of inspiration. For until we begin to see the small things for what they truly are, we will never understand the much larger mysteries of the universe.

Acts and Affirmations
Don't feed the material demons this holiday season. Buy as many of your gifts and decorations from the little guys: smaller charities and locally owned businesses that directly benefit from your dollars. Patronize cottage industries, collectives, and farmer's markets where you know that the money is being used wisely and in a socially responsible way. That way you'll know your purchases are going toward a good cause that will make the world a better place, not just increase corporate profits.

December 15

The laws, the life, and the joy of beauty in the material world of God, are as eternal and sacred parts of His creation as, in the world of spirits, virtue; and in the world of angels, praise.
—John Ruskin, *Modern Painters*, 1843–1860

In ancient times, pagans of Britain believed spirits resided in every living plant. They honored the holly as the only broadleaf evergreen to keep its beautiful foliage through the cold northern winters. This was a sign that the spirits of the frost that killed plants collectively resided in the holly waiting for spring. Crimson berries were even more evidence of this, and the old practice of "bringing home Christmas" was originally the cutting of such evergreens to invite these spirits to take up lodging in the comfort of warm pagan homes.

Acts and Affirmations

You may not know that the traditional candle at the center of a wreath of holly is actually a pagan custom. Share one of the oldest pre-Christian traditions in Eastern Europe—the lighting of a single large candle surrounded by fresh holly. This practice is actually an ancient solstice rite that promised the spirits of the plants (holly) that the sun (candle flame) would soon be reborn after the dark days of midwinter.

December 16

To northern peoples the holly was the type of the Burning Bush, and so a symbol of the chaste Maiden, chosen to be the Mother of Christ, whose being glowed with the sacred fire of the Holy Spirit. The holly was indeed sacrosanct, and never to be otherwise regarded.

—William Muir Auld, *Christmas Traditions*, 1931

In Christian times, holly was rededicated to the new religion. It was associated with Mary and the birth of the Christ child. The holly spines represented the crown of thorns, and the red berries the blood of the inevitable crucifixion. What was once the candle to symbolize the light of the newborn solstice sun surrounded by holly became the light of the world, Mary's newborn son. Holly became so empowered by Christianity that sprigs from churches became a talisman against the forces of darkness, so powerful this time of year.

Acts and Affirmations

If holly is used to decorate your church this Christmas, be sure to ask for sprigs of it before it is all taken down at Epiphany. It has long been believed that church holly is sacred and may be hung in the home for the remainder of the year as a protective symbol. It makes an auspicious addition to the household or garden shrine.

December 17

It is the love of God that sends the winter days when I am cold and sick, and the hot summer when I labor and my clothes are full of sweat: but it is God Who breathes on me with light winds off the river and in the breezes out of the wood. His love spreads the shade of the sycamore over my head and sends the water-boy along the edge of the wheatfield with a bucket from the spring, while the laborers are resting and the mules stand under the tree.

—Thomas Merton, *Seeds of Contemplation*, 1949

This is the season of love, when we tear down our walls and become filled with charity. The winter is a gift to the farmer, a season when he is forced to spend a long time indoors while his body repairs itself from the rigors of the more active months. Although in recent times the holiday season has become associated with a shopping frenzy that drains energy and finances, traditionally it was a season of housebound closeness, of relaxation and feasting. The love of God indeed sends the winter days as respite for the gardener, too, so let us spend them enjoying the people close to us.

Acts and Affirmations

If you have fruit trees, prune off branches about three feet long to bring indoors and arrange in a large vase. The warmth will make the buds flower out of season. Flowers are most welcome during the January doldrums, after all the fanfare of the holiday season is over. They are nature's promise to you that despite the cold and snow spring is still very much alive deep inside the plants.

December 18

Though thou art poor and hast no gold to bring, though ice-bound earth no Heaven-sent flowers bestows, yet give thy heart this Noel to thy King. This is the Legend of the Christmas Rose.

—Emile Belmont, *Noel Roses*, nineteenth century

A poor girl of Bethlehem was moved deeply after finding the Christ child in squalid conditions. She cried and prayed to find some way to duly recognize the great event. Angel Gabriel heard her and asked why she was crying. The girl replied that in winter there was not one flower to offer the baby. Gabriel took her hand and led her into the night, where she was enveloped by a golden light. The angel touched the earth with his staff and on every side sprang the blossoms of the Christmas rose (*Helleborus niger*). She gathered some in her little hands and laid them before the child in the manger.

Acts and Affirmations

If you go picking the Christmas rose this season, be sure to do so the way ancient Greek naturalist Theophrastus instructs: "One should draw a circle around the Hellebore, and cut it standing towards the East and saying prayers, and one should look out for an eagle, both on the right and the left; for there is danger to those that cut, if your eagle should come near, that they may die within the year."

December 19

Chinese Winter Solstice Festival

If you want to stop being confused, then emulate these ancient folk: join your body mind and spirit in all you do. Choose food, clothing and shelter that accords with nature. Rely on your own body for transportation. Allow your work and your recreation to be one and the same. Do exercise that develops your whole being and not just your body. . . . Serve others and cultivate your self simultaneously.

—Lao-tzu, Chinese philosopher, sixth century B.C.

The art of voluntary simplicity is embodied in the Tao and in Lao-tzu's oral teachings. There is so much to glean from wisdom many centuries old. Simple foods are best grown in the garden. Clothing should be comfortable, of natural fibers, and offer freedom of motion. And shelter that is small and comfortable and easy to take care of frees you of the daily drudgery of housekeeping. Above all, let gardening become both work and recreation. This practice will help you discover that all good things come from the soil, and the simple life is the only sure way to obtain them.

Acts and Affirmations

Celebrate the solstice by ordering a takeout Chinese dinner. Ask for pork-filled dumplings, which are believed to bring good fortune and health in the future. Be sure to eat the meal with red chopsticks, which are reserved for special occasions. Honor your household gods or shrine with offerings of fresh oranges, flowers, lighted candles, and Chinese incense.

December 20

At the nativity season when the sap of all other Thorns is at its lowest point, the Holy Thorn, regardless of the severity or mildness of the temperature, revives, leafs and flowers usually within the very twelve feastful days, and frequently it would seem upon the very night of the nativity itself.

—Alfred E. P. Raymund Dowling, *The Flora of the Sacred Nativity*, 1900

There are many different legends of the Christmas season that explain why certain trees and shrubs blossom in the middle of winter. This occurrence is always perceived as a divine sign that the solstice is rife with magic and supernatural events. Perhaps the most wonderful of these legends is that of the hawthorn tree at the medieval Glastonbury Abbey in England (see page 418). It is remarkable that both pagan and Christian cultures recognize this holy sign, for it underscores the fact that they share a belief that nature is a manifestation of God.

Acts and Affirmations

I will strive to see all natural phenomenon with fresh eyes. Though they may be explained by science, it is far more inspiring to believe in miracles and wonders. I admit that there is a separate reality at work, and I wish it to fill my life with a deep sense of the sacred.

(Crataegus Praecox)

glastonbury hawthorn tree

Glastonbury, England, is close to the legendary Arthurian island of Avalon, but the thorn tree arrived there long before Arthur's time. After the death of Christ, it is believed that Joseph of Arimathea ventured to the British Isles to spread the faith. He made landfall at Glastonbury, but he was so exhausted that he stuck his staff into soft earth before collapsing. It remained there, took root, and grew into a tree, which miraculously blossomed right at Christmastime (the native hawthorns bloomed in the spring). It was believed that blooming sprigs of this tree were spiritual talismans, and they were paraded through the winter countryside where all could witness the miracle. Later an abbey was built at Glastonbury beside the thorn tree. Eventually botanists labeled it *Crataegus praecox* and suggested that it was a species transplanted from the Holy Land. Descendants of that tree still exist in Glastonbury today.

December 21

Oh Jesus and Mary, Archangel Saint Michael, captain of the heavens—captain of the earth—generous prince—captain of the moving cloud—captain of the shining clouds! Accept these candles and keep the wind, the storms, the hail from ruining our fields!

—CONTEMPORARY NAHUATL PRAYER

These words of Mexican rain petitioners are chanted to protect against rain and hail damage to the crops. The old men climb up the mountains to special caves, where they pray and chant for many days, just as the Aztec priests climbed the steep steps to the high temples to pray to the ancient gods. We hear the voice of the old religion and words of Christianity integrated into the rites that have existed for many centuries. They illustrate that, though the religion may be denied the culture, the culture will never truly release its claim on its spiritual traditions.

ACTS AND AFFIRMATIONS

In Mexico the traditional food of Christmas is the tamale, cornmeal dough enclosing meat and sauce and wrapped in corn husks. Women come together to make them in a festive holiday party. Made ahead of time, large quantities can be steamed for the holiday family feast. Join in and celebrate the holidays with Mexican gifts of Christmas: tamales and poinsettias. Although tamales are sold at supermarkets, buy them at a Mexican grocery or restaurant for more authentic flavor!

December 22

DIES NATALIS INVICTI SOLIS (THE BIRTHDAY OF THE UNCONQUERED SUN) (VARIES)

May Shamash the sun god give you your heart's desire, may he let you see with your eyes the thing accomplished which your lips have spoken; may he open a path for you where it is blocked, and a road for your feet to tread. May he open the mountains for your crossing, and may the night time bring you the blessings of night, and Lug your guardian god, stand beside you for victory.

—THE EPIC OF GILGAMESH, third millennium B.C.

The sun god was among the first gods recognized by humanity. This great source of light shining over all lands governed plant life and made the seasons. Every culture recognized its power by celebrating the four great solar occasions of the year: two solstices and two equinoxes. The winter solstice marks not the death of the sun but its birth, and the Christians overlaid the old solstice rites with their own great birth festival, so that gradually these became integrated into the Christian traditions.

ACTS AND AFFIRMATIONS

On this day the sun rises low in the southern sky but falls into perfect alignment with Stonehenge and all the other stone circles in Great Britain. To witness the sunrise this day is an ancient practice that is both holy and beautiful. If you are fortunate enough to have clear skies, go outdoors and watch that ball of light rise above the distant horizon, and offer thanks that it has survived rebirth.

December 23

There are spirits of the sylvan and spirits of the open, natural interpreters of the woods and interpreters of the fields. The true spiritual descendants of the Druids are a small minority. How many of us, while loving trees, are also lovers of the woods, we are much at loss there.

—EDITH M. THOMAS, *Men and Trees*, 1910

Druids are the unheralded source of our best-loved holiday traditions. Their sacred trees were hung with offerings to the spirit that dwelled within. They believed the mistletoe that lived in the canopies of the most ancient trees was more sacred than anything. The fact that it is rare to find mistletoe in Christian churches during the holidays is proof that this pagan symbol was not adopted by the new religion. Are we gardeners the true spiritual descendants of the Druids? Just look around at our plants for the answer.

ACTS AND AFFIRMATIONS

Mistletoe became a widely recognized sign of sex and fertility. It was delivered by Apollo into the care of Venus, the Roman goddess of love. The practice of kissing under the mistletoe was a sign that honored Venus and rejected warfare. In the spirit of the great pagan civilizations, use mistletoe generously throughout the house. Hang it high above the ground to preserve its powers, and kiss one another often. It is an offense to Venus to simply discard mistletoe after the holidays, so save the dried sprigs for protection throughout the new year.

(PHORADENDRON SEROTINUM)

mysterious mistletoe

It was called "a different twig" by the Celts because it remained green while the great oaks shed their leaves in winter. But what makes mistletoe truly different is that it is a parasitic plant. Birds spread the seeds, which lodge in the bark of a deciduous hardwood tree to root into the living tissue of its host. Evergreen mistletoe is far more apparent when trees are leafless in winter, and Druids believed that the spirit of the tree receded into the mistletoe. This imbued it with considerable powers, which would vanish into the earth if any part touched the ground. The cutting of mistletoe required severing with a golden blade or one other than iron, and the sprigs had to be caught before falling to the ground. This custom of cutting mistletoe when it was most powerful at the dead of winter dates back long before Roman times and comes down to us as the most ancient of all our holiday traditions.

December 24

CHRISTMAS EVE

> *The Cock crowed* Christus natus est *(Christ is born); the Raven asked* Quando? *(When?); the Crow replied* Hac nocte *(This night); the Ox cried out* Ubi, upi? *(Where, where?); the sheep bleated out* Bethlehem; *and a voice from Heaven sounded* Gloria in Excelsis *(Glory on high).*
>
> —ANIMAL'S DECLARATION OF THE NATIVITY, 1631

St. Francis of Assisi first introduced barnyard animals into the culture of the nativity. He brought sheep and donkeys into churches to stage a live version of Christ's birth. This was quite a controversial move at the time, but Francis showed that the animals were blessed by being the first to witness the Savior's birth. Though the people of Israel failed to honor this night, the animals stabled there fell to their knees in homage. The innocence of animals is what endears them to us, and on this night they deserve a special recognition.

ACTS AND AFFIRMATIONS

It is an old Irish tradition to honor your pets and livestock on Christmas Eve, for the animals were the first to witness the newborn Christ.

Choose sprigs of herbs, holly, or mistletoe to tie onto their collar this night, and be sure to leave them special treats. It was once thought that all animals kneeled in homage at midnight, while the families were away at midnight mass.

December 25

CHRISTMAS DAY

Christmas Eve came to the lonely home of a forester. Outside the winter wind howled but inside the woodsman and his family spent a happy evening. Just before retiring someone knocked on the door and the father answered it finding a child shivering outside. He was welcomed by the family, warmed, fed well and bedded down for the night. Early the next morning all were awakened by a choir of angels caroling in the heavens. Before them the boy stood transfigured into the Christ Child. He took a twig from a fir-tree, planted it in the ground and said: "I have gladly received your gifts, and here is mine to you; this tree will never fail to bear its fruit at Christmas and you shall always have abundance."

—GERMANIC FOLK TALE

The Christmas tree as we know it is a combination of pagan and Christian influences over thousands of years. It is a natural desire during the darkest time of winter to have trees blossom, and so people decorate them with colorful ornaments in imitation of this natural phenomenon. Ball ornaments evolved from the Mediterranean tradition of attaching citrus fruit and pomegranates to the tree. Icicles and candles are a legacy of the north. To create a tree that is filled with evocative symbols and ornaments, we too become part of this ancient midwinter legacy.

ACTS AND AFFIRMATIONS

Today choose a small mirror and nestle it on your decorated mantle, on your home shrine, or even in front of the kitchen sink. This centuries-old tradition is designed to help you see yourself clearly, and in doing so consider whether you have been generous enough with your charity this season. If you can see no sign of greed there, take the mirror down. But if it evokes a sense that you could have done more, go and give. Only when you can look at yourself comfortably can you put the mirror away.

December 26

O God! Make free this barren, shackled earth, so deadly cold,
Breathe gently forth thy spring, till winter flee in rude amazement, fearful and yet bold.
—Thomas Campbell, nineteenth century

Life is warm and beautiful, but in winter there is little to remind us of this fact in the view outdoors. Barrenness is all around the garden, and skeletons of once leafy plants stand stiff and cold. This winter landscape is like the human heart when the pain of loss or the million tiny sufferings of daily life make us draw inside ourselves. There we live in isolation until we decide to be painfully reborn by struggling through our healing. Only then will we become strong and fruitful again, like the warming days of spring.

Acts and Affirmations

Let me be inspired by the deciduous shrubs in my garden. I see in them the barrenness that I feel when sad or lonely, but they teach me that this is but a fleeting season of my life. In the wake of adversity, all things heal stronger than before if given enough time.

December 27

All things change, nothing is extinguished. . . . There is nothing in the whole world which is permanent. Everything flows onward; all things are brought into being with a changing nature; the ages themselves glide by in constant movement.
—Ovid, *Metamorphoses*, first century

The only constant we can ever count on in this world is change, and there is no better place to illustrate that point than in the garden. Unlike static architecture, gardens are evolving creations. This is perhaps the most compelling aspect of making and tending a garden: that each new growing season brings a host of subtle changes. We are changing daily as well. Age brings new questions and answers to the mystery of life.

Acts and Affirmations
Always view your garden as being a child. When new, it is an infant that requires all your time and attention. When it begins to grow up, you train it to grow straight and strong. As it matures, you may stand back and admire the plants as they reach their full beauty. Let these changes help you look forward to each new season when plants prove the truest measure of your lifetime.

December 28

May we not once in the year remember the earth in the food that we eat? May we not in some way, even though we live in town, so organize our Christmas festival that the thought of the goodness of the land and its bounty shall be a conscious part of our celebration? May we not for once reduce to the very minimum the supply of manufactured and sophisticated things, and come somewhere near, at least in spirit, to a Christmas husbandly fare?

—Liberty Hyde Bailey, *The Holy Earth*, 1915

Liberty Hyde Bailey viewed the art of farming as a quasireligious act and felt that farming well was akin to obtaining grace from heaven. He contends that most people have never experienced the intangible yet fulfilling rewards of growing one's food. To him, the preparation of the Christmas meal was like a sacrament. To purchase the holiday meal at a grocery store—or worse, to go out to a restaurant—distances us from the land and loses the whole idea of the feast as a reflection of good farming. If you experience an elusive feeling that something is unearthly about your holiday feast, perhaps it is this separation from your agricultural roots that is nudging your subconscious.

Acts and Affirmations

Give next year's holiday feast true meaning and value by planning your garden with an abundance of root and leaf crops. Take the time to extend your harvest by canning chutney and pickles, jellies, and other delectables for a diverse and meaningful homegrown feast.

December 29

Many of the phenomena of Winter are suggestive of an inexpressible tenderness and fragile delicacy. We are accustomed to hear this king described as a rude and boisterous tyrant; but with the gentleness of a lover he adorns the tresses of Summer.
—Henry David Thoreau, *Walden*, 1854

Winter's tenderness and fragile delicacy are often overwhelmed by the unpleasant experience of cold. Yet in this season there is great beauty, such as the patterns of ice crystals that form on windowpanes or the way snow rests so perfectly on the layered limbs of a fir tree. Though there is little color and the scenery sometimes resembles an old black-and-white photo, there is even wonder in the myriad shades of gray. Winter's phenomenon of quiet change is indeed gentle, and the cold is welcome to the plants that need it to rest before the labor of regrowing their green tresses for summer.

Acts and Affirmations

God: Help me to transcend the discomfort I feel when it is very cold outside. Let me see the fragile beauty and learn to appreciate every feature of the dormant landscape. I ask that you give me eyes to see the glittering crystals, each subtle shade of gray, and the rare forms created in my garden under snowfall.

December 30

Books alone, however well written, or richly stored with facts, cannot teach all that is necessary to be known about the subject; they can only act as a guide. Hence it is that during the present month we must examine the work of the past, and note down errors of practice that have led to failures for rectification; so as to go forward with additional experience and a firm resolve to merit success in the new year.

—T. W. SAUNDERS, *The Garden Calendar*, 1887

Books alone cannot tell us all about gardening any more than they can convey all there is to learn about the spirit. Both are learned over time, with much looking back over our successes and failures. The accumulation of experience is vital to both, for only through error can we learn the deepest truths. See your weaknesses and mistakes in the garden not as mere failures but as part of the requisite process of learning.

ACTS AND AFFIRMATIONS

The best New Year's resolutions are those that make us more spiritual people by attending to things of the soul rather than of the physical world. A resolution to set aside a few hours each week or a few moments each day to spend in the garden may make you deeply happy. A resolution to learn more about horticulture may make you wise in the garden and in life. A resolution to share your love of plants with others expands your soul. And a resolution that brings you closer to nature, be it in her wild places or in the cultivated ones, will bear the fruit of consciousness as the circle of the seasons turns once again.

December 31

NEW YEAR'S EVE

The most noteworthy thing about gardeners is that they are always optimistic, always enterprising, and never satisfied. They are forever planting, and forever digging up. They always look forward to doing better than they have ever done before. "Next year . . ." they say, and even as they pronounce the words you become infected by their enthusiasm, and allow yourself to be persuaded that the garden will indeed look different, quite different, next year. Experience tells you that it never does; but how poor and disheartening a thing is experience compared to hope! Let us continue to be sanguine even at the cost of future disillusionment.

—VITA SACKVILLE-WEST, *Country Notes*, 1939

Hope and *faith* are the two most beautiful words in our language. Hope is the feeling that what we want is obtainable. Faith is the trusting confidence that it is indeed obtainable. All of us hope that our lives and our gardens get better every year. But it is the degree of our faith that fuels determination to continue on even in the wake of a small failure. For to become a better gardener, we must learn the lessons from every dead tree, from each withered flower or seedbed that refuses to sprout. It is hope that urges us to continue gardening, and faith that keeps us walking down that often crooked road toward the light that is the future.

ACTS AND AFFIRMATIONS

Resolve to make next year's garden bigger and better than ever. Spend the next few weeks sending for gardening catalogs, and make a point to get all your plants ordered early. Now is the time to round up supplies and tools as well. With prior planning, you can spend more time at the end of a shovel than at the end of a checkout line later on. You'll also have much more contemplative time on those spring weekends in the new season ahead.

Jewish National Fund
42 East 69th St.
New York, NY 10021
(800)542-TREE
http://www.kkl.org.il
To have a tree planted in Israel in your or someone else's name, send $10 per tree to the Jewish National Fund.

Seeds of Change
P.O. Box 15700
Santa Fe, NM 87506-5700
Free catalog.
Heirloom flowers and vegetables, including amaranth, unusual sunflowers, maize, and fava beans.

Native Seeds/Search
526 N. Fourth Ave.
Tucson, AZ 85705
Catalog $1.
Heirloom seed varieties from Native American crops of the Southwest and northern Mexico. Best source for maize and native tobaccos. Choice gourds, tepary beans, amaranth, and sunflowers.

Ethnobotanical Catalog of Seeds
J. L. Hudson, Seedsman
Star Route 2, Box 337
La Honda, CA 94020
Catalog $1.
Written for more experienced gardeners; no illustrations. Best source for daturas both native and tropical, plus many other hard-to-find shamanistic plants. Includes the Zapotec seed collection, featuring rare indigenous crops of southern Oaxaca, Mexico.

The Thomas Jefferson Center for Historic Plants, Monticello
P.O. Box 316
Charlottesville, VA 22902
Catalog $2.
A valuable resource for early American heirloom flowers and vegetables.

Seed Savers Exchange
3076 N. Winn Rd.
Decorah, IA 52101
International membership of seed-saving gardeners and farmers who make their annual seed crops available to other members through a single publication.

Lourdes Water
Missionary Association of Mary Immaculate
P.O. Box 96
San Antonio, TX 78291-0096
Free Lourdes water vials, but a small donation to cover costs is appropriate.